A
CARPET RIDE
TO KHIVA

CHRISTOPHER ASLAN ALEXANDER

A
CARPET RIDE
TO KHIVA

SEVEN YEARS ON THE SILK ROAD

ICON BOOKS

or their agents

Distributed in the UK, Europe, South Africa and Asia
by TBS Ltd, TBS Distribution Centre, Colchester Road,
Frating Green, Colchester CO7 7DW

Published in Australia in 2010
by Allen & Unwin Pty Ltd,
PO Box 8500, 83 Alexander Street,
Crows Nest, NSW 2065

Distributed in Canada by
Penguin Books Canada,
90 Eglinton Avenue East, Suite 700,
Toronto, Ontario M4P 2YE

ISBN 978-184831-125-1

Typesetting in 11pt Plantin by Marie Doherty

Printed and bound in the UK by
CPI Mackays, Chatham ME5 8TD

Contents

About the author

Christopher Aslan Alexander was born in Turkey (hence his middle name) and grew up there and in war-torn Beirut (as a boy, his understanding of a shell collection was more the weapon variety). He spent his teenage years in England before escaping for two years at sea. Chris studied media at Leicester and became the first white boy in the university gospel choir.

After a year working for the students' union, Chris moved to land-locked Central Asia, volunteering with Operation Mercy, a Swedish NGO. While writing a guidebook about Khiva, he fell in love with this desert oasis – which boasts the most homogeneous example of Islamic architecture in the world – and stayed.

www.acarpetridetokhiva.com

To my team-mates in Khiva, my Uzbek family, friends and colleagues. And especially to Madrim:
Katta minnatdorchilik bildirib, do'stligimiz abadiy bo'lishini tilab qolaman

List of Illustrations

Author's note

I have used the terms 'carpet' and 'rug' interchangeably. Pedants will argue that one is larger than the other, but this distinction is rarely acknowledged in modern-day usage.

Most Uzbek words appear in the glossary and are generally pronounced phonetically. The exception is the 'kh' sound which is always pronounced the way Scots pronounce the 'ch' in the word 'loch'. I have written most Uzbek words phonetically, their pronunciation often different from the same word in Farsi or Turkish.

Technical terms from carpet-weaving and design can also be found in the glossary.

For the most part, I have used people's real names except when to do so might endanger them. The views held in this book are my own and in no way reflect those of Operation Mercy, UNESCO or the British Council.

Prologue

Tashkent transit lounge

I'd always imagined that if I wrote a book about the carpet workshop and my time in Khiva, it would be written, or least begun, in the workshop itself. I'd sit in my office – a cell in the Jacob Bai Hoja madrassah – and write about the beginnings: the transformation of a disused and derelict madrassah into a centre for natural dye-making, silk carpet-weaving, and exploration into long-forgotten carpet designs. My laptop would be plugged into the rickety socket in my corner office cell next to the phone that rang incessantly, occasionally with carpet orders but usually with mothers passing on shopping lists to their daughters, or amorous young men unable to meet a young weaver in public but happy to court over the phone. I'd sit there typing as the light filtered through the arched plaster latticework, forming hexagonal pools of light on the stone floor. Perhaps Madrim would sit next to me, magnifying glass in hand, bent over a copy of a 15th-century manuscript, examining a carpet illustrated within its pages, partially obscured by a Shah or courtesan.

I'd look around our small office that once accommodated students of the Koran, now filled with a carved wooden table and chairs, beautifully constructed by my friend Zafar and his brothers; the wall niche that once held a Koran, now crammed with books and laminated carpet designs; the sleeping alcove, supported by thick ceiling beams, now storage for fans or electric heaters.

Sounds would filter through the small wooden door: the thumping of weavers' combs on the weft threads that mark the completion of each new row of silk knots; the rhythmic pounding of oak gall being crushed in the large brass mortar by Jahongir, our chief dyer; the loud *thwack* of dried silk skeins beaten hard against the wall, removing the entangled remains of powdered madder root or pomegranate rind. Over this, the sound of an argument between loom-mates from one cell, laughter from another, competing Uzbek, Russian and Turkish pop music, and the voice of Aksana giving a guided tour.

But this book will never be written in my office, or anywhere else in Khiva. Next to me, a bag full of gifts for the weavers and dyers who have become my family sits unopened. I am in the transit lounge in Tashkent. This is the furthest I can get, having been refused entry into Uzbekistan. I feel rumpled and tired, and have spent the last few nights sleeping on newspaper. More than that, I feel a crushing sense of loss, a dull ache around my heart that sometimes shifts to a constriction in my chest. I'm not sure how long I will be stuck here for, what I've done wrong, or whether I will ever return to the desert oasis I now call home.

Tashkent, November 2005

1

The walled city of Khiva

*It was now near midnight and the silent, sleeping city lay bathed
in a flood of glorious moonlight. The palace was transformed.
The flat mud roofs had turned into marble; the tall slender
minarets rose dim and indistinct, like sceptre sentinels watching
over the city … It was no longer a real city, but a leaf torn from
the enchanted pages of the Arabian Nights.*

—J.A. MacGahan, *Campaigning on the Oxus,
and the Fall of Khiva,* 1874

'The amazing thing about working in Khiva, or anywhere
else in Uzbekistan, is what you might end up doing,' Lukas
explained during a recruitment phone call. 'You'll find yourself doing things you're not qualified to do and would never
have the opportunity to do elsewhere. You just do them
because no one else is.'

Over the next seven years I often thought back on these
words, whether holed up in the British Library poring
over medieval Persian manuscripts, debating Timurid carpet
designs with an Oxford professor, stripped naked and radiated at a former Soviet youth camp, crawling through worm
droppings in an attempt to record the silkworm's life-cycle,
accused of drug-smuggling while attempting to bring sacks
of natural dyes out of Afghanistan, or running for cover as an
anti-Western riot engulfed the Kabul carpet bazaar.

I had no background in textiles or carpet-weaving and
no inkling that this would become my main focus in Khiva.

1

In fact, my only background in carpet-weaving had been a rug-making kit I was given as a child. The rug still languishes, unfinished in an attic somewhere, after I managed to impale the weaving hook into my nose, mid-thrust. It was now 1998 and I had recently graduated from a degree in mass communications, which didn't seem very relevant for life in a Silk Road oasis. Lukas thought otherwise, and was excited to have someone work alongside him. We would be writing the content of an online guidebook about Khiva, requested by the Mayor of Khiva to boost tourism. Lukas was working for Operation Mercy, a Christian humanitarian organisation, and they seemed happy with my qualifications.

There were many reasons to ignore Khiva and look for volunteer possibilities in more hospitable climates. It was a remote desert oasis with freezing winters and simmering summers; I knew that conditions would be basic, and everything that I'd heard about Central Asian cuisine had been overwhelmingly negative. I would have to learn a new language and culture, and had never been particularly good at foreign languages. Operation Mercy didn't pay volunteers – who were expected to raise their own expenses – and an initial commitment of two years felt far too long. My supportive parents reminded me of a note posted in the staff room at my old school for teachers on swimming duty: 'Beware C. Alexander. Jumps in deep end but cannot swim!'

I considered other options, but kept coming back to Khiva. I had been specifically invited there with a project waiting for me that fitted my skills. I appreciated the humanitarian and Christian ethos of Operation Mercy and was impressed with their current work in Khiva among the blind. There was also something very alluring about Khiva and the Silk Road.

I was born in Turkey at one end of the Silk Road, and my parents held a fascination with China at the other end. I was intrigued by the peoples of the Silk Road, particularly those of the former Soviet Union. At school I had studied Soviet Politics, though the course was renamed halfway through due to the Soviet Union's collapse. Before this, I had naively assumed that the term 'Soviet Union' was simply a Communist term for Russia, and had no idea of Tatars, Tajiks, Azeris, Kazakhs or any of the other peoples who called the USSR their home. Now I might be living among them.

It was also at Bedford School that I first heard about Captain Frederick Burnaby. He had attended the school and there was a house named after him. Burnaby, reputedly the strongest man in the British army, was a Victorian hero. Bold, brash and assured of England's God-given superiority over everyone else, he decided to travel to Khiva in 1876, largely because the Russian authorities had forbidden foreigners access to Central Asia, which they now considered theirs. Burnaby travelled overland on horseback in the middle of winter and narrowly avoided freezing to death en route. He was granted an audience with the Khan, who was shocked to discover that the great Britannia was ruled by a woman. Burnaby had plans to travel through the Turkmen city of Merv and into Afghanistan but was apprehended by the Russian authorities and ordered home. However, his travels gave him enough material for a bombastic bestseller: *A Ride to Khiva*.

I didn't want to travel to Khiva but to live there. I wasn't sure what to expect and whether any of Burnaby's encounters with 'the natives' would be similar to my own. In one respect, though, we were to prove similar: we were both single

Englishmen in a culture of arranged marriages, which baffled Khivans as much today as it had back then.

'Which do you like best, your horse or your wife?' inquired the man.

'That depends upon the woman,' I replied; and the guide, here joining the conversation, said that in England they do not buy and sell their wives, and that I was not a married man.

'What! You have not got a wife?'

'No, how would I travel if I had one?'

'Why, you might leave her behind and lock her up, as our merchants do with their wives when they go on a journey.'

'In my country the women are never locked up.'

'What a marvel!' said the man. 'And how can you trust them to so much temptation? They are poor weak creatures and easily led. But if one of them is unfaithful to her husband what does he do?'

'He goes to our mullah, who we call a judge, and obtains a divorce, and marries someone else.'

'What! You mean to say he does not cut the woman's throat?'

'No; he would be hanged himself if he did.'

'What a country!' said the host; 'we manage things better in Khiva.'

Captain Frederick Burnaby, *A Ride to Khiva* (1876)

With Burnaby's book to guide me, I knew what Khiva had once been like but had no idea what over a century – most of it under Soviet rule – had done to change the cultural landscape. My initial commitment of two years would extend to seven, before being cut short by deportation. A place I knew only through the eyes of a long-dead British soldier would become home. The bizarre would become familiar, and the exotic would become normal. Soon I would daily roll up my mattress on a balcony that overlooked the minarets and madrassahs of Khiva's old city, glowing in the dawn sun, growing used to these scenes from the pages of *The Arabian Nights* through which I'd slipped.

Khiva would leave a huge imprint on my life: toughening me up, humbling me with regular examples of sacrificial hospitality and kindness, broadening me with new friendships and very different perspectives on life. I would find myself not only living on the Silk Road but immersed in a world of silk, discovering indigo blue, madder red, pomegranate gold and the subtle shades of life in a desert oasis. Random strangers would become my second family and an eclectic assortment of characters would be woven together to form a thriving workshop of weavers, dyers and embroiderers. People I might simply have photographed if passing through would become the tapestry of my life. Khiva was a place I would come to love; and then, unexpectedly, Khiva was also a place that would eventually break my heart.

First, though, there was a compulsory two-month language course in Tashkent, the capital. I had savoured the exotic sound of this name, only to discover a drab, charmless city with no centre, no heart and little visible history. Tashkent had been levelled during an earthquake in the 1960s and rebuilt by the Soviets in swathes of concrete. There was still a sizeable Russian community in the city, making it a contrasting place of mosques and mini-skirts, Russian rap and Uzbek folk music. Tea-houses full of bearded men wearing skull-caps and shrouded in smoke from skewers of sizzling *shashlik* evoked a timeless image of the Silk Road. Next door, a new Korean pizza restaurant attracted upwardly mobile young Russians and Uzbeks with the Backstreet Boys blaring from the entrance over the clink of vodka glasses.

I found it hard to define Tashkent Uzbeks, who seemed able to flit between traditional and more Soviet ways of thinking and living. While I was scrabbling for a towel at the presence of a female cleaner in the men's swimming pool changing rooms, young Uzbeks around me would think nothing of sauntering past naked to collect their locker key from another female attendant. The world of sport, I learnt, was a Soviet one with no place for bashfulness. Yet these same youths got dressed, caught trolley buses or trams, and arrived home to a different world where parents planned arranged marriages for them, where food was cooked by the subservient wives of older brothers and the day began with ritual washing and dawn prayers. It was a society looking for identity, marooned somewhere between Mohammed and Marx.

The government had moved dramatically away from the Kremlin after independence. The Russian-speaking first secretary of the Communist Party reinvented himself as President Karimov of Uzbekistan. He learnt Uzbek and, despite his initial pleas to maintain the Soviet Union, marked the first of September as Independence Day. He encouraged the building of mosques (although in the fumbling early days of independence one mosque inauguration had scandalised its Saudi patrons with vodka served by skimpily-dressed waitresses) and the revival of Uzbek history, language and culture.

But by the time of my arrival in September 1998, the government seemed to be questioning its embrace of all things Muslim as radical Islam gained popularity, particularly in the densely inhabited Fergana valley to the east of Tashkent which made up a quarter of the population. Having served as an efficient wedge between Tashkent and Moscow, Islamism was now the largest competitor to the government and its power monopoly.

My days were spent in language study. I had only two classmates, Catriona from Scotland – a teacher also joining Operation Mercy in Khiva – and an enthusiastic American whom we dubbed 'omni-competent Sarah'. She had arrived in Tashkent two months previously and as far as we were concerned, was already fluent.

We learnt phrases such as, 'This is a pen', and 'Is this a pen?', attempting to apply them practically in the teeming bazaar just outside our classroom. Hawkers of stationery nodded solemnly in agreement, 'Indeed, it is a pen.'

Our teachers – two women – spoke little English, which was good for forced language practice but didn't help us with the many questions we had about Uzbek culture and traditions.

We learnt how to get around the city. Tashkent boasted a tastefully designed metro, each station themed after an appropriate Soviet hero or after cotton, which seemed to be the main value of Uzbekistan as far as the Soviet authorities were concerned. We learnt to understand Cyrillic, despite new edicts attempting to move the country towards a Latin script. Laboriously pondering the first couple of letters on hoardings, we'd suddenly recognise words like *gamburger* or *got-dog*. Borrowed English words beginning with 'h' were translated into Russian with a 'g' instead, giving rise to places such as

Gonduras or Gong Kong and a pantheon of new personalities including Gitler, Gercules, Gamlet, Frodo the Gobbit, Attila the Gun and Garry Potter.

I was placed with an Uzbek family who lived on the outskirts of the city. Their house was backed by a courtyard full of chilli plants, aubergines and tomatoes; the pit toilet at the bottom of the garden guarded by a bad-tempered sheep. There were three sons in the family and the middle one attended the University of World Languages, speaking some English. While the small, rotund father of the house wore a traditional black skull-cap embroidered with chillies to ward off the evil eye, his sons wore jeans and tracksuits and were all keen to emigrate to America. I learnt to enjoy greasy bowls of noodle broth called *laghman*, and to cup my hands in prayer at the end of each meal. My host parents were kind and hospitable but also very concerned for my safety, wringing their hands each evening if I appeared fifteen minutes later than my promised return time.

After two weeks in Tashkent, smothered by my host family, struggling to make any sense of the language and missing home, I slipped into self-pity. It would take over an hour to get home from language class in crammed buses, which seemed the perfect place for melancholy. Standing wedged between two stout Uzbek women, pungent armpits in my face, I wondered if I'd made a terrible mistake in leaving England. A chicken, one of three forlorn birds trussed in a shopping bag near my feet, pecked my ankle sharply. Khiva took on the allure of a promised land: the concrete claustrophobia of Tashkent replaced with a skyline of glittering minarets; a place with no overcrowded buses; a place where chickens could roam free.

∾

I had imagined arriving in Khiva, after a long, arduous journey, to see its exotic skyline beckoning like a mirage across the desert. In reality, my first glimpses of the city, at three o'clock one blustery November night, were the few metres illuminated by headlights after an eighteen-hour drive. There was no sense of exuberance, merely the opportunity to collapse on the piled cotton-filled mattresses that Lukas and Jeanette, my hosts, had prepared for me.

Lukas and Jeanette, a Scandinavian couple, had lived in Khiva for two years and in Tashkent before that. They both spoke good Uzbek and had adapted well to life in Khiva. Jeanette wore a headscarf as all married women should, and baggy pants under long, brightly-patterned dresses. Her distinctive gold hooped earrings studded with nuggets of turquoise were typical of those worn by local women but had been a birthday present from Lukas rather than the usual marriage gift. She tried to sweep outside her house every morning and keep up with the cultural expectations of her neighbours. On some days she managed excellently, but on others the challenges of home-schooling her eldest daughter and raising three children in such a different environment from her own would overwhelm her.

They lived in a modern part of Khiva in a concrete two-storey house that doubled as our office. Their faith and commitment to the blind children they worked with had kept them in Khiva despite the challenges and isolation. They both taught children how to use white canes, increasing their independence and freedom. They were also attempting to change the attitudes of teachers at the blind-school who had been trained in the Soviet science of *Defectologia* – an approach to disability that was caring but isolating, ensuring that those with disabilities existed in a cosseted parallel world of institutions, away from their able-bodied family and friends. Lukas was struggling with the corrupt school director, who was building a palatial new house for himself with money meant for the blind children under his care.

Both Catriona and I were keen to visit the blind-school, but first we wanted a general tour of the town – and especially the Ichan Kala or walled city, dubbed by UNESCO 'the most homogeneous example of Islamic architecture in the world'.

Our tour took us down one of two main roads that ran the length of the modern town, past the blind-school, the park and a rusting ferris wheel which I assumed, wrongly, was disused. At first sight, Khiva had a shabby, provincial and slightly disappointing feel to it. It was only as we turned the corner at the bottom of the road that the Ichan Kala loomed in front of us. The bulging mud-brick walls wound around a crowded centre of madrassahs, mosques, minarets and mausoleums like a large bronze snake basking in the autumn sun. Nearing the walls, we could see their crenellations and the impressive watchtower, giving the appearance of an elaborate sandcastle.

Four enormous, turreted gates led into the inner city from the four points of the compass. We approached the Grandfather Gate and Jeanette introduced us to a plump woman who sold entry tickets. We would pay admission this time but, seeing as we were living in Khiva, wouldn't pay again. This was, after all, one of the main thoroughfares for getting to the bazaar.

Wherever we went, we were greeted with a chorus of 'Toureeest! Toureeest!' As time went by, I learnt to expect this accompaniment, along with 'Good morning' at any time of day or night, and the occasional 'Fuckyoo' from gaggles of daring boys. We were also greeted with cries of 'Aiwa', which

I assumed to be a local variant of 'hello'. Its origins were actually in the first capitalist television adverts shown in Uzbekistan after the Soviet Union's collapse. Aiwa electronics featured an ad with two passers-by, both carrying Aiwa products, waving a cheery 'Aiwa' to each other with the tagline, 'The whole world speaks Aiwa.' The greeting was practised on the first tourists who visited Khiva, and they – assuming as I had that it was a local greeting – responded with enthusiastic Aiwas, establishing its authenticity. These first tourists had also arrived armed with pens, which were now considered an expected gift from all foreigners accosted on the street. Often children would shout 'A pen, a pen!' at me, sounding much like I probably had during my language course in Tashkent.

We walked past a series of small stalls selling souvenirs – a huge mud-brick wall to our right and an impressive madrassah to our left. Next to this was a large, squat tower layered with beautifully glazed bricks in shifting shades of green, turquoise and brown. This complex, built by Mohammed Amin Khan after a particularly lucrative pillaging of Bukhara, was on such an opulent scale that parts of the city walls were removed for its accommodation. Rivalry between the Khiva Khanate and the neighbouring Emirate of Bukhara was a reccurring theme in both Khiva's history and its modern-day attitudes. Mohammed Amin Khan planned a minaret taller than any other, dwarfing the one in Bukhara, but never completed it. Some claimed that this was because the Khan realised that those calling the faithful to prayer would gain a tempting bird's-eye view of his harem. Others believed that the Khan had plans to assassinate the architect on completion of the minaret – ensuring that the Bukharan Emir could not commission him to build an even larger one. The luckless architect, fearing for his life, jumped from the minaret, turned into a bird and flew away.

'Well, seeing as we've paid for our tickets, we might as well be tourists for the day,' decided Catriona, heading towards a stall selling papier-mâché puppets. I was drawn to one selling carved wooden Koran-stands and boxes in different shapes and sizes. Having greeted the stall owner in Uzbek, I discovered that he spoke excellent English and that his name was Zafar. He praised my Uzbek, amazed at my simple phrases. I was used to flattery in response to my limited efforts, particularly in Tashkent where few foreigners strayed from Russian.

'You've only been here six weeks and already you speak more Uzbek than all these Russians who were born here!' a Tashkent taxi driver had declared once, glaring at a passing mini-skirted Russian. 'What are you giving me money for?' he demanded as I got out of the car. 'You are learning our language, you are our guest. Please do not offend me with money.'

Far more impressive was Zafar's English, which was self-taught and fairly fluent. He was about my age, with a ready smile and a quick wit. We got chatting as Catriona and Jeanette haggled at the neighbouring stall, and as we left he invited me to visit his home. Zafar would become a good friend and would play a significant role in my carpet journey.

Jeanette took us next to the Kunya Ark, or old fortress. We entered through another huge, carved wooden gate, past a magnificent *iwan*. These roofed, three-walled structures acted as primitive air-conditioners, capturing cooler northern breezes and circulating them. Most were simple but this one was part of the Khan's palace, held up by immense fluted pillars decorated with intricate carving. The three walls were completely tiled, with stalks, leaves, blossoming lotuses and peonies winding around each other, covering each wall in mesmerising complexity. This was a place I would return to later, to discover potential carpet designs.

We wanted to view the whole of the walled city from the watchtower. Entering through a darkened doorway and fumbling our way up a steep staircase built into the mud-brick walls, we emerged blinking in the sunlight to a spectacular view. Ahead of us the large green dome of the Pakhlavan Mahmud mausoleum glinted, and behind it was the shapely, tapered minaret of the Islom Hoja madrassah. This was the second-largest minaret in Central Asia and, with its bands of dazzling tiles, it made a fine desert beacon for weary travellers to fix their eyes upon. Sunlight flashed off the distinctive blue, white and turquoise tiles adorning the portals of each madrassah. Beyond a central group of larger buildings were flat-roofed mud-brick houses clustered like a Christmas-card Bethlehem, and in the distance I could just make out the first dunes of the desert. The only thing missing was a flying carpet or two.

I stayed with Lukas and Jeanette in their tiny spare room upstairs, next to the larger room we used as our office. Over the next few weeks our guidebook team established a routine. Lukas still had his other responsibilities at the blind-school but would meet us in the morning for planning and researching the guidebook. I valiantly waded through a few Soviet guidebooks that had been translated – nominally – into English. In the afternoon Catriona and I would visit each site of interest to learn as much as we could about it from local guides and museum attendants.

Lukas encouraged us to view all opportunities to speak Uzbek as 'work' and good language practice and to seek them out as much as possible. Most of the museums were housed in madrassahs and presided over by women bundled in layers of acrylic cardigans with angora headscarves, knitting colourful socks and slippers to sell to tourists. These museum 'wifies', as Catriona referred to them, became our first friends. They assumed that we were married to each other, but – after our vehement protests – concluded that we were merely conducting an affair. We quickly learnt that there was much more segregation between men and women in Khiva than in Tashkent.

Khiva's madrassahs varied in size. Most were now museums but some had been converted into hotels, woodwork shops, even a bar. Originally they were residential colleges for learning the Koran, each following the same basic design: an elaborate front portal leading into a courtyard, with a tree for shade and a well for water. Radiating from the courtyard were cells in which students studied and slept. Some had a mosque and minaret attached and some didn't.

Sitting inside the madrassah cells, making conversation with the museum wifies, we realised just how different the dialect in Khiva was. They smiled at our stilted, textbook Uzbek, explaining how they would say the same thing completely differently in Khorezmcha, their own dialect.

We weren't the only ones struggling with pronunciation. The wifies warmed to Catriona's name, adapting it to the Russian 'Ekaterina', but 'Chris' proved more tricky – particularly with the English 'r'. After attempts at 'Cliss', 'Cwiss', and even the occasional 'Christ', I presented my middle name, Aslan, as an alternative.

'But that's not your real name,' declared one of the ladies. 'Aslan is an Uzbek name.'

I was born in Turkey, I explained, and my parents had given me a Turkish middle name, much to the delight of their Turkish friends.

'And this is also in your passport?'

I nodded and from that point on everyone in Khiva referred to me as Aslan.

I felt claustrophobic living and working in the same place. The house felt too small for Lukas and Jeanette and their three small children without their having to give up a bedroom for me, so I started looking for a place of my own to live. I was glad to have tasted life with an Uzbek family in Tashkent, but had no wish to repeat the experience. There were no newspapers to advertise accommodation for rent, so I placed posters around town. I watched expectantly as an old Uzbek man in a long, quilted robe tore off a phone number from the poster, certain that a deluge of housing options would soon come my way. Unfortunately, my poster-placing spree coincided with Lukas and Jeanette's phone line breaking for ten days.

I made my first trip back to Tashkent, helping Lukas collect equipment donated to the blind-school. During the month I'd stayed in Khiva, Tashkent seemed to have magically transformed itself. Now it was a paradise overflowing with English-speaking foreigners, hot water on tap, nice restaurants and shops brimming with variety. I wondered why I'd never appreciated these things before.

There was also Tezikovka – the weekend flea-market. Anything from toilets and potted plants to dismembered fridges, second-hand books and pets were laid out on the streets for sale, and if you were lucky you could sometimes buy back your own, previously stolen, property. The bazaar began after independence as the large Jewish population of Tashkent started selling off their possessions before departing for the promised lands of Tel Aviv or Queens, New York. I bought myself a large red flag of Lenin covered in Communist slogans and then – in a moment of weakness – found myself the owner of a lime-green parrot who I named Captain Frederick Burnaby.

Returning across a desert whipped by bitterly cold winds with nothing but the occasional squawk from Burnaby to relieve the boredom, my enthusiasm for Khiva waned. We arrived to a grey and overcast city approaching winter. I placed Burnaby and cage in the corner of my little bedroom, where he perched glowering. All attempts to teach him how to mimic the traditional greeting 'Assalam-u-Aleykum' were met with hostile silence and the occasional lunge.

This time, my arrival in Khiva had none of the mystery or excitement of before. I tried to remain positive. I knew about culture shock and that the honeymoon phase in a new culture would lead to the despondent phase as the novelty wore off and the differences niggled. Knowing didn't really make much difference to how I felt, though. I looked for the positive and for events to look forward to. We had all been invited to a circumcision party in Urgench (a town about twenty miles from Khiva, and the capital of our province of Khorezm), which would be my first cultural celebration and might even lead to making some local friends.

While in Tashkent, I'd been mortified to discover that weddings, circumcisions and christenings were held at five o'clock in the morning. Dragged out of bed by my Tashkent host-brother, we'd attended the *beshik toy* of a neighbour celebrating a new birth. Mother and child were absent from the proceedings, as both were still vulnerable to the evil eye – a curse caused by jealousy or the unwitting complimenting of a child. We sat at plastic tables covered in food and I nodded off during a lengthy monologue from the mullah, shaken awake and confronted by a large bowl of greasy *plov*. This national dish of rice, carrot-shavings and raisins was topped with lumps of mutton and fat. Central Asian sheep have large, overhanging bottoms where fat is stored for winter. This prized fat, known as *dumba* (with a powerful taste I never acquired), divides each piece of meat on a stick of shashlik, and is generously pushed from guest to guest when eating from a shared mound of plov.

It was a relief to learn that celebrations here in Khorezm took place, more sensibly, in the evenings. Our hosts in Urgench were Rustam and Mukkadas. This couple – good friends of Lukas and Jeanette – were the pastor and his wife of the only Uzbek Christian church in the region. Despite official harassment and regular visits from the secret police (formerly the KGB), they had been told by the authorities to register their church but were then denied registration by the same authorities on the grounds that there was no such thing as an Uzbek Christian; that they were both Uzbek and Christians was apparently inconsequential. Considered a threat by the local government, they were also ostracised by their family and community on account of their faith, and accused of turning Russian. Both of them were determined to maintain their cultural traditions, and keen that their community recognise that they were still Uzbek and proud to be so. Circumcising their sons was a natural part of this, so a trip to hospital and the deed was done.

We arrived outside Mukkadas and Rustam's simple mud-brick house at sunset, greeted by the two young boys who hobbled awkwardly, wearing specially-made loose pyjamas. Boys were always circumcised aged three, five or seven, and often brothers or cousins were done together to save on costs. Each guest would congratulate them and stuff bank-notes into their clothing. The weather was freezing, but the abundance of plastic trestle-tables and chairs made it clear that the celebrations would take place outside. I was looking forward to meeting Rustam and Mukkadas, but they were both busy organising food and Lukas went to help them. Catriona and Jeanette were led to a women's table, while I was seated beside a group of young men from the neighbourhood. They nodded in my direction but were more concerned with pouring shots from a bottle in a paper bag, disgusted that their hosts had not provided vodka – their main motivation for being there.

I picked up a slice of melon and discovered it had frozen. A live band blending keyboards and pre-programmed percussion with traditional stringed instruments and a large hand-held drum performed a deafening repertoire, accompanied by a professional dancer in a glittery outfit covered in jangling metal tassels. Plates of plov arrived and I gratefully ate with my right hand, the rice and carrots warming my fingers. Groups of women – their faces animated by gossip – sat bundled in cardigans and scarves. A table of men nearby were busy toasting each other. My valiant attempts at small talk with other men on my table had petered out into awkward silences. I felt alone; an unnecessary appendage to the established community around me.

This feeling persisted over the coming weeks. Other than brief forays to museums, I was stuck in the office, succumbing to a blend of boredom, listlessness and loneliness. Remembering my encounter with Zafar the wood-carver and his invitation to visit, I returned to his stall, but it was shut up for winter. The mud-brick madrassahs and city wall that had glowed bronze in the autumnal sun were now grey and lifeless. Even the bazaar had lost its sparkle. Mounds of bright red peppers, yellow melons and stacks of fresh herbs were succeeded by lacklustre piles of drooping root vegetables. The gaudy sequin-and-glitter dresses worn by local women were now subsumed in layers of grey woollen shawls, the men all wearing uniform black leather jackets.

I found colour only in Khiva's history. Bundled in blankets, over which the occasional mouse scuttled, I curled up in bed reading tales of treachery, intrigue and political manoeuvring between imperial Russia and Britain. Khiva was to play a crucial role in pushing the Russian empire south towards India – their ultimate goal – and experienced three Russian invasions.

The first invasion in 1717 had ended in almost complete annihilation of the Russian troops. Battling against the Khan's army and running short of water, they welcomed the Khan's offer of a truce and discussion of terms. The wary Russians were welcomed into the city, the Khan apologising for the paucity of lodgings and explaining that the troops would be separated into smaller groups for more comfortable accommodation. The Russian generals were suspicious but were overridden by their commander – an Azeri convert to Christianity – who understood the sanctity of hospitality and did not want to cause offence. Once divided, the Russians were promptly slaughtered – a remnant surviving and put to work with Persian slaves building the Mohammed Ghazi Khan madrassah.

The perfect pretext for a second invasion was provided by the returning diplomat-cum-spy Captain Muraviev. He visited Khiva in 1820 and discovered the city's bustling slave trade, bolstered by captured Russians. Most of the slaves were Persian Shi'ites – considered worse than infidels by the Sunni Turkmen and Khivans. Turkmen raiders captured them, forcing any Christians or Jews among them, who were considered 'People of the Book', to convert to the Shi'ite faith first, making them infidels and thus worthy of slavery. Those who survived the long desert march were sold in the Khiva slave bazaar. Persian slave girls were the most popular additions to harems, while a young Russian male was considered the hardest-working and worth four camels.

Captain Muraviev narrowly avoided slavery and imprisonment himself. He held audience with the Khan and was kept for a number of months under house arrest. During his first day in Khiva, he had seen the pitiful faces of Russian slaves in the crowds as they stared imploringly at him. The slaves made contact with him secretly through a message hidden in the barrel of a gun he'd sent for repairs:

'We venture to inform your Honour that there are over 3,000 Russian slaves in this place, who have suffered unheard of misery from labour, cold, hunger etc. Have pity on our unhappy situation and reveal it to the Emperor. In gratitude we shall pray to God for your Honour's welfare.'

Later, Muraviev met one of the unfortunate slaves personally.

The old man's name was Joseph Melnikov; he had been 30 years in slavery, was the son of a soldier, and had only been married a week when he was seized by the Kirgiz near the fortress of Pretshistinsk and sold as a slave at Khiva. After 30 years of bitter bondage, when by daily and nightly work he had at length scraped together sufficient money to purchase his freedom, his master cheated him by accepting his savings, and, instead of setting him at liberty, selling him to someone else. (Captain Frederick Burnaby, *A Ride to Khiva*, 1876)

The Russians had found their pretext, but waited until 1840 before acting. Summoning a vast army, they planned to attack Khiva in winter, fearing the scorching desert summers. Unfortunately they chose the coldest winter for decades and soon their army was decimated by scurvy, snow-blindness, hypothermia and wolves. Eventually they turned back, suffering massive casualties without even a glimpse of the walled city.

It was clear that the Russians would not admit defeat, and the English stationed in Persia dispatched Captain Abbot to Khiva, hoping he could persuade Allah Kuli Khan to release the Russian slaves (now a mere 300 or so) and destroy any pretext for another invasion. Captain Abbot – a rather dour and mournful character – failed to impress the Khan and narrowly avoided being buried up to the neck in the desert, a suggestion made by the Khan's spiritual advisor. With no news from Abbot, a dashing young officer by the name of Richmond Shakespeare was sent to Khiva. He used his charm and eloquence to convince the Khan of an imminent Russian threat – despite their recent defeat – and the need to free all Russian slaves.

Reluctantly the Khan complied, even releasing favour- ite slaves from his harem. The liberated Russians followed Shakespeare in a joyful exodus across the desert to Russian territory. The Tsar – privately livid – offered public gratitude to the British for this liberation, buying the Khanate of Khiva 30 more years before the Russians finally invaded successfully under General Kaufmann in 1873.

Trading Persian and Kurdish slaves continued into the 20th century, ending only under the Bolsheviks. Slaves were not the only source of Khiva's ethnic diversity. Alexander the Great had conquered Khorezm, his armies taking local wives and leaving a blond-haired, blue-eyed legacy. Invaders from the East had done likewise, and Mongolian features were also present. Some Khivans could pass for southern European, while others would look at home in China or Indonesia.

Of the variety of mosques in Khiva, only one was allowed to function. This had been the way during the Soviet era, and the Uzbek authorities were wary of Islam and keen to main- tain Soviet standards of control. The working mosque stood beside the Strongman's Gate next to the fish-selling area of the bazaar. A row of painted clocks announced the times for praying *namaz* – performed by pious Muslims five times a day, facing Mecca. Beside them was a government 'wanted' poster of *wahabis* or Islamic fundamentalists. I arrived there with Catriona, unsure whether or not infidels were welcome to explore. We were soon put at ease by the gold-toothed mullah who was delighted that foreigners wanted to know more about the origins of his mosque.

A walnut trader from Khiva, the mullah explained, had once discovered a large bag of gold coins at the bottom of one of his sacks. Assuming the money was cursed, he took the coins to the Khan. The Khan's advisors – also fearful of a curse – advised the Khan to order a new mosque built with the money in order to alleviate any bad luck. The walnut trader had the money returned and was granted a plot of land. The mosque took shape but the walls were only half-completed by the time the coins ran out. The resolute trader announced to the city that he would exchange a walnut for each brick provided for the mosque. And this, concluded the mullah, was how the mosque was completed.

I wanted to ask the mullah about religious freedom, but my language was limited and he grew uncomfortable at the subject. We did find out that during the Soviet era, a complex system of informants had kept tabs on attendees. This system still flourished and anyone younger than an *aksakal* or white-beard was suspected of potential radical tendencies and risked inter-rogation or worse.

Khiva's Friday mosque – with similar status to a European cathedral – was built to accommodate the entire adult male population of Khiva. Its low wooden ceiling was supported by hundreds of carved wooden pillars, with a lamp-post in the middle of this pillar forest bathed in sunlight from the overhead window. The mosque was no longer a place of prayer and was frequented largely by tourists and illicit young couples who had discovered that the steep, dark minaret staircase made an ideal location for passionate embraces. Unless one wheezed loudly while climbing to the top, it was quite common to catch couples hastily separating and brushing down rumpled clothing.

Gone were the days when the minaret had served for dispatching women suspected of improper behaviour. Adulterous women were trussed in sacks and thrown from the top. A captured Turkmen rebel had also been hurled to his death, but a combination of crosswinds and his billowing baggy trousers ensured that he survived the fall. This was obviously the hand of Allah and the people assumed he would be spared. Instead, the merciless Khan had the luckless rebel taken back up to finish the job.

There were other draconian punishments illustrated in Khiva's historic jail, now a macabre museum. Two forlorn-looking mannequins were incarcerated, surrounded by paintings depicting ways in which they might be sent to the next world. The Hungarian traveller Arminius Vambery witnessed Turkmen rebels having their eyes gouged out, the sword wiped clean on their beards as they groped around in blind agony. Adulterous women not hurled from a minaret were placed in a sack of wild cats which was then beaten until the women were scratched to death, or were stoned, as witnessed by Vambery:

The man is hung and the woman is buried up to the breast in earth near the gallows, and there stoned to death. As in Khiva there are no stones, they use Kesek (hard balls of earth). At the third discharge, the poor victim is completely covered with dust, and the body, dripping with blood, is horribly disfigured, and the death which ensues alone puts an end to her torture. (Arminius Vambery, *Travels in Central Asia*, 1864)

Captain Muraviev, who had been so touched by the plight of his enslaved compatriots, wrote about the form of execution in vogue at the time of his visit.

> Impalement is carried out in Khiva with still greater cruelty than attends it in Turkey. The stake is of wood and has a rather blunt point, and, in order that the victim may not die too soon, his hands and feet are firmly bound. As soon, however, as the stake has entered pretty deep into his body, they are released again, when the tortured wretch increases his sufferings by his violent struggles. (Nicolai Muraviev, *Journey to Khiva through the Turkmen Country*, 1822)

Khiva's history, though grisly, seemed for the moment more interesting than its present. In search of excitement, I determined to explore the bazaar further. I learnt where the illicit money-changers loitered – their pockets bulging suspiciously – and where to buy gaudy wooden chests painted in bright magenta and turquoise with 'May your wedding be blessed' written on them. Not everything for sale was as it appeared. A stall sold rough wooden pipes that had nothing to do with smoking. They were inserted between a baby's legs before it was swaddled and strapped into a cradle, funnelling pee into a clay jar below.

Another stall sold packets of dark green mulch that looked like desiccated spinach. I assumed it was a spice of some kind but was told it was *nuzz*. Sprinkled onto the palm of the hand and tipped back into the cavity between teeth and bottom lip, this blend of tobacco and something stronger caused a mild high, slurring of the speech and suppression of appetite. Used by all taxi-drivers, it rendered them incomprehensible to my untrained ear. After fifteen minutes or so, nuzz lost its potency and was spat out. This proved dangerous when sitting in the back of a taxi, and on one occasion a large expectorated globule blew back, spattering my face.

I made friends with Kamil, a carpet-seller who trawled the closer villages in neighbouring Turkmenistan for carpets, providing generous bribes to the border guards and selling the carpets to tourists for enormous profit. I was useful – able to translate English books on carpets into a pidgin Uzbek of sorts – and Kamil taught me more about Turkmen carpet designs. Although not part of the local mafia/government, he'd done well for himself, buying influential friends and a smattering of wives whom he'd installed in different houses around town. Polygamy was officially illegal but many richer men took mistresses and referred to them as second wives.

My experience with Kamil helped me learn more about Turkmen carpets and begin to appreciate indicators that affected a carpet's value, such as the knot count per square centimetre. I also realised that within a few years, there would be no more old carpets to sell off. I wondered what it would take to set up a workshop producing new carpets of a decent quality to sell to tourists. It wasn't something I gave much thought to. After all, what did I know about carpets? A few years later, when asked by tourists visiting the workshop where I'd studied carpets and textiles, I'd look back and remember my very basic tutelage.

My accommodation prospects brightened. I discovered a beautiful old courtyard house within the walled city just next to the Khan's fortress and watchtower. It was empty but owned by the Ministry of Culture who used it sporadically as a guest-house. I could rent the main living room for the princely sum of around $10 a month, sharing the bathroom and kitchen with an occasional guest from Tashkent. I was keen to move in as soon as possible, but the landlady insisted I gain approval first from the Ministry of Culture in Tashkent. I persuaded Lukas to visit them next time he was there, sure he would charm them with his fluent Uzbek.

'Maybe it will be possible,' had been the response. 'But first you must get these other permissions.' This sounded straight-forward, but I failed to understand that I had been given an Uzbek 'no'. Preferring not to say no directly, the hope was that I would be put off by the demand for permissions and look elsewhere. It was only later that I understood this, learning to spot the expression of vagueness immediately assumed by any official when asked questions to which the answer was negative, or the dreaded *hozer* in response to a 'when' question. We were taught in language class that *hozer* meant 'now', but swiftly learnt that its practical application could mean anything from five minutes to eternity.

Catriona and I continued to collate stories for the guidebook, and Isak – a German-speaking guide – proved particularly helpful. Standing before two life-size photographs of the last Khans of Khiva, he told us stories of their lives. The elder of the two was Mohammed Rakhim Khan, a poet known by his pen-name 'Feruz Khan', and ruler at the time the Russians successfully conquered Khiva in 1873. He had retained his position but was stripped of his armed forces, expected to pay a huge war indemnity to the Tsar. He was Khan when Burnaby made his ride to Khiva, hosting the Captain and astonished that such a great nation as *Inglizstan* might be ruled by some woman called Victoria.

Feruz Khan had been a benevolent ruler and popular with his subjects. His trusted Vizier, Islom Hoja, was a progressive thinker committed to improving the lot of the common man. The Tsar invited his new vassal to St Petersburg and the Khan left his medieval Khanate, returning with tales of wonder at the modern world. His new, purely decorative telephone was given pride of place, and a pianoforte was installed in the palace with a courtier instructed to learn how to play it. The Vizier Islom Hoja was similarly inspired and returned with grand schemes to modernise Khiva. He set about building the city's first hospital, its first secular school (which even admitted girls) and a post office – dreaming that one day Khiva might be connected to the world by telegraph.

Islom Hoja was a respected Vizier and honoured by the Khan, who arranged a marriage between their children. However, his fortunes changed with the death of the Khan. The Khan's first-born was a hopeless opium addict and passed over in favour of Isfandir, who wasn't much better. The new Khan – preoccupied with his harem and dancing boys – left the running of the Khanate to the Vizier. This arrangement worked nicely until Tsar Nicolai invited the Khan and his entourage to St Petersburg.

At the first official reception the Khan, unaccustomed to meeting virtuous ladies uncovered, was introduced to the Tsarina. His frank sexual proposition was judiciously translated as: 'The Khan, enamoured by your beauty, humbly requests a portrait of your likeness to show his harem the superior beauty of the European woman.'

The Tsarina, delighted, provided the Khan with a portrait, and the smouldering Khan was promptly packed off to the nearest brothel. The Tsar, hearing of such lewd conduct, was furious and refused to appear in the official photographs marking the occasion. Meanwhile, Isfandir contracted syphilis, a disease then unknown in Khiva, and returned to the Khanate where his physicians assured him that cleansing would occur if he slept with 40 virgins. The Vizier – fearful that his own daughter might get infected – intervened, quarantining the Khan from any further sexual exploits until he was well again, making a powerful enemy in the process.

Isfandir was determined to do away with his interfering father-in-law; but he needed allies, who were hard to come by due to the Vizier's popularity. He consulted the mullahs, who were also keen to see an end to the Vizier and his modernising ways, which threatened their own power base. A plot was hatched and a messenger dispatched ordering the Vizier to come to the Khan's palace immediately. The mullahs arranged for bandits to lie in wait for the Vizier, robbing and murdering him. The Khan immediately rounded up the bandits, executing them before they could protest that they were merely following orders, and conveniently tying up the loose ends.

Still, there were people in the Khan's palace who knew the truth – and one of these was Isak's grandfather. Corroborating his story, Isak pointed out a yellowing official photograph taken in St Petersburg with the Tsar notably absent. Next to this was the portrait of the Tsarina given to Isfandir. Catriona wanted to know what happened to the last Khan.

'You must not worry about Isfandir,' Isak reassured her. 'A few years later, he too was assassinated.'

The Bolsheviks were fearful of former royalty staking claims to Khiva, and exiled the next in line to the throne. He returned from Ukraine after independence with his children and grandchildren. His offspring, speaking only Russian and Ukrainian, wandered around Khiva in jeans, marvelling at this exotic and foreign place that they might have ruled had history turned out a little differently.

By the beginning of March, I had lived with Lukas and Jeanette throughout the long, cold winter and we were all desperate for me to move out. Lukas was bogged down with endless bureaucracy required by the government for Operation Mercy work and, despite my nagging, had not followed up the permissions I needed to move into my dream house. I decided to take matters into my own hands and contact the Ministry of Culture myself. Enlisting the help of an English-speaking guide, we visited the post office and made our call. A terse conversation ensued, during which the guide simply nodded. Afterwards he turned to me and said: 'They just say "no". You simply cannot live in that house.'

This was both emphatic and unequivocal. I had no alternative plans, but had to move out of Lukas's house as his parents were visiting soon. I was anxious and irritated; although I'd made it through the winter, it had been about surviving, not thriving, and I was still unsure whether coming to Khiva had been a mistake.

However, my housing crisis would result in an unexpected encounter in the Khan's derelict palace that was to change my fortunes in Khiva considerably for the better.

2

A home by the harem

Uzbek people like to drink tea very much. This is not just a simple fact about statement of devotion of one country population, because Uzbek people's love for tea is something different than German's love to beer or Finn's to coffee. It does not just like for tea, if they talk they drink tea, anyone who was in Uzbekistan can continue this file of associations for ever and ever.
—Uzbek Air magazine, Winter 2005

My quest for a new home began with a long list of criteria which rapidly grew shorter after each unsuccessful house visit. Often one of the numerous barrack-like flats near the carpet factory became available. They were all identical in layout but in varying states of disrepair. In one case the door to the kitchen opened into thin air; a woman in the flat below peeling carrots looked up as I was pulled back from the brink by my host.

'I don't understand,' I began. 'Why are you showing me this place when there is no floor? Where am I supposed to cook?' My unshaven host stared disinterestedly at the yawning chasm as I saw myself out.

Another house fulfilled my criteria in terms of location. It was right in the heart of the walled city beside a large madrassah. However, it was basic to say the least – little more than a shack. The outer layer of mud and straw adobe had washed away in places to reveal crumbling mud bricks. The front door opened into a small room that did have a floor – give or take a couple of floorboards – but little else. I dwelt on the positives, noting the presence of wiring which implied electrical capabilities. An even smaller room that might serve as a bedroom opened off the main room but there was no kitchen or bathroom, just a small pit latrine outside.

'What would I do,' I ventured to the owner, a corpulent middle-aged man bulging out of his greasy tracksuit, 'about getting water? There doesn't seem to be any plumbing.'

He airily brushed away such concerns, explaining that two streets away was a well. Was I not strong? Could I not buy buckets? I realised that any concerns at a lack of bathroom would be similarly dealt with, for could I not use the local *homom* – the traditional bath-house used by most Khivans who didn't have bathrooms?

I decided that water, gas and electricity were non-negotiable, although I accepted the unlikelihood of living in the walled city. It was rumoured that rooms in the Nurulabeg Palace beside the park had been renovated for use as offices. I wasn't sure if they would be habitable, but then most of the potential houses I'd visited weren't either, and the idea of living in a palace appealed. I decided to pay the place a visit.

From the outside, the palace looked rather like a prison, with huge walls lacking windows or doors, and just one giant set of carved wooden doors leading into the interior. It was set up as any other Khan's palace would be, with a guest court-yard, a harem courtyard, and a courtyard in the original sense of the word: for holding court. I walked into the first, which was decaying, derelict and serenely beautiful. Fluted carved wooden pillars graced the upper level of open balconies, and a huge iwan of white plasterwork faced northwards. There were some rickety steps leading up to a room behind the iwan which would be delightfully cool in summer. Instead of the rotten floorboards carpeted in bird droppings I imagined my own palatial bedroom.

Downstairs, I entered the main rooms. Crumbling ceiling plaster revealed patches of mud brick and a few voids gaping to the balcony above. The original splendour of the plaster-moulded walls and painted wooden surfaces could still be seen in places. It was, however, quite clear that this courtyard would be uninhabitable unless a huge amount of expensive restoration took place.

I moved on to the next courtyard, which was less impressive but did have a well. I could tick off my requirement for accessible water. The rooms were all locked, but cupping my hands I peered through the smeared windows at dingy interiors, bare of furniture or floorboards. I heard a polite cough behind me and turned to greet a middle-aged man with closely cropped grey hair, a row of gold teeth and pronounced crow's-feet. He was smiling and we introduced ourselves, discovering that we both knew Lukas. His name was Koranbeg and he was responsible for restoring Khiva's ancient monuments. I noticed the way that he simplified his language for me without sounding patronising and found myself warming to Koranbeg immediately.

I explained, in halting Uzbek, that I didn't have any *tanish bilish* – connections – so was finding it hard to get somewhere to live.

'I must go away from home. Lukas, his parents are will come soon. No space for me. Now I looking for new house. Here, *remont*? New home for me here, maybe?' I looked at him hopefully.

'No, there has been no *remont* here. Now, there is no money for these things.' I must have looked dejected, as he continued: 'But, have you seen the first courtyard? My grandfather was the

Khan's master craftsman and he decorated all those walls and ceilings. Now, each year they just get worse.'

I nodded, and we stood in silence for a minute. I was about to thank him and leave, when Koranbeg made me an unexpected offer.

'I understand that it is very difficult for you foreigners without *tanish bilish* here in our country, and yet you are our guests and you have come to help us. I have lots of *tanish bilish* and I will help you find a house. Come and live in my house until we find somewhere for you to live.'

This was to be the defining moment of my integration into the community. A complete stranger had offered me a place in his home. I had no idea what his family were like, where his house was or what condition it might be in. He, in turn, knew almost nothing about me and yet welcomed me as a guest.

My natural reaction was to refuse and protest that I could manage by myself, even if this wasn't true. But, putting pride aside, I found myself shaking his hand and scribbling down his phone number, arranging to visit him the next day. I had walked into a derelict palace and found a place to live after all.

The next day Jeanette called Koranbeg to find out exactly where his home was, and what time I should come over to visit. She hung up and turned to me smiling. 'Did he tell you where he lives?' she asked. 'Right next to that house you were so desperate to live in, beside the Khan's harem in the heart of the walled city.'

Beaming, I offered up a silent prayer of thanks. 'A house by the harem …' I enjoyed the sound of it, imagining the generations of young men who'd lived in the house before, dreaming of the sequestered beauties just a wall away.

That afternoon I followed Jeanette's directions and entered the walled city's northern gate, turned right and followed the snaking, crenellated wall as it curved left. At the bottom of the street was the Khan's harem, topped by the watchtower. Before this – the last house on the left – was number 57, Koranbeg's house. It was a large, two-storey mud-brick building with a flat roof and balconies. One of the neighbours was bent over a glowing round oven, slapping dough against its sides with only her headscarf visible. Some children kicked a football around on the street and hailed me with the usual 'Toureeest!' followed by clicking motions and 'Photo! Photo!'

I knocked on the door and was welcomed by a thin, sallow woman in a gaudy house dress over baggy trousers. She was, I assumed, Koranbeg's wife. She smiled enquiringly, flashing an upper row of gold, and I sensed instantly that she had no idea who I was. Koranbeg had obviously not mentioned his encounter with me.

'Assalam-u-Aleykum' I began. 'Is Koranbeg *agha* here?' She shook her head and I asked if I might come inside and speak with her.

'Of course, please come in, you are welcome,' she replied, ushering me to a corpuche (a long seating mattress) next to a low table. I sat down cross-legged and she scurried into the kitchen, emerging with a pot of tea, some flat rounds of bread and a bowl of jam. I wasn't really sure how to approach the subject of her husband's invitation, and decided simply to recount our conversation in the Nurulabeg Palace. She nodded, smiling and hiding any surprise or annoyance she might have felt towards her husband.

'My name is Zulhamar,' she said slowly. 'When would you like to move in? Would you like to see our house?'

We had been sitting in a small dining area next to the main entrance, and now she opened a door that led into a huge room full of scaffolding. Workmen were busy with the ceiling – a blizzard of interlacing stars and complex geometrical designs rendered in three-dimensional painted plasterwork. The walls were a mock-baroque plaster confection tinged with gold-leaf. The effect – while not to my taste – was truly palatial, belying the humble mud-brick exterior.

'My husband is responsible for the restoration of the Khan's ceilings, and now he wants to make our ceiling also look nice,' Zulhamar explained simply.

I smiled up at the workmen, and Zulhamar called one of them down.

'This is Madrim,' she explained. 'He is my husband's youngest brother.'

Zulhamar asked Madrim to show me upstairs, as it would appear unseemly for her to escort a man to a bedroom. Madrim was short, brawny and in his early thirties. With his thinning light brown hair and Caucasian features, he could have passed for southern European. Zulhamar, on the other hand, looked more Eastern, with slanted eyes, dark hair and yellow skin.

Upstairs, Madrim showed me the bedroom. It was large and unused, having been recently painted, and led out to a walled balcony with a panoramic view of domes and minarets and the Khan's watchtower. It was perfect.

Downstairs, Zulhamar was making lunch for us. I attempted stilted conversation with Madrim, who was shy but polite and clearly struggled with my pidgin Uzbek and strange accent. I remembered suddenly that I hadn't mentioned I was vegetarian and hurried to the kitchen.

'I sorry, I vegetarian.'

'No problem,' said Zulhamar. I wasn't sure if she knew what I meant.

'As a result, I not eat meat,' I tried.

Zulhamar looked shocked. 'But what do you eat if you don't eat meat? Where do you get your strength from?'

'Yes, I eat eggs,' I finished lamely. Shrugging at such strange eating habits, she began frying six eggs in a generous amount of cotton-seed oil.

I returned the following evening with bags, ready to actually move in. Burnaby the parrot stayed at Lukas and Jeanette's for the first week, in order not to push my eccentricity too much too soon. I hadn't realised the significance of my arrival date: it was the night before Navruz. I knew little about this celebration, except that it marked the beginning of spring and the new year and was the most important festival in the calendar.

A moon-faced, willowy girl of around fourteen greeted me demurely and led me to my room. They had placed a mattress on the floor and strung up some gaudy-looking orange and purple patterned curtains. Other than that, the room was large and bare, which was fine as I expected to stay only for a few weeks before moving into one of the many houses Koranbeg had assured me he knew about.

The girl said something about *sumalek* and beckoned me to follow her. Zulhamar and some other women were gathered around a huge steaming cauldron, stirring its contents with long paddles. Koranbeg sat with the men and a few stately-looking grandmothers on a raised platform covered in cushions and corpuches. He called me over and introduced me as his English guest, Aslan.

Male neighbours, relatives and friends offered their hands to be shaken, while women simply nodded, placing their right hand on their hearts, asking after my health, my work and my family. These pleasantries were followed by a series of questions that I became quite adept at answering due to their repetition: What was I doing in Khiva? How old was I? Was I married? Why wasn't I married? When would I get married? Did I have any brothers and sisters? What was my religion? Did I pray to paintings like the Russians? How much did I earn? What was the price of a kilo of meat or a loaf of bread in England? Where was life better: here or there?

There was some disagreement as to the precise location of England, some maintaining that it was next to America, others convinced that it was in London. I decided to ask a few questions myself and enquired after Koranbeg's children. He called over the girl who had answered the door, introducing her as his eldest, Malika. I found out later that she was quiet but stubborn and quite capable of mischief. Aware of her place in the family order, she was respectful for the most part towards her father, joked easily with her mother while cooking or cleaning together, sparred with her younger brother Jalaladdin, and terrorised or mothered her youngest brother Zealaddin depending on his behaviour.

Jalaladdin was an awkward, skinny twelve-year-old with the beginnings of an Adam's apple and a squint – his left eye slightly askew. For some reason, Koranbeg seemed ashamed of his eldest son, speaking to him roughly, always expecting more of him and rarely showing him any praise or affection. These were lavished instead upon Zealaddin, a young, bright-eyed boy of seven, who looked like his mother but with his father's lighter skin colouring. He had the cheekiness and confidence his older brother lacked, and while his brother could do no right, he could do no wrong.

I knew nothing of the family dynamics at that point, or who was a relative, who was a neighbour and who was both; the evening was a blur of faces for the most part. While some guests sat and chatted, others took a turn with the paddle, stirring the large cauldron constantly to ensure its contents didn't stick to the bottom and burn. Somehow, the women seemed to end up doing most of the stirring while the men considered it their role to throw an occasional log on the fire. I asked what sumalek was made from and received a long and incomprehensible answer to which I nodded, pretending to understand.

Tea and spring clover-filled ravioli were served to those of us seated on the platform. The sun set, leaving a chill in the air. Smoke from the fire mingled with the steam from the sumalek and one of the old grannies began to rock cross-legged and sing, others joining her. Bats ricocheted around the crenellated silhouette of the city walls and a group of children charged past with Zealaddin in the middle of them. For the first time I began to feel less like a tourist and more like a guest. It was a magical evening, celebrating not only the new year but a new chapter in my life.

The following morning was my first Navruz and I wandered around town with Catriona and Andrea – a team-mate who had returned from six months in Germany. The weather was pleasantly warm and a plethora of stalls had sprung up selling watery ice-cream, clover ravioli and other delicacies. The souvenir shops were open once more and I met Zafar, who recognised me. He invited me to his home again and I eagerly accepted, agreeing on a date and writing down his address. The rusting ferris wheel – which we'd previously assumed was derelict – cranked into life and gaggles of girls screamed and flirted with schoolboys, ignoring the stunning views of Khiva's walled city that unfolded behind them. I had survived my first winter in Khiva, had a place to live and an invitation to Zafar's house. Life was improving.

The light green fuzz that appeared over the fields grew rapidly as the weather warmed, replacing the desert-brown monotony of Khiva's winter landscape. Trees budded and blossomed, and fresh herbs appeared in the bazaar. I settled into my new home, overjoyed at the presence of an indoor toilet and accustoming myself to Soviet textbooks in lieu of toilet paper. At first I was treated with deference by Koranbeg and Zulhamar, all of us trying a little too hard. Gradually, the atmosphere became more relaxed; the family would quarrel or joke in my presence, and I play-fought with the boys.

The three children slept together in the living room, with a niece from the village who was studying in Khiva. Each morning they rolled up their mattresses and stored them in a neat corner pile, draped with a synthetic Chinese tapestry. Zulhamar and Malika were excellent cooks and kindly indulged my vegetarianism, introducing me to dishes such as *shwitosh*, a green noodle made with dill and served with yoghurt and stew, or semi-circular fried pastry parcels of vegetables.

Koranbeg and Zulhamar weren't old enough to be my parents or young enough to be my equals. I wasn't sure what term to use for them, but settled on *agha* and *abke*, meaning 'older brother' and 'older sister'. They tried to simplify their language for me, and as I grew in my comprehension of Uzbek, I learnt more about them both. Zulhamar was originally from the village of Yangi Arik, or New Canal, where people were, she assured me, more honest and hard-working than the inhabitants of Khiva. Her father had died when she was still young, so Zulhamar had looked after her numerous younger siblings as her mother went off to work. Zulhamar cooked and cared for the family and learnt how to weave carpets and *kilims* (woven floor coverings). They had moved to Khiva so her mother could work in a factory, and there Koranbeg's mother, their neighbour, had noted how industrious the young Zulhamar was. It came as no surprise when a match-maker was dispatched to their house and a marriage arranged with Koranbeg.

'He was very disappointed to be marrying a village girl, especially as he'd just come back from studying in Tashkent,' she recalled. 'He didn't like me at all, I was too thin and too dark, and we hardly spoke for the first few years. Anyway, I was too busy, the only daughter-in-law in the house, cooking and cleaning and then weaving carpets late into the night. My mother-in-law was a hard woman, and I was more submissive than the other daughters-in-law who joined us later. I think he was going to divorce me as I kept having miscarriages, but finally after three years of marriage I gave him Malika.'

Having shown my photos of home to Koranbeg, he rummaged in a wardrobe for a large plastic bag containing an ageing army photo album. During his two years of army service he had, like most Uzbeks, been sent to other parts of the Soviet Union. His tank unit in Kazakhstan all got frostbite in the sub-zero temperatures, and it was here that he learnt to drink vodka, eat pork and speak Russian. After army service he attended college in Tashkent – much skinnier in those days – sporting bushy sideburns and flares.

There were unsmiling portraits of Koranbeg and other students in Red Square, Moscow on an educational trip, and pictures of him on scaffolding learning to restore ceilings, applying gold-leaf to a section of moulded plaster. His wide education and experience had left him with a broader understanding of the world than his wife, and a keen respect for foreigners. Zulhamar, though mocked by her husband for her lack of worldly knowledge, was an astute judge of character and had a dry sense of humour and a good head for business.

I soon met the rest of Koranbeg's family. He had two younger brothers and a sister. Madrim, his youngest brother, worked incredibly hard to finish the painted wooden ceiling in the guestroom. A man of few words, he was strong, shy and industrious. The middle brother Abdullah, however, was a constant source of concern for both Koranbeg and Madrim. Despite the fact that Koranbeg's formidable mother was installed at Abdullah's house to keep an eye on him, he still managed to come home drunk most evenings.

Both Koranbeg and Zulhamar had lost their fathers. Zulhamar's mother was small, round and jolly, always well dressed in the tent-like style that suited larger women. She treated me with the affection of an exotic pet, patting my knee reassuringly whenever I looked blank – unless her favourite Mexican soap opera was on, which then consumed all her concentration. Koranbeg's mother was a fine-looking but fierce woman. She was the only person around whom the youngest boy Zealaddin behaved himself and, though barely into her sixties, catalogued a long and mournful list of ailments whenever she visited; this interspersed with barked orders to Zulhamar and the children for tea or an extra cushion.

Koranbeg told me about his restoration work, which largely centred around ceilings and wall tiles. It was an honour, he explained, to follow in the footsteps of his grandfather who'd built some of the original ceilings now being restored. He and his team had recently completed their largest project, a rushed affair to prepare a number of buildings for the 2,500-year anniversary of Khiva's founding. This date, along with Bukhara's 2,500-year jubilee which would take place a week later, had been dreamt up by some local historians at the government's insistence.

On the day itself, President Karimov arrived with an assortment of ambassadors and the UNESCO director in tow. The people of Khiva were all told to stay in their homes for security reasons, forbidden to take part in the celebrations. Snipers perched on the roof of Koranbeg's house scanning the horizon, while Koranbeg and his family had to watch the events taking place less than 100 metres away on television. He had still not been paid the thousands of dollars owed him for all the work he and his men had done.

'I have offered bribes to the right officials. I told them they could even take 30 per cent of the money owed us, but still I haven't seen one *som*. It is a bad thing to tell my workers who worked so hard, "I know that you must feed your families, but I have no money for you."'

I was amazed at such treatment, although I later became, if not inured, at least unsurprised by such tales. Corruption was an accepted part of everyday life and most people expected to pay a bribe to get a job, a bribe to obtain their salary, and a bribe to get it paid in cash to avoid an even larger bribe needed to extricate their money from the bank. Abdullah – the way-ward middle son – had a similar story to tell. He had landed a lucrative contract working on the President of Karakalpakstan's mansion. It was a huge job and he took a band of men from Khiva up to Nukus, capital of the semi-autonomous region, to help him. He paid for the labour and materials himself, fully expecting to be reimbursed by the President. The work fin-ished, he waited for his wages, but was fobbed off each time with promises that the money would be available soon. By the time I left Khiva seven years later, Abdullah had still not been paid, despite three or four trips a year to demand what was owed. Each time, he would return to Khiva dejected and get himself drunk.

Life with my Uzbek family revolved around meals which, in turn, revolved around television. Although actual entertainment was relatively scarce, the family seemed inured to the tedium of songs and sonnets about glorious motherlands, schoolchildren reciting epic poems dedicated to the President, the montages of historic mosques and madrassahs, new factories, happy work-ers hand-picking cotton, collective farm bosses marvelling at the size of the melon harvest, etc.

World news consisted of disasters culled from the BBC or Euronews, juxtaposed with happy domestic news of another factory opened or a record wheat crop. Russians joked that if you wanted to see heaven on earth you should watch Uzbek TV – and to see hell on earth, you should actually visit.

What made television watchable for most Uzbeks were the dubbed soap operas from Mexico or Brazil. The most success-ful *telenovela*, entitled *Esmeralda*, was an implausibly melodra-matic tale of a rich blind girl, swapped at birth with a young village boy who grew up as heir apparent. Blind Esmeralda met and fell in love with him but then a dashing young doctor restored her eyesight, leaving a protracted dilemma as to which lover she should choose. It was shown every night at nine, and life ground to a halt as the nation gathered around their television sets. Guests left wedding banquets early, and buses to Tashkent timed their evening stop at a tea-house so as not to miss an episode. In summer I walked home with the dubbed voices of José Armando and Esmeralda drifting through the open doors of each house I passed.

The first series of *Dallas* also proved a popular hit and sparked increased bazaar sales in shoulder pads and bright, polka-dotted fabrics. All of Khiva was rapt, ignoring the bad dubbing, laughing and weeping with the characters. I became something of a prophet, foretelling Bobby's imminent demise.

'Aslan, don't say such a thing!' Zulhamar gasped, spitting to ward off any bad luck I might have incurred. Yet a few months later Bobby died as predicted. Zulhamar and some of our neighbours tearfully discussed the funeral around the local well, noting that no one wore white for mourning, there was no weeping over the coffin, and they even allowed women to attend the burial. My successful prediction was also considered, and I became something of a television seer, predicting Bobby's return to life. This was flatly denounced as impossible, for hadn't he just died? There were also gasps of horror at the prospect of JR being shot. On our street, drama – whether dubbed and on screen or played out in a domestic squabble next door – was all real.

I felt it was time to develop a more active social life and make some friends, so I took up Zafar the wood-carver's invitation to visit his house. He lived in Kosmabot, just outside Khiva, and his house was easy to identify, as there was a pile of huge tree trunks against his front wall. These were black elm – a hardwood getting scarcer due to disease. I asked him if they planted new saplings to replace the trees felled. They didn't. But he assured me they would never chop down one of these ancient trees if there was so much as a leaf still growing, for that would be a terrible sin.

I was ushered inside and took off my shoes as Zafar poured water over my hands from a copper jug that had been warming on a stove at the entrance. The warm water from my hands drained into an ornate copper basin and I remembered the golden rule not to flick but to wring the water off my hands, as each drop flicked would become a *jinn* (devil).

We went through to the guestroom, where the walls were spray-painted in bright lime green with wallpaper-effect red roses. Every Khiva guestroom wall displayed either a giant plastic gold wristwatch clock or a Mecca clock garlanded with plastic flowers. Like most guestrooms, there was little furniture other than a long, low banqueting table surrounded by corpuches and a TV and stand.

The table – barely visible beneath its contents – groaned with the weight of food. In the centre congregated bottles of wine, vodka and vivid soft drinks. Next to these was a large bowl of fruit and a stack of round, flat Khorezm loaves, and radiating from these were small plates of cookies, cakes, salads, nuts and dried fruit. There were two large empty bowls, at odds with the general excess. They were for slinging tea dregs, apple cores and sweet wrappers – an elegantly simple solution to waste disposal.

I made the mistake of eating too much of what were, after all, mere starters, and felt quite full by the time large platters of plov were brought through. Zafar's brothers joined us and I was introduced to them in turn: Javlon, Jasoul, Jahongir, Jamshid.

'How many brothers have you got?' I asked, as yet another appeared.

'Can you guess how many people live in our house?' was Zafar's playful reply. 'There are 24 of us!'

He numbered off each married son and corresponding wife and children. Each married brother had a separate room where he and his wife and children would sleep. The younger brothers and sisters all bundled into one large room at night, sleeping on corpuches which were then stacked up on top of a chest during the day.

'So what do you do if you and your wife want to, you know ...' I asked, not sure if this was too personal a subject. Zafar grinned, explaining that they just learned to stay up well after the children were asleep and be quiet about it.

As we ate, Zafar's rotund father joined us and was soon back-slapping me as he poured out shots of vodka. One presumption of mine had been that people in Muslim Uzbekistan wouldn't drink. These, however, were post-Soviet Muslims; three men could happily dispatch two bottles of vodka and still go to work the next day. I hate vodka but felt obliged to at least down the 50 grams that Zafar's father had cajoled me into drinking. But before that, Zafar asked me to make a toast, his father roaring approval and adding more vodka to my drinking bowl.

After more plov and toasts (I toasted with tea, after Zafar told his father that I had an allergy to vodka) Zafar offered to show me their workshop. I was presented with plastic slippers and a torch as we went out into the garden, detouring for a toilet-stop where I banged my head hard on the lintel to the pit latrine.

The workshop was simple and some of the apprentices were still there, working late into the evening. Zafar's eldest brother was the *usta* or master who oversaw the workshop and was responsible for the main carpentry. The second brother drew out the arabesque designs needed for each item, and the apprentices and younger brothers did the actual carving. They started on cutting-boards, which were easiest, and worked up to ornate boxes, Koran-stands and larger items of furniture. The patterns were transferred from paper to wood by making hundreds of pin-pricks along the contours and then pouring black powder through the holes onto the wood.

The brothers demonstrated how different tools created different effects and offered to let me try. I declined, anxious not to destroy anything, but wanting to learn more, keen to explore other products that they could also sell to tourists. Had they considered collapsible coffee-tables that tourists could take home with them? Or carved plate mats, napkin rings, bookends, framed mirrors?

Zafar watched politely as I scrawled down a design for inter-locking coffee-table legs while enthusing about the possibility of carved wooden chess-sets. Helping artisans develop their products for a tourist market, and acting as a bridge between the two cultures, seemed a perfect blend of creativity and business – and a lot more appealing than spending my days writing up a guidebook. I left my table design with Zafar, suggesting that he might like to experiment with it.

I asked him about the collapsible coffee-table the next time we met up, and he smiled awkwardly. I realised that there was no incentive to experiment with something new that might not sell when he already conducted a brisk trade in chopping boards and boxes. Instead I offered to sell some of his stuff in Tashkent next time I was there, as I knew lots of foreigners who would appreciate his work.

An English lady in Tashkent bought several boxes and a cutting board and enquired whether Zafar produced anything else. Well, I explained, he was considering a range of collapsible carved coffee-tables, and was she interested in being his first customer? Back in Khiva, I handed Zafar his money and the few items I hadn't sold, and told him that there was an order for a coffee-table and drew out what it should look like. I'd discussed a price with Liz, the English lady, and it was a lot more than Zafar made on boxes and book-stands. Soon the coffee-table was completed and orders came in for more, as Liz's friends all wanted one. Next came ornate shelves with pegs, mirrors and telephone-stands. Zafar's brothers were kept busy and now had a lucrative sideline for the winter months when few tourists visited Khiva.

Lukas noted my new 'hobby', which he approved of as long as it didn't interfere with writing the guidebook. We had originally hoped to finish the book within six months, but it seemed to expand continually as we discovered more information that could be included.

My language improved, with plenty of practice answering the same stock questions, whether in a shared taxi, at the barbers or in the bazaar. Where was I from? How old was I? How much did I earn? What was I doing in Khiva? Where was my wife? Why wasn't I married? At this point, if the questioner was young and male, there was more probing. Was I circumcised?

Did I prefer Manchester United or Newcastle? Did I like Uzbek 'bad girls', and which was my favourite brothel? Inevitably all questions returned to the subject of money. How much was a teacher paid in England? What was the price of a loaf of bread, a kilo of meat, a car? Was life better there or here?

At first I answered this last question as diplomatically as possible, explaining that some things were better in England, such as higher wages and less corruption, while other things were better in Uzbekistan, such as the importance of family and hospitality. Later, tired of an oppressive government and unremitting propaganda, I simply explained that life was much better in England as no one had to pay a bribe for a job, or worry about arrest for what they believed. This naturally led to questions regarding the best way to get into the UK and what work opportunities there were for Uzbeks.

I became friends with Rustam and Mukkadas, the pastor of the Urgench church and his wife. At this stage they were still happy to let foreign Christians worship with them, although later on, as the government became more anti-religious, they requested that we stop attending their meetings for fear of reprisals. I visited them in their tiny little house with Catriona and we would enjoy language practice, hospitality and friendship.

We learnt about the challenges they faced from all sides, as Uzbek Christians. Their friends and relatives ostracised them for abandoning Islam, while Russian Christians couldn't understand why they wanted to read the Bible and conduct liturgy in Uzbek. On top of this the government continually harassed them, accusing them not only of abandoning Islam but also, paradoxically, of being Islamic militants.

I visited the Korean church in Urgench one Sunday, which met in a run-down shack with marker-penned stained-glass windows and a rickety old piano. Koreans with names like Boris or Svetlana arrived in jeans and mini-skirts and the whole service was in Russian. I enjoyed it, despite understanding nothing, but could see why Uzbeks wanted something that fitted more with their own culture.

The Koreans of Central Asia had been deported en masse from eastern Siberia and North Korea in the 1940s by Stalin. They arrived with nothing but gradually worked themselves out of poverty, adopting Russian language and culture to the extent that the current generation spoke no more than a few words of Korean. They had retained their cuisine, though, and every bazaar had a section where Koreans sold spicy *kimchi* salads and dog fat – a popular medicine for flu.

Life became difficult for all religious communities, including the Koreans, when bomb blasts in February 1999 were blamed on wahabis or Islamists, resulting in a government purge and a crackdown on mosques around the country. No one was sure if these attacks were genuinely the work of fundamentalists or whether they were staged by the secret police to justify a wave of crackdowns.

Rustam and Mukkadas were patient with our halting Uzbek and gracious about our linguistical blunders, of which there were many. Perhaps the most colourful was when Catriona attempted to describe what church was like in Scotland and how men and women weren't separated but all sat together, singing and sometimes clapping. Rustam looked horrified and it took us a while to establish that Catriona had mistakenly used the word for toilet instead of church.

My problem was with similar-sounding words, and I often asked for chopped-up train to sprinkle over my chips, or made enquiries about the onion going to Tashkent at the train station. I also caused a few raised eyebrows at checkpoints as I offered to show policemen my potato – a mere vowel away from 'document'.

It was through Rustam and Mukkadas that I met Bakhtior, who became one of my closest friends. Short, dark and muscular, Bakhtior was a wrestler. He had an Afghan grandfather, which accounted for his colouring, and a murky past, having run a gang in his home town that specialised in roadside hold-ups. He was well known by the police in his town but had then become a Christian through a university friend. He left his life of crime and was promptly arrested as a suspected Islamic fundamentalist. He told the authorities that he had, in fact, become a Christian, which seemed a good enough reason to continue harassing him.

I began to feel at home in Khiva, and particularly at home living with Koranbeg and his family. I'd acquired a kilim for the floor in my room and had taken down the garish curtains. The myriad of potential houses for rent, once promised by Koranbeg, had failed to materialise and instead he and the family encouraged me to stay on. However, I found a house for rent in the walled city and decided to visit it. It was simple but liveable, but as I wandered through the empty rooms, I realised suddenly how much I'd appreciated living with a local family, and how lonely I'd feel if I moved out.

I sat down with Koranbeg later that day and broached the subject of my future accommodation. He urged me to stay with them, to which I agreed as long as I could pay rent. So far, he had refused all payment, saying that I was a guest and that it was an honour to host me. I told him that it would bring me much shame if I was not to contribute towards the family expenses as he had taken me in as part of his family. Mollified, he reluctantly agreed to this proposal.

My home by the harem was now permanent, and I was feeling a lot more settled. The next challenge was to survive my first summer in the scorching desert heat.

3

The madrassah

*The people of Khiva, as all the Soviet people, take an active part
in socialist up-building, indulge in socialist emulation aimed at
fulfilling and over-fulfilling state plans, at raising labour efficiency
and quality … Its true masters – the working class – begin their
working day to the beat of the Kremlin chimes.*
—N. Gatchunaev, *Khiva Soviet Guidebook*, 1981

'It's a dry heat, a dry heat.'

I kept repeating this mantra, but as the thermometer crept above 40°C and continued, I accepted that dry or humid, the weather was unbearably hot. We had no air-conditioning in the office so I would douse my T-shirt in water and put it on wet, the table-fan by the computer on full blast.

The walled city was even worse – the huge mud-brick walls retaining the heat – and my bedroom was impossible to sleep in. I dragged my mattress up to the roof, joining the boys under the stars and enjoying the occasional night breeze. Getting up early felt unnatural but this was the only time when I had any energy. The summer days were long and the sun set around eight at night. I would return from the office, the slanted rays turning the Ichan Kala walls bronze. Girls spattered water from buckets around their house to settle the dust and take the edge off the heat. Grannies sat in the shade of a tree gossiping, and as the evening wore on, families dragged their televisions outside ready for the evening meal.

Despite the heat, Zulhamar was mortified that I showered with cold water and was convinced of my imminent sickness. I assured her that English people were immune to the evils of cold water, and sure enough I remained alive and well. Cold water, breezes or ice-cream were all perilous and the sources of colds and other ailments. Koranbeg's mother would bundle up in cardigans drinking hot cups of tea to protect her health, while I simmered in just a T-shirt. Soon, showers, both hot and cold, ceased as we experienced a drought.

Koranbeg had a water pump outside but one of the neighbours broke it, so I bought a plastic canister and located the well closest to our house. There were gasps from neighbourhood girls that a man should attempt to draw water and they were quick to offer their services. I waved away their offers and they watched in amusement as the bucket clattered against the sides of the well, emerging quarter-full. Ears reddening, I tried to master the art, eventually tottering off with a full canister which I placed on my balcony. It warmed up during the day, and that evening – the high walls of my balcony screening me from prying eyes – I enjoyed a warm outdoor shower.

Life took on a steady rhythm. I spent the evenings with my Uzbek family or visiting friends, at weekends hanging out at the souvenir stalls with Zafar and the other sellers. We would try to guess the nationalities of tourist groups, and I was privy to any disparaging remarks about them in Uzbek. I discovered that Zafar had never visited the Friday mosque a mere 50 metres away. Worse, there were even two carved wooden pillars inside made by his brothers during the building's restoration which he had never bothered to go and see.

At the end of September, Catriona made a cake to celebrate our first year in Uzbekistan, and soon after that Lukas and Jeanette left suddenly due to ill health. I continued to work on the guidebook but was more drawn to my sideline in wood-carving. I was also interested in kilims – hand-woven flat-weave floor coverings, popular in the villages where people couldn't afford factory-made carpets. If the quality, size and designs could be improved, I was convinced there was a market for them.

That Christmas I returned to the UK and took a kilim with me, hoping to find someone interested in ordering more. In true Central Asian style, a friend of my cousin knew someone and we met up and discussed a partnership. He was importing dried fruit from Uzbekistan and was happy for us to add some kilims to his containers of apricots and sun-dried tomatoes.

The kilim designs of Khorezm were too busy for a UK market, so, back in Khiva, I drew up some simpler designs in fewer colours and took them to Miriam, who ran a kilim work-shop in a nearby village. Despite muttering at the difficulty and ugliness of each design, Miriam soon had her looms in action with pleasing results. I paid her a premium rate, on time, and insisted on good quality. The kilims arrived successfully in the UK and sold well, and we decided to double our order for the following year.

During the second year of exporting kilims (this was by now my third year in Khiva), I visited Miriam's workshop to see how our order was progressing, and she assured me that she had her women working on them fourteen hours a day. This reality, along with the dingy lighting, didn't fit with the 'fair trade' ideals I had rather naively held. If I wanted to provide better working conditions I would need to establish my own workshop, although this seemed highly unlikely at the time.

Meanwhile, Andrea, our German physiotherapist, had established a successful community-based rehabilitation project which had attracted the attention of UNESCO. They asked her to speak at a conference about inclusive education and afterwards she chatted with Barry Lane, the Uzbekistan director of UNESCO. One casual mention of the kilim project and his eyes lit up. They wanted to set up a school for natural dye-making and carpet-weaving in Khiva but hadn't found anyone to implement the project. Would I be interested, he wanted to know, and when could he come up to Khiva and meet me?

Barry called me and explained more about the proposed school of carpet-weaving. A similar workshop had just been set up in Bukhara, about 250 miles away, and an American carpet specialist was providing training. The Mayor of Khiva had already agreed to provide a madrassah for our use and UNESCO had funding for start-up costs. My dream project had effortlessly fallen into my lap, and I assured Barry that I was looking forward to working with him.

Barry visited the following week with Komiljan, his Uzbek translator and assistant. Barry was in his fifties with a neatly clipped white beard and equally clipped speech. It was clear from the start that he was accustomed to giving orders and having them carried out without question. Our main task was to decide which madrassah would make the best workshop.

'The Mayor offered me any madrassah I want,' Barry explained, 'but I don't want other people chucked out, so we'll just be looking at ones that aren't in use right now.'

The Mayor of Khiva, it transpired, owed Barry a few favours and agreed to provide us a madrassah rent-free on the condition that we pay for its renovation. We had an hour or so before the Mayor's arrival and I offered to show Barry some of the modern carpet workshops dotted around Khiva. He blanched at the proposal, well aware of the poor quality, lurid colours and synthetic fibres being used. The whole concept of hand-made carpets had not sat well with Soviet ideology, as the labour-intensive process required someone poor enough to produce them and someone rich enough to buy them. Instead, the bulk of carpets were made in factories, and most Khivans still preferred a standardised factory carpet over a hand-made kilim for their floors.

The Mayor arrived – sober and obviously keen to impress. We were ushered to the door with promises of wonderful madrassahs, whichever one we might fancy. The first madrassah on show was the Kutluq Mohammed Inaq madrassah, and I had noticed during my guidebook research the significant cracks in the turrets on either side, and the odd angles at which they jutted out. I was sure the Mayor hoped Barry would choose this madrassah and save the local government a small fortune in restoration. The brickwork on this one was beautiful, and as one of the larger madrassahs it contained two storeys of student cells. We passed between the carved wooden gates into a corridor with doors to the right and left and archways leading to the main courtyard. An enormous old woman with a rolling gait and a perpetual grimace was there nominally to collect tickets, swathed angrily in headscarves, skirts and vast baggy pants. She had not been informed of our visit.

Barry investigated the room to our right, pushing open the small, carved wooden door, and quickly retreated, retching, at the stench. The Mayor, alarmed, peered into the gloom where curled dollops littered the floor of what had become a makeshift toilet. I stared at the old woman I knew to be the perpetrator, having once interrupted her mid-squat.

'My God! This is a madrassah and they let old grannies shit all over it!' Barry muttered. Komiljan did not translate.

Handkerchief to his mouth, Barry led us inside. It was a magnificent room with an enormously high ceiling that had once been a winter mosque for the students living here. The plaster was crumbling and extensive building work was needed, but this didn't detract from its overall grandeur.

'This would make a good show room, wouldn't it?' I ventured. 'We could hang all the carpets up on the walls and install some spotlights.'

'We'd have to get rid of this appalling stench first,' Barry observed from behind his handkerchief.

The opposite room was slightly smaller and smelt a good deal better, and we warmed to the place. Out in the courtyard we poked our heads down some stairs leading to a cool, spacious cistern, and then looked into some of the empty cells around the courtyard.

'They're not that big, but I think we could probably fit at least two looms into each one,' said Barry. 'Let's have a look at the corner cells – they're generally a lot larger.'

He went over to a corner cell and opened the door part-way – enough to see a dirty mattress on which a girl hid her face as a naked young man attempted to wrest the door shut.

'Good God!' Barry was visibly shaken. 'That old witch has turned this place into a brothel! This is a madrassah, for God's sake! A historic site, a holy site, and she shits all over it and rents out rooms by the hour!'

Komiljan, keen to avoid a scene with the Mayor who was pottering in one of the other cells, blissfully unaware, hurried us out to view our next site.

We turned past the Islom Hoja minaret towards the Pakhlavan Mahmud mausoleum – Khiva's holiest site. Pakhlavan Mahmud, known by Khivans as Palvan Pir, the Strongman Saint, was buried here. He was a curious combination of poet, hat-maker and wrestler, said to be the strongest man in Central Asia. Today he was the patron saint of barren women, who would come from afar and weep at his tomb, cupping their hands in prayer and making offerings of diamond-shaped fried dough called *borsok*.

The Mayor stopped outside the mausoleum and presented us with the madrassah opposite it. This was the oldest madrassah in Khiva and had been built by slaves including a remnant from the first unsuccessful army of invading Russians. Today, the Shir Gazi Khan madrassah was famous among Khivans not for its history but for its bottled conjoined twins. The madrassah had been converted into a museum of medical studies during Soviet times, although it was the freak-show value that attracted the punters. All that was left of this display was a glass container in which the pickled twins lay, joined at the hip. The rest of the museum was now incongruously devoted to the republic of Karakalpakstan, leaving just the courtyard empty and free for us to use. Giving it no more than a cursory glance, Barry felt it would be unsuitable to share a workspace with an existing museum. What we really needed was a whole building to ourselves.

The Mayor led us away from the Pakhlavan mausoleum, up some stairs and past a few small wood-carving workshops and an orchard. We stopped outside a simple madrassah portal studded in green Zoroastrian butterfly tiles. This was the perfect location for a workshop, as all the tourist groups walked along this street and we wouldn't have to lure the guides away from their established routes. One of the Mayor's entourage unlocked the madrassah door for us and led us inside. This courtyard was small compared with the others, but I liked the size. I tried to imagine it without the flotsam of rubbish strewn all over the place, picking my way between dusty broken bottles and boxes, wondering why a battered motorbike side-car had been left there. Ten cells radiated from the courtyard and we peered into each one. Most of them had thick wooden beams supporting a sleeping niche above. Barry was concerned that this might pose a problem for the looms.

'If we're going to have the looms purpose-made, I can make sure that they're not too tall for these cells,' I offered.

In one corner was a small cell that I thought would make an ideal office; and in another, a spacious room that had obviously been the winter mosque. Flanking it were two dim little rooms that would provide useful storage space. A larger room to the left of the entrance way was nearest the gas pipes, making it an obvious choice as the dyers' workshop. In the centre of the courtyard was a drain, but there was no well.

'You'll have to arrange for a water pump to be drilled in the courtyard,' Barry declared. 'We'll also need electricity and electric sockets in each room. I want there to be adequate light for the weavers, and we'll need the gas pipe so that we can heat the rooms.'

We both knew, without anything said, that we had found our workshop.

Outside, I stood back to take in the madrassah. It was dwarfed by the huge green bricked dome of the Pakhlavan

Mahmud mausoleum and the towering minaret of Islom Hoja behind it. The madrassah – our madrassah now – was named after Jacob Bai Hoja (whoever he was) and built in 1873, the year Khiva was successfully invaded by the Tsar.

It was perfect.

Thanking the Mayor, and commissioning a restoration budget from the chief architect, we returned to my house to discuss matters further. It was now late October, and we hoped to begin training the following March or April, once spring had begun and the weather was warm enough for fermentation dyeing. This also gave me time to finish the guidebook, oversee the madrassah restorations and buy the looms, dyes and other paraphernalia. Barry handed me a list that his American consultant, Jim, had drawn up for the sister workshop in Bukhara. It read like a coven wish-list: 'Six large copper cauldrons, 25kgs oak gall, 25kgs madder root, 30kgs pomegranate skins – dried …'

I would do my best to find all these dye-stuffs, and also a master dyer. Quite where I'd find one, given that the art of natural dyeing had faded out, I wasn't sure.

'What we need,' suggested Barry, 'is someone who's already a craftsman, who knows colour and design and has some basic artistic talent.'

I asked Koranbeg, who was sitting with us, if he knew of anyone through his work contacts. He thought for a moment.

'I have a brother, Madrim. He is unemployed right now because there are no more contracts for restoration work. He is a very hard worker and he is an excellent craftsman with many years of experience in restoring the Khan's ceilings. He understands colour and patterns very well.'

I wasn't keen on employing one of Koranbeg's relatives, hoping to avoid the usual nepotism prevalent in Khiva. Still, I had no other suggestions and Madrim, once summoned, seemed to be keen; he was given an address in Bukhara where Jim was conducting a training session and told to join them there the following day. Madrim was to become our master dyer and the untiring manager of the workshop.

The next few weeks were devoted to the long list Barry had given me, as I worked out what items of equipment needed construction – including looms, drying racks and skein-winders – and which items needed purchasing. In the midst of this, events took place on the other side of the world with an effect that would ripple out as far as our workshop in Khiva.

Koranbeg, while lurching home after a heavy drinking bout, had tripped on the uneven stone paving outside our house, breaking his leg in the process. He was now ensconced in a huge cast with Zulhamar fussing over him. She'd installed him in the downstairs bedroom and even moved the television there. It was one evening in September that, idly flicking channels, he watched world events unfold.

Calling for me to join him, I rushed in to see CNN footage with Russian dubbing. The headlines read: 'America under attack!', with a shot of a plane hurtling into a skyscraper and bursting into a fireball. The scene cut to the newsroom in Moscow where an ice-queen presenter who rarely had a hair out of place had just dropped her earpiece and was looking flustered.

I asked Koranbeg what was going on and he explained that no one knew for sure but that a large building for trade in New

York had been hit by two planes. At first they thought it was an accident, but after the second plane crash it was clear that this had been planned. People were jumping off the buildings and many were trapped inside by the blaze. Just then, with a loud yelp from the Russian commentary, we watched as the buildings disintegrated, spewing huge clouds of dust everywhere. We both sat stunned, wondering if a third world war had just been unleashed.

More reports came in about other planes: one had hit the Pentagon and another was thought to have been aimed at the White House. I asked Koranbeg to check the other channels in case there was more news. The other Russian channel was showing a film and the two Uzbek channels were showing nothing but cotton harvest propaganda. It was harvest-time and Uzbekistan's largest export was being hand-picked by happy workers, who briefly stopped to assure journalists that this year was a bumper crop and that they were sure to fulfil their quota. Serious-looking factory bosses stood in front of large machines vomiting what looked like stuffing onto huge mountains of raw cotton.

I'd become inured to state devotion to the cotton plant. 'Cotton-picker' was the name of the main metro station in Tashkent, the national emblem was emblazoned with cotton, and all over the capital a three-bolled cotton head appeared on the sides of buildings, on walls and even on most teapots and drinking bowls. Still, the dramatic events unfolding in New York might have seemed worthy of briefly interrupting the cotton news. Instead the event was ignored by the Uzbek media, until a week or so later it became clear that Islamic fundamentalists based in Afghanistan had been responsible. At this point, the Uzbek government realised the propaganda value of 9/11.

After heavy criticism by Western human rights groups for the arrest, torture or killing of suspected radical Muslims, the government could now claim that they were simply doing their bit for the 'war on terror'. Footage of happy cotton workers was replaced with endless replays of the planes smashing into the Twin Towers, followed by sermons expounding the evils of radical Islam and the need for its eradication.

Further good news for the government came later that year as America invaded Afghanistan. While the moderate opposition groups in Uzbekistan had been largely exiled, imprisoned or assassinated, the radical Islamic Movement of Uzbekistan had conducted a violent guerrilla campaign to overthrow the Karimov regime. Their main training centres were in northern Afghanistan and they were thought to receive funding from Al Qaeda, making them targets for an American army seeking revenge.

A flurry of anxious emails from home arrived, enquiring when I'd be leaving Uzbekistan. This seemed an odd suggestion, as not a lot had changed in Khiva. However, most people in the UK watched footage of angry crowds of flag-burning, effigy-stamping, bearded fanatics chanting outside the homes of Westerners in places like Pakistan and assumed it must be the same for me. In reality, most Muslims in Uzbekistan had far fewer rights and freedoms than in the UK, and anyone remotely radical had either been arrested or had disappeared to northern Afghanistan. Young men were detained for merely sporting a beard, such was the persecution of anyone suspected of radical intentions. Anyway, most people in Khiva were far more interested in what was happening in the Brazilian soap opera than the war raging just a border away.

Hysterical American parents of Peace Corps volunteers demanded an immediate evacuation of their children from Uzbekistan, with little regard for any actual danger. The Peace Corps capitulated, despite protests from most of the volunteers that this was an unnecessary knee-jerk reaction. Each volunteer was given 24 hours to get to Tashkent. They could take one small item of hand-luggage with them – their other bags being sent on later. Andrea and I helped a heartbroken Peace Corps couple wind down their affairs. They loved Khiva and didn't want to leave. Soon we were once more the only foreigners in Khiva.

The Taliban were defeated and the rebuilding of Afghanistan began. It was at this point, in March 2002, that the ripple hit our workshop: Jim, our trainer, decided to pursue far more lucrative UNESCO contracts in Afghanistan. Barry was livid but powerless, and unsure whether anyone else could take Jim's place. This left a big question mark over who would train us. Barry was looking into alternatives but wasn't feeling too positive.

I made regular visits to the madrassah, overseeing its restoration and pretending I knew what I was doing. I'd commissioned Zafar the wood-carver to build four wooden looms and another wood-carving friend, Erkin, to work on drying racks, storage shelves and a skein-winder. Zulhamar, my Uzbek mum, helpfully located a mammoth double loom that stood idle in a nearby factory. Once repainted it took pride of place in the winter mosque room, which was the only place large enough for it.

My biggest headache was locating copper cauldrons needed for the natural dyeing. The coppersmiths at the bazaar would beam at my request and rummage through their piles of dismembered samovars, teapots and water-pipes. I obtained a battered old cauldron that needed patching, and a magnificent piece with inscriptions around the rim and large handle-rings. It took a trip to coppersmiths near the Chorsu bazaar in Tashkent to locate two more, as well as madder root and oak gall – both needed for making red.

The list of items still needed wasn't getting any shorter, and I decided to employ Madrim two months before our training began, to locate industrial thermometers, a magnifying-glass, weights, scales and more. We needed several large earthenware pots for fermentation dyeing, which proved problematic as most potters weren't used to making anything quite so large. The buying of silk, heaters and walnut husks had been left to the workshop in Bukhara, as they were also making their own purchases of these, and we arranged to come down and pick them up.

The trip there, tightly wedged in a crowded van driven as if the road contained no pot-holes, was relatively uneventful. We stopped in a tiny oasis made up of a few trees, a vegetable patch and a small tea-house. This one was home to an aggressive colony of ducks who quacked incongruously in the middle of the desert. They gathered expectantly around our plastic table on the veranda and were soon wolfing down pieces of bread and taking cannibalistic delight at the scraps of fried egg I threw their way.

Further on we drove through the petrol oasis. I wasn't sure of its real name, but at this fork in the road there were some scraggy trees and some cobbled-together dwellings. Young boys in ragged clothes hawked petrol freshly smuggled from Turkmenistan. Petrol-filled Fanta bottles balanced on bricks beside the road – like offerings to the god of urine samples – indicated that petrol was for sale.

The journey to Bukhara always felt long and tiring, and my first thought on arrival was to head for the homom. There was one for men and a separate one for women in another part of Bukhara's old city which I'd seen once from the outside a year earlier when my sisters had visited Uzbekistan. Both were keen for a good scrub, but I had been shooed away near the door, leaving them to fend for themselves. Sheona was self-conscious about entering the homom naked, and had opted for a towel, but this – she told me afterwards – was whisked away by a sturdy matron who ushered her, squealing, into the washing area. Well scrubbed, Helen was first to receive a massage. She described it as a painful series of pinches from a large, middle-aged woman who placed the sole of Helen's foot squarely between her drooping bosoms and began pummelling her legs. Helen watched, dismayed, as the tan she had surreptitiously acquired on my secluded balcony sloughed off.

The men's homom, on the other hand, was familiar territory. We stripped off and opened the heavy wooden door, blasted by thick, humid air. Inside the dimly lit chamber, men sat on stone slabs shaving, steaming or dousing themselves with pans of water. Old bearded men gossiped on the marble slabs, their leathered faces abruptly whitening where their turban tan-line began. Young men scrubbed each other's backs while a flabby middle-aged Bukharan was contorted into some surprising positions on a central slab by a masseuse, the scent of balm hanging heavily in the steamy air. There was a cooler chamber for general chatter, and next to this an antechamber where men shaved their armpits and pubic hair in a timeless alternative to deodorant. Some men were naked, others wore a wrap-around sheet of cotton. There was no fashion, no indicator of what century we might be in, just hot stone slabs, the murmur of conversation, the sound of sluicing water and bowls of spiced tea.

Emerging a few hours later refreshed and invigorated, we made for the Bukhara carpet workshop. I knew the area fairly well and had been told that the Eshani Pir madrassah was past the synagogue in the warren of alleyways that make up the old town. We wandered down an alley between a surprisingly well-stocked Soviet-style grocers and an internet café for tourists, then past the synagogue. Glancing through the large gates, I noticed a few old men sitting around inside. Until a few years ago there had been a thriving Jewish community in Bukhara that had existed there for centuries. Although as non-Muslims they were heavily taxed and forbidden to ride horses, wear belts or marry non-Jews, they had flourished. Now the lure of Tel Aviv and New York proved too great and the only Jews left were the elderly, living comfortably on remittances sent back by children and grandchildren. There were also the *challa* – Jews and their descendants who had converted to Islam and were rejected by the Jewish community yet never truly accepted by the Muslims.

We were welcomed by Fatoulah, the chief dyer of the workshop, a short, plump, wide-hipped man in his late forties with an ingratiating manner. He was keen to make a good first impression, as Barry had decided that our only option in Jim's absence was for two of his Bukharan progeny to come to Khiva and train us. One trainer would be Fatoulah, the other Ulugbeg, a cocky young Tajik with a bulbous nose who was to provide the weaving tuition.

We were given a tour of the workshop and examined some of the photos of miniatures that Jim had provided, intricate carpet designs visible in each picture. Fatoulah had purchased the items on our list and had saved bribe money at the silk factory by ordering for both workshops simultaneously. He'd also found a large brass pestle and mortar which we would need for pounding the dyes. We made arrangements for the training sessions, which would take place over six weeks, and set off back to Khiva.

There were at least three police checkpoints on the desert road, and I'd learnt how to negotiate them. I'd written an official letter on Operation Mercy stationery, explaining our purpose of travel and stamped and signed by my director. If this didn't dissuade a bribe-hungry policeman, then my first course of action was to feign linguistic incompetence.

'Problem,' an officer would declare, pointing at my passport gravely.

'Problem? No problem,' I would reply, smiling innocently. 'Everything good. Thank you, now I going.'

The officer would size me up, weighing the time it would take to inform me of my supposed offence – assuming that I understood the rules of bribery and knew that I should be the one to offer a 'gift' (prevented from leaving until I had done so). This was usually considered too much like hard work. My passport was tossed back through the window and we could continue.

This was a far better course of action than getting lippy – which had once cost me a complete search of all my belongings, emptied onto a table in the roadside booth. I had only avoided a strip-search by abject apology and calls for international friendship and understanding. Policemen wanting to put me in my place would often reprimand me for wearing a seatbelt.

This was a reckless danger for, if we crashed, how would I easily free myself?

Whether it was checkpoints, metro stops or even the bazaar, the important thing when accosted by police was to avoid their booths, where the mitigating influence of a crowd was absent. I'd once been caught urinating beside a rubbish-tip in the Osh bazaar in southern Kyrgyzstan. The police, ignoring the local urinators who always used this spot, considered me a prime opportunity and were keen to take me to their booth and extract as much money as possible.

I protested loudly, expressing my shock that, as a guest, no one had told me where the toilets were, and what were guests in this country supposed to do when they needed to 'rest'? Was this the hospitality I should expect, to resort to urinating in dirty places and then to be fined for it? A crowd formed, and with the nation's hospitality called into question, I was escorted to the public toilets – not much better than the rubbish-tip – and allowed to go.

Back in Khiva, Madrim oversaw the final stages of madrassah restoration while I set about identifying apprentices. I had given a lot of thought to the subject of employment, wanting to get it right. We would make dyeing a job for the men, as it required heavy lifting and we wanted to give men employment as well as women. More challenging was how to create a workshop that ran on ethical principles. I knew that Uzbek businesses survived only by greasing the right palms. So much money was lost in bribes that employees were often not paid on time, if at all. I wanted our workshop to be seen as a school or a charity, and I wanted to find apprentices seen by the community as needy.

I met the official responsible for government pensions and explained that I wanted to identify widows, orphans and disabled people who would be capable of learning carpet-weaving and dyeing. I was given a long list which he then went through, crossing off the names immediately of those he considered incompetent, dishonest or too remote. This whittled it down considerably. There were no phone numbers – most of them didn't have phones – so I would have to track them down.

The first house I visited was home to a girl paralysed from the waist down. She was, apparently, already a carpet-weaver. Her father welcomed me in and we sat down on dirty corpuches as I ate the obligatory mouthful of bread. Bread was sacred: never thrown away, dropped or placed patterned-side down. It was also a symbol of friendship and always broken, never cut, and offered to all guests irrespective of how long they visited for. Even if I called at the door of a neighbour to let them know that someone had called them on our phone, they would appear with a round of bread and expect me to break off a chunk before running to take their call. This particular bread was crawling with flies and far from appetising and the home looked poor and barely held together.

With a brittle smile I explained the purpose of my visit; but instead of enthusiasm, the girl's father seemed unhappy to allow his disabled daughter to work. Who would bring her to and from work? Who would take her to the toilet? Who would be willing to sit in the same room as her?

At this point another daughter, bringing tea, spoke out.

'Father, I could take my sister to work each day. Perhaps there is also work for me. You know that I can weave well.' She looked up, smiled quickly and hurried back to the kitchen.

Her father paused for a moment and then made up his mind.

'Just take my first daughter. She's strong and healthy and it will be good for her to leave the house.'

Her name was Umida, which means hope. It was only months later that I heard her story from one of the other weavers. She'd been married but her father-in-law kept trying to rape her. No one else in her husband's household was willing to help her, so she had run away. As a divorced woman her only chance of remarrying was with another divorcee. Employment at the workshop gave her status and kept accusations of sponging off her family at bay.

Next on my list was a disabled boy called Davlatnaza. He lived in the walled city, not far from the madrassah, in what I'd initially assumed was a shed for animals. The crumbling old house was dingy and dirty. His mother and father were overjoyed that I might consider giving work to their disabled son. After all, he had recently married and should have more to offer his wife than a disability pension. His young wife silently emerged at this point, wearing a headscarf as required of all married women, and served us tea from a cracked old teapot. She was Russian and had just left the orphanage. Men with disabilities were unlikely to find wives, but orphanage girls – assumed not to be virgins – were available for anyone. I asked her if she too would like to join her husband in working for us. She nodded, unable to speak in the presence of her mother-in-law, and scuttled away.

Sanajan was a widow in her late thirties with three children to care for, having lost her husband in a car accident years ago. She was already a weaver and would be happy to join us. Another house visit within the walled city yielded a young deaf boy who signed up for work as a dyer. His sister, Nazokat, was already a weaver and also signed up. In the old neighbourhood beside the Grandfather Gate, I eventually located Toychi. A dilapidated but beautiful iwan with a cracked wooden pillar led to a small hovel. Here, a formidable matriarch clutched me to her bosom at the news that I might give her poor son work; his father had died less than a year ago. Toychi, dark, playful and impudent, simply sat and smirked until chastened by a withering look from his mother.

My list of workers grew. Needing more skilled women, I decided to hunt down some portrait carpet-weavers. There were sisters, I was told, who lived next to the pool outside the Grandfather Gate: they wove portrait-rugs. I could ask anyone, and they would provide me with directions.

I approached a basic little house with music drifting from a room with three looms inside, and was welcomed by a thin, cheerful and slightly cross-eyed girl in her early twenties who grinned and introduced herself as Zamireh. She was very happy that day, she explained, as her mother would be arriving back from Russia. Zamireh ran a small carpet-making business and was responsible for her five sisters and a brother while her mother was away. She hadn't seen her mother in almost a year. As one of the few remaining employment options, trading was becoming increasingly popular. The men – like Zamireh's father – would go to Russia as manual labourers, and the women would trade.

I began an explanation of the workshops but was interrupted by shrieks from outside. Zamireh's mother had obviously returned and Zamireh leapt up and threw herself at her as she entered the main room. Everyone talked at once, the girls recounting family news and neighbourhood gossip, the mother doling out gifts for each daughter. After ten minutes or so I coughed politely and explained that I would come back at a more convenient time. There were protests from Zamireh's mother, particularly when the offer of work was mentioned.

'No, no! Please sit down. Look! Zamireh is a clever girl. She understands business. See! We have three looms, she works hard every day and her sister Shirin is also good. Of course they will work for you! Take them, they are yours.'

Zamireh and Shirin just beamed. I asked Zamireh where she had learnt her skill and she leapt up to take me down the street to her *usta*. This generic term applied to anyone who was a master or expert in something, whether plumbing or wood-carving. Ulugbibi, her usta, wasn't there. Instead I talked with her mother-in-law, who had been weaving for decades and had herself trained Ulugbibi.

The following evening I returned, discovering that Ulugbibi's sister-in-law was also the museum 'wifie' at the Zindon jail. Neither she nor her own sister had married, and they lived at home. Ulugbibi herself was a pretty woman in her early forties. Judging by the way her sisters-in-law looked at her, I sensed that this was not a harmonious household and it came as no surprise when Ulugbibi jumped at the opportunity to work with us and escape the house. She would also have the prestige (and increased pay) of being one of our two weaving ustas.

I'd already found the other usta, trained by Zulhamar, my Uzbek mother.

'She's very docile and hard working!' I was assured. I visited her house, also in the neighbourhood near the Grandfather Gate and typically squalid. A squat, cylindrical mother of two, Safargul wore a black and magenta acrylic cardigan over a neon-green house dress. She didn't say much, but having seen her work – and on Zulhamar's recommendation – I offered her the position of our second weaving usta.

Soon I had four dyers, two weaving ustas and eighteen weavers. Then there was Madrim, who was to be our dye usta and was already operating as assistant director. The last looms were completed and hauled into the madrassah and now we were ready for our first gathering.

We began with a tour, starting with the dyeing room, with its cauldrons and gas rings. At this stage the walls were glowing white, although they would soon be spattered in a rainbow of colours. We moved on to the different weaving cells and the girls who already knew weaving nodded approvingly at the monolithic double loom Zulhamar had purchased for us. I ran through a list of rules, emphasising that stealing would be met with immediate dismissal, there would be no bribe-taking, we would pay wages promptly on the last Friday of each month, and no boys were allowed to loiter here pestering the younger weavers. The weavers listened with downcast eyes, a few suppressing a smile at this last rule. We were not to refer to ourselves as a business or factory, as this would rouse the appetites of bribe-hungry officials. We would be known as the Ghali Maktab, meaning 'carpet school'. Our Bukharan trainers would arrive that evening and we would begin training the following day. Were there any questions?

As I'd expected, it had proved difficult to find the Bukharans accommodation, as they were determined not to waste money in a hotel. Fat Miriam from next door had eventually agreed to take them, as she needed the money. She'd been the second wife of a man who had deserted her when she lost her looks, and was now dependent on a son in Russia from whom she hadn't heard for a while. If the Bukharans didn't mind sharing, she would give them a room, although the window looked out on Khiva's only two camels. They belonged to a fat, jolly man with a melon belly who charged tourists for posing on or beside a camel – and the camels spent each evening at Miriam's house just a short walk away. She fed them and mucked out their stall, selling the wisps of camel wool to local women who twisted them around cardigan buttons to ward off the evil eye.

Our trainers, Ulugbeg and Fatoulah, arrived and were unimpressed with both the camels and the accommodation. Ulugbeg went for an evening walk to check out the local girls and see if they were as beautiful as all the girls in Bukhara. He casually mentioned at this point that he was now engaged. Fatoulah was tired and went to bed, and I returned home to prepare myself mentally for our first day of training. Fatoulah had given me a wad of photos, graph-paper designs, and some articles in English written by Jim that I wanted to look through.

The following day our training began. Ulugbeg preened and flirted with the prettier apprentices as he distributed pieces of graph-paper with simple motifs on them. The weavers' first task was to copy these designs into notebooks. Most of the girls managed well and over the next few days graduated to harder designs. Those who had woven before found it easiest. The purpose of this exercise was to familiarise the apprentices with how carpet patterns work and how to read a design.

I scanned the courtyard where girls sat on corpuches, hunched over their notebooks, scribbling. The boys were busy with Fatoulah and Madrim, weighing out skeins of silk to be dyed. Four of the cells were now crammed with looms, and the storage cells were full of bales of silk and sacks of natural dye ingredients. The whole place buzzed with activity and it felt as if everything was finally coming together as an actual workshop.

There was no time to sit back and relax, though. We needed six beautiful Timurid designs ready before we started weaving. Jim had left some completed designs with the Bukhara workshop but these wouldn't be enough. I had no background in carpet-designing – but then I had no background in starting a carpet workshop, and yet the beginnings of one were forming outside.

It was time for me to explore the world of carpet designs and Timurid miniatures.

4

From calligraphy to carpet

The scene is of a meadow – a rich tapestry of shrubs and flowers with barely room for grass to grow. I recognise dandelions with their jagged leaves and yellow flowers, and what appear to be wild strawberries. My eyes wander to a grey poplar standing tall as it juts out of the picture frame past swirls of Persian poetry in flawless calligraphy. It fills the top right-hand corner of the page with beautifully detailed, individually painted leaves. Behind the tree, a stream snakes across the vellum, flowing from a spring nestled in the base of a rocky outcrop that sweeps above the meadow like an arid wave.

In the foreground, a turbaned black eunuch stands guard over his mistress with a perfume bottle in his hand. Maidservants sit on the grass, having laid out a platter of cool sherbets in tall copper vials. One plays a nai flute, another a tambourine. There is also a lyre player and a musician who claps and sings. Their mistress Shirin is unaware of the music, her mind on other matters. She stares, transfixed, at a portrait found nailed to the tree. The portrait is of a handsome young man, Husrov, and the artist is obviously a master. Out of the picture frame, and unknown to Shirin, the artist Shapur remains hidden in the undergrowth, watching.

It is Shapur who has set the wheels in motion for a tragic romance as familiar today in the East as the story of Romeo and Juliet is in the West. Blessed with the ability to evoke images through both paintbrush and the spoken word, Shapur has intoxicated Husrov with his description of Shirin, a virgin princess. He has never met her, but already the fires of love burn strong in his heart and he commissions Shapur to paint his portrait, capturing the essence of his soul and his love for Shirin.

As Shirin gazes at the portrait of Husrov, she feels a stirring of passion in her bosom. Never has the essence of a man been so cleverly captured. She has fallen in love, not with a man, but with a painting.

∽

And so have I.

I stare transfixed at this magnificent illustration from the medieval Persian poet Nizami's *Khamsa*, painted half a millennium ago (see colour plate 10). Running a magnifying glass slowly over the page, I discover more detail, hidden from the naked eye, marvelling at each individually painted leaf, each fold and crease of the handmaidens' robes. But my eyes rarely stray for long before returning to the carpet that Shirin sits on.

Although part of it is obscured from view, enough can be seen to appreciate its stunning design. The border immediately marks out the rug as being from the time of the Timurid dynasty in 15th-century Persia. Gold interlacing motifs that were once letters of Kufic script, now evolved into stylised motifs, adorn a rich crimson background. The field design (the area within the central rectangle framed by the border) is made up of tessellating hexagonal star-flowers. The balance of colour is masterful and yet it flouts many of the conventions of colour in practice today. Each flower is framed in orange, containing a green centre pierced with a yellow circle, and surrounded by a blue hexagon. These hexagons are entwined in a complicated geometry of white interwoven threads on a vivid red background. They create a pleasing interlaced-knot effect and tessellate in six different directions to join up with other star-flowers.

Sadly, over time, this style of carpet design suffered from the caprice of fashion, as arabesque medallion designs from the later Safavid dynasty eclipsed the more geometrically staid Timurid carpets, leaving no trace of them except in illustrations to poems and epics. But I see these pictures as blueprints, ready to be woven to life once more.

Most of my journey into the world of miniatures took place eight months after the carpet workshop opening, back in England. Ironically, despite the famous Bukhara school of miniature painting, there were far more books on miniatures, as well as actual originals, in Britain. Cambridge University Library was a short bike-ride away from my parents' house, and I holed up there, combing through anything I could find on the subject, quickly realising how little I knew. Even my assumption that the term 'miniature' referred to size was wrong. The name actually comes from a reddish-orange pigment, *minium*, that was popular with Persian and Mogul miniaturists.

For the miniaturists themselves, it must have been a risky business, painting representative art in a culture where all images of living beings were considered idolatrous. Miniaturists were not considered artists in their own right, but an extension of the manuscript workshops that included calligraphers and makers of calf-skin vellum pages. Their work was unsigned and anonymous, although some – determined to leave their mark – would hide a tiny signature somewhere in each illustration. These workshops developed a highly structured process for painting miniatures. Apprentices would spend months repeating the form of a horse, a tree or a prince in love. These standardised images were then assembled together to form an overall picture. The approach to painting was much closer to that of functional crafts, aiming for excellence and detail without the need for expressions of individuality.

The religious stricture on representative art was not simply ignored by the miniaturists, who feared the bouts of fervent iconoclasm they could provoke. Instead, self-imposed restrictions were introduced to appease Islamic conservatives. The centre of a miniature, for example, would never contain a human being, as only Allah could ever occupy this position. Many miniatures portrayed religious events, including scenes from the Bible and the Koran. In one, Potiphar's wife pats a particularly attractive Timurid carpet, attempting to entice Joseph onto it. He flees her seductions, his head – as with all depictions of Prophets – aflame with a fiery halo. In the case of Mohammed, the most venerated of Prophets, his face was always covered with a curtain, as to attempt his likeness would be a terrible wickedness.

Particularly helpful for us was the convention that miniatures should be painted from the perspective of a minaret. This resulted in a curious blend of bird's-eye view and side-on perspective. It meant that carpets would appear on the page as simple rectangles without receding perspective, in exquisite detail, making the perfect colour blueprint.

The prohibition on representative art affected all artisans, whether workers of stone, metal, wood or cloth. Instead, artisans found their expression in arabesque swirls, maze-like interlocking letters and a myriad of geometrical designs. Nor were these designs restricted to one medium. Dazzling calligraphy and intricate arabesques from the frontispieces of Korans and other manuscripts would inspire masons building a new mosque or madrassah to imitate these same embellished arabesques in tile and mosaic work. These buildings would, in turn, end up in painted form as miniaturists copied them into their depictions of courtly or religious life. I noticed that sometimes the same designs that appear in Timurid carpets are found in other miniatures as ceramic wall-tiling.

I wanted to find out more about Timurid carpets. They followed the tradition of most carpets, consisting of a central field design framed with a border. I was learning how to spot their distinctive fields, typically consisting of repeating *guls*, interlaced with banded knots rather than the later medallion design most associated with classical oriental rugs. The main giveaway that a carpet was Timurid was in the border, which consisted of stylised letters, evolved and embellished to appear like Celtic knots in some cases. I preferred Timurid designs to their more floral successors, but what had led to this transition in carpet patterns? Had the freer style of calligraphy led some miniaturists to experiment with new carpet designs in their pictures, which were then copied by the carpet-weavers themselves, or had this transformation occurred first with carpet-weavers and been merely mirrored by the manuscript illustrators of the time? There was no definitive answer or even much scholarly work on the subject, though a footnote in one carpet book mentioned an article on Timurid carpets and I tracked it down at the University Library. Heaving the dusty hardback edition of *Ars Islamica* (1940) onto a table – noticing that it had last been taken out five years previously – I paged through to the essay on Timurid carpets by an American, Amy Briggs.

She refuted the suggestion that Timurid carpets were merely works of a pen and had never actually been woven. If the Timurid tilework, carved wooden doors and buildings – many of which are still standing – had been painted in faithful realism, then why would the carpets have been mere experiments in geometrical calligraphy and not a rendering of the real thing?

There was no actual proof, though. While the tiles, doors and buildings of the 15th century had survived, these carpets hadn't withstood the constant tramping of feet and the scourges of moth and damp. In fact, there was just one known carpet fragment from the Timurid era, now part of the Benaki Museum collection in Greece. Jim had given the Bukhara workshop a photo of the fragment and a graph-paper design that we had improved.

I loved the Benaki fragment's striking interplay of burgundy and gold and was excited at the prospect of reviving it. The ustas had assured me that the absence of a third colour would make it fairly easy to weave. The only drawback was that we weren't sure what its original border had looked like, experimenting instead with a border popular in many Timurid designs.

Amy Briggs made mention of the fragment in her essay, and the unique era in carpet design that flourished during the Timurid period. I wanted to discover more about Amir Timur, its founder.

Timur means 'iron' in Uzbek, and as a barbarous warlord he didn't seem an obvious patron of the arts. Known in the West as 'Timur the Lame' – the result of an arrow wound to his leg – later corrupted to Tamerlane, he was born in 1336 near Samarkand, in the south of modern-day Uzbekistan. I'd been there a number of times and climbed the turret of the crumbling White Palace he'd had commissioned. Despite its dilapidated state, enough mesmerising Timurid tilework remained to keep me entranced for quite some time as I climbed the uneven stairway, causing a major blockage of Uzbek schoolchildren trying to squeeze past me and continue their noisy ascent to the top. Here again were the same interwoven knot patterns so characteristic of Timurid carpets, and bands of tiled Kufic script in relief mimicked the carpet borders.

Like his predecessor Genghis Khan, Timur excelled on the battlefield, with a penchant for mass annihilation. He ruled by terror, so that even the most heavily fortified city would quake at news of his approach. He ordered towers of skulls assembled outside the cities he wished to punish, and – I read, eyes widening – would build towers out of the living bodies of prisoners, cementing them together with clay and brick into weakly writhing structures. Reputed to have killed more people than Stalin and Hitler combined, he seemed an odd choice as national hero of Uzbekistan, particularly as he's famed for saying: 'If you see an Uzbek, kill him.' In fact it was the Uzbeks who eventually drove the Timurid empire into oblivion, although they weren't the same people as the hotchpotch of ethnicities within Stalin-drawn borders referred to as Uzbeks today. Nonetheless, the new Uzbek state, desperate to forge an identity after Soviet rule, decreed Timur to be the embodiment of Glorious, Independent Uzbekistan.

I had been to the Amir Timur Museum in Tashkent – an enjoyable piece of national propaganda linking the glorious reign of Timur with that of President Karimov. My favourite feature of the museum was the impressive domed ceiling. I would point out to guests the quotes from Timur in both Uzbek and English that rimmed it, drawing their attention to one – 'In justice is our strength' – in which the gap between the words 'In' and 'justice' wasn't quite wide enough.

Near the Amir Museum was the Amir Timur metro station, where the police patrols were particularly voracious for bribes.

Beyond the metro was the Amir Timur park and in the centre of it a huge statue of Timur on horseback, replacing a smaller statue of Karl Marx that was taken down after independence. Timur appeared everywhere, and regular low-budget TV costume dramas depicted his strong but fair rule over glorious Uzbekistan.

However, I knew very little about the real Amir Timur and the role he had played in the creation of Timurid miniatures. I discovered that when he wasn't massacring large swathes of his enormous empire, Timur focused his efforts on transforming his capital, Samarkand, into a breathtakingly opulent demonstration of wealth and grandeur. The city was built by slave-artisans, the only survivors of his many conquests, and they brought with them a variety of artistic traditions. Here, in the series of tombs known as the Shah-i-Zindah, are the most exquisite tiles in Central Asia, and again the same *naqsh* or patterns found in Timurid carpets weave their way into the ceramic tiles, which are also 15th-century.

This still didn't explain Timur's interest in miniatures. He was, after all, a man who liked to think big, whether building or butchering. According to legend, he was once approached by the master calligrapher Umar Al-Aqta, who had devised a minute 'dust' script that allowed the entire Koran to be written on a book the size of a signet ring. Timur was unimpressed. The calligrapher, keen to impress the Amir, realised that it was all about size. He returned some time later with a cart groaning under the weight of a huge Koran, the like of which had never been seen before. Now he was talking the tyrant's language and was promptly welcomed into the court and lavished with favour.

What made Timur a champion of miniatures was his desire to leave a narrative mark and a written history of his mighty conquests. During his lifetime he had fostered an enormous personality cult. Still, the largest mosques and palaces and towers of skulls wouldn't ensure a legacy unless it was written down. He recognised the lasting importance of the written word and poured resources into his royal *kitabtkhana*, literally 'book room', ensuring that the finest vellum-makers, leather-workers, book-binders, scribes, calligraphers and miniature-painters were put in his employ. Manuscript workshops became an integral part of Timurid expansion, and after Amir Timur's death his sons continued this tradition. Most notable was the kitabtkhana run by his son Shah Rukh in Herat, where many of the miniatures we were now using had been painted.

As I familiarised myself with the history of miniatures, I realised that books were no match for the original miniatures themselves. Many of the books were unable to capture the sheen of gold-leaf and failed to display the detail of the originals. I discovered that two simple but elegant miniatures came from the same manuscript and were now in the Royal Asiatic Society in London, so I decided to visit their library. Unsure about protocol, I arrived without a letter of introduction, armed simply with a workshop photo album. I was obviously too clueless to be a manuscript thief and, after enthusiastically showing my photos to the librarian, was offered a seat while their Timurid manuscripts were sent down.

Surrounded by heavy oak bookcases, with the patter of rain against the window, I prised the first manuscript open, worried that it might crumble or fragment in some way. Instead the sheets of vellum, half a millennium old, were as supple and smooth as when the book was bound. I was disappointed at the absence of a frontispiece – then realised that I had opened the book at the end and not at the beginning. Flicking through, I found a miniature with a carpet design I recognised. The scene was a courtly one and, with no English inscription next to it, I could only guess which particular Shah or Sultan was sitting on the throne and who the other men standing before him might be. As for the carpet they stood on, it had a beautiful golden field with a simple overlapping octagonal design that tessellated across it in red. Was I the first person in 500 years to open this page with the intention of bringing the carpet within it back to life? Back in Khiva, this design proved popular, and our first carpet sold while still on the loom to an Australian oil magnate working in Kazakhstan.

Poring over the other manuscripts, I discovered another design, elegantly simple with a tracing of gold octagonal fili-gree on a largely green background. This surprised me, green being a holy colour in Islam and not often used in carpets to be trampled underfoot. I had my own theory as to why green was less often used in carpets. Despite the dominance of green in the plant world, no plants or vegetable dyes yield more than a murky olive. Instead, skeins of silk are double-dyed – first yellow and then blue. Colour consistency is much harder to achieve, making green less favourable to work with.

Staring at the original miniatures, I was amazed again at just how minute the detail was. Most of them were scarcely larger than the average paperback, and brushes as fine as one or two hairs were often employed. It was no wonder that miniatur-ists often went blind, although many of them continued their careers, their practised hands remembering the form of each image. I left the Royal Asiatic Society with photos and drawings of each carpet design, eager to see them transformed once more into tangible warp and weft.

My next stop in London was the home of an Oxford professor of carpet history. Arriving at Jon Thompson's house I was greeted by the stereotypical professor, resplendent with luxuriant moustaches and half-moon spectacles. I had barely stepped through the doorway before we were both down on our hands and knees, examining and discussing the rug in his hallway. It was woven as part of the Dobag project, reviving natural dyeing in western Turkey. Jon told me about his involvement with the German chemistry teacher Harald Boehmer, founder of the Dobag project. Boehmer, intrigued by natural dyes, wondered what it was about them that appealed to him so much more than the same shades in chemical colours. With chemical analysis he discovered that the harmony of natural dyes is partly due to the presence, for example, of madder red, which also contains elements of blue and yellow that the conscious eye doesn't see.

We entered Jon's study, where I could happily have camped for a week, working my way around his impressive collection of carpet books. Finally I had found someone who might answer my questions.

'So, Jon, this Celtic-looking knot pattern that appears on so many Timurid carpet borders – where did it come from? Did the Celts somehow end up in Central Asia? I know the Vikings travelled far further east than anyone used to think. Or did manuscripts somehow end up in Celtic monasteries? Or maybe ...'

I was instantly admonished by Jon. 'Now Christopher, if you wish to study carpets, one fundamental lesson you must learn is not to make assumptions about design similarity and design causality. That said, the world of Timurid carpets is a fascinating one and little explored. I expect you know about Amy Briggs. There's really been so little scholarship since then, and yet Timurid carpets have been the foundation and starting-point for a wide variety of carpet types.'

We continued our discussion as I showed Jon my album of photos of carpets we had already produced.

'Ah, now this one here is interesting. You didn't tell me you'd produced a Lotto. You have done well with that deep red. Extra oak galls in the madder bath, or forays into cochineal?' he asked. I didn't think we would find cochineal beetles in Central Asia, or the particular cacti they fed on, so our attempts at red had been limited to powdered madder root and oak gall.

'Yes, I'm glad you've made this connection, Christopher,' he continued. 'This really is an example of carpet causality. You know, I assume, that the carpet type is named after the Renaissance painter Lotto, who often included such carpets in his paintings. Look at the border and you can see how it still mimics Kufic script much more closely than some of the classical Timurid carpets do. Of course, we can only speculate, but it seems likely that, just as the Timurid empire sucked in artisans from a vast area, so they later dispersed, taking with them Timurid carpet themes. This Lotto rug was probably woven by a weaver influenced by Timurid carpets, and maybe even trained in a Timurid workshop. The weaver was from Anatolia and the rug must have found its way from eastern Turkey through the bazaars and eventually to Florence.'

These discoveries in England all lay in the future, and weren't of much help as we prepared our first carpet designs. Ulugbeg the Bukharan had assured Barry of his proficiency as a designer, but it quickly became apparent that he had no real aptitude and he excused himself, eager to return to his admiring circle of apprentices. Both Safargul and Ulugbibi, the two weaving ustas, were busy with the looms, so I decided to try my hand at designing.

I began unwisely with a particularly difficult hexagonal design that tessellated in six different directions. Jim had given us his version of the design, but the hexagons were stretched and the design didn't look much like the original. Rueing my geometrical incompetence and aggressively rubbing out another failed attempt, I noticed Rosa peering over my shoulder. A serious half-Russian fresh from school, she had no experience in carpet-weaving and I was surprised to see her interest. She'd finished copying the designs Ulugbeg had given the apprentices, so I handed her a ruler and protractor, dredged up some hazily recollected principles of trigonometry and let her get on with it.

Zamireh, a portrait-weaver herself, came to watch Rosa at work and pointed out a few inaccuracies. Soon she was working on the interlocking stylised letters that would frame the central field. A day or so later, with a few minor changes, the design was complete. We called it, rather lamely, 'Alti Buchek', which means hexagon.

At that stage our collection of miniatures left by Jim was small. There was one with a tantalisingly beautiful carpet border that we couldn't use – Husrov lay on top of it, blood spurting from his neck as an assassin plunged a dagger through it, the field pattern totally obliterated. In another miniature Rustam, the hero of Persian mythology, reclined on a rug, obscuring most of it but leaving just enough of the repeating field design for us to copy.

Soon we had our completed hexagonal pattern, the design called 'Rustam', and a design based on the Benaki fragment. Zamireh had begun work on a design which we simply called 'Shirin'. She'd already requested that this be the rug she wove with her sister Shirin and her deaf friend Iroda. The design was reminiscent of medieval European wallpaper: a series of henna-coloured, leafy crosses interlaced with golden scroll on a rich green background. It came from a miniature entitled 'Shirin awaits news of Husrov'. I made a few changes to another design Jim had left us, which we called 'Mehmon', meaning guest, as there were a few unidentified men kneeling around the carpet in the miniature and we couldn't think of a better name.

The apprentices had finished copying out carpet designs and were now ready to begin weaving. Safargul and Ulugbibi had divided the girls into threes, with at least one experienced weaver for each loom. The looms themselves varied in size and shape, as some were wooden and some metal. However, the basic principle was the same. Each had smoothed wooden crossbeams or rotating metal bars at the top and bottom of a frame that could be tightened or loosened to control the tension of the warp threads (the vertical threads that form the backbone of a carpet).

Safargul was warping one of the looms, passing a ball of thick silk thread around the top and bottom beams and plucking at the threads like a harpist to test their tension. Each rotation of the warp thread was counted out; and each crossing of vertical warp and horizontal weft was represented as a square on the graph paper that our designs were drawn on. These 'cartouches' were propped on the crossbeam of every loom for the weavers to read, like a map.

The boys had begun experimentation with different dyes and our new drying-rack was covered in a spattered rainbow of different colours. The fermentation vats in the cell next to the dyers' room were filled with tepid water, jam, apple cores, uncooked dough and raisins, and already emitted a reassuringly evil smell. Fatoulah the Bukharan promised us that vivid reds and blues would result.

Safargul hung some of the dyed skeins of silk on our warped loom, and we were now ready to begin our first carpet. The girls gathered round and watched Ulugbibi and Safargul as they sat at the low weaving bench, intoned 'Bismallah' (in the name of God), and then began weaving a thinner continual strand of silk between the tense warp threads. This horizontal thread was the weft, and between weft threads woven through warp threads would be the rows of knots. Once the first row of weft was completed, the women yanked down on the hed-dle – a horizontal wooden pole that separated the warp threads into odd and even on either side of it. When the heddle was brought down, it moved the position of the even and odd warp threads, allowing the weft to be passed through again, and then thumped firmly against the first weft thread with a heavy wooden carpet comb.

So far, the two centimetres of carpet looked like roughly woven cloth and were not very impressive. However, once this first chunk of kilim fringe was woven, Ulugbeg stepped in and showed the experienced weavers how to tease out strands of dyed silk, twisting them into rough threads, and then hooking them between the warp threads with a hook-knife, lopping off the knot close to its base to avoid wastage. As he began the first knot of our first carpet, the weavers threw handfuls of sweets over him with the wish that our work would go sweetly. Our experienced weavers were transfixed: this process was familiar and yet new to them, as their own curved carpet-knives had no hook, and this was a new double knot, rather than their familiar half-knot.

Zamireh watched deep in thought as Ulugbeg slowly knotted each twist of silk so the girls could see the process.

'Wouldn't it be easier to make the knots like this?' she asked, her fingers flying as she rapidly hooked a knot and began another one.

'How did you do that?' Ulugbeg asked incredulously.

'I was just watching you, and it seemed to make more sense to bring the silk around, like this, and then hook it behind the warp threads,' she explained.

It was clear to all that her way of making the same knot was far more efficient. Continuing the row, Zamireh, the apprentice, began teaching Ulugbeg, the supposed Bukharan master. I felt a flush of pride at our talented bunch of weavers.

Fatima, Sharafat and Nargisa began work on this first rug, counting off the squares of colour on the graph paper. Fatima – as any Khivan would know from her name – was a twin, and later her sister Aisha also came to work with us. Fatima lived just around the corner in a crumbling mud-brick house with a beautiful iwan. A skinny, stooped woman in her late thirties, she had an acerbic personality and a passion for gossip. Sitting at her loom became punishment for lax apprentices who needed some discipline.

Next to her was Sharafat, a friendly and starkly unattractive woman of considerable size. She had crippled her right leg as a child, and had stayed at home (a tiny, run-down hovel) receiving a meagre disability pension from the government. Staring at her huge, meat-cleaving hands with sausage-like fingers, I was unsure how well she'd weave, but the hook-knife helped enormously. Fatima seemed pleased with her progress and was surprisingly patient. Sharafat later developed a reputation as a bit of a drinker at workshop celebrations. Plied with bowls of vodka, she'd be first on her feet, uninhibited by her crippled foot. Moving her bulk with surprising grace and dexterity, she'd make eyes at the dyers and shimmy her shoulders for them, causing hoots of laughter from the weavers as the dyers paled or reddened.

Sitting on Fatima's other side was a girl called Nazokat who had just finished school and whose father had died, forcing her to find work fast. She generally worked well, but had a fiery temper that led to regular spats with Hoshnaut, one of the dyers.

I watched the three girls at work, twisting wisps of indigo silk and then knotting it around the warp threads and cutting it, feeding through weft threads after each alternate row. These were banged into place with the heavy comb-beater and then trimmed with special silk shears that I was unable to master.

Surrounded by all this silk, I decided it was time to find out more about this fibre that had changed the course of history.

5

Worms that changed the world

*A good deal of silk is manufactured in Khiva. The whole oasis is
planted with white mulberry trees and in every house we found
two or three rooms full of the busy little spinners feeding off the
leaves … The whole work of spinning, dyeing and weaving is often
done in one family by one or two persons … Going along one or
two streets in Khiva you will find the walls covered in yarn silk,
hung out by the dyers to dry, and if you do not look sharp, you
will find your clothes bespattered with red and purple, from the
dripping masses over your head.*

—J.A. MacGahan, *Campaigning on the Oxus, and the
Fall of Khiva,* 1874

Once more, skeins of silk dripping rainbow colours hung on
racks or were flung against the madrassah wall, where they
would catch and stick until fished down with a pole by one of
the dyers. We had reintroduced the art of natural dyeing – once
the preserve of Bukharan Jews – and felt proud of our first
efforts. Not all the traditional cottage industries had disappeared during the Soviet era. The art of sericulture – the raising
of silkworms – had been left largely intact and was more prolific
than ever. Each spring, entire villages gathered around the mulberry trees that lined every roadside, hacking down branches of
fresh leaves to feed to their worms.

Not all mulberry trees had edible leaves. Some were allowed
to develop sticky white fruit, collected in large sheets positioned
under each tree. My favourite mulberries were the dark *shor
toot*, or sour mulberries. Sold in the bazaar by the cupful and

swimming in their own juices, they were deliciously tart. Their juice stained badly, and later we experimented with it as a dye. It produced a beautiful, vivid purple that quickly faded in sunlight to a drab grey.

Mulberry trees used for feeding silkworms were easily distinguishable by their shape – a thick, sturdy trunk which grew to chest height before fanning out into smaller, spindly branches that were cut back each year. Driving past them in winter they looked like rows of severed hands, fingers splayed.

Tropical countries like India could grow worms all the year round, but in Uzbekistan they were reared only in spring, feeding on fresh new mulberry leaves. I wanted to produce an album of pictures documenting sericulture in Khorezm, hoping it might inspire tourists and other potential carpet clients to buy one of our rugs. Zulhamar's brother-in-law lived out in Yangi-ariiq village and was responsible for incubating and hatching silkworms for their collective farm. One evening, over supper, I asked my host family if we could perhaps visit him. The response was enthusiastic and the next day we piled into Koranbeg's red Lada for a family outing.

We found Nuraddin under a large apricot tree in his garden and he leapt to his feet, hand on heart, to greet us and offer green tea. Having worked through the essential preliminary enquiries after health, family, work and livestock, Zulhamar disappeared inside with her sister to catch up on the latest village gossip, and Koranbeg explained the purpose of our visit. We were in no hurry and would be expected to eat an early lunch before anything more taxing.

I excused myself and wandered down to the bottom of the garden, where a small mud-brick shed with a sack-cloth covering the entrance marked the toilet. Inside, next to the hole, was a rusting bucket full of hard pieces of clay. These lumps of clay were a common substitute for toilet paper in most villages, except during the cotton season, when clumps of raw cotton were used. I'd never quite worked out the mechanics of wiping with a rock, and was content to use old newspapers or the grey crepe toilet paper available in the bazaar.

One of my foreign friends had been berated in a village as she removed some toilet paper from her bag, about to head down the garden. 'Don't you know that the Holy Koran was written on paper?' they demanded. 'How can you possibly use paper for such unholy purposes?' Thinking quickly, she replied: 'Yes, but our Holy Ten Commandments were written on stone so I couldn't possibly use lumps of clay either,' and continued down the garden path.

After lunch, Nuraddin took me inside to see his silkworm incubator. A bed, covered in a mosquito net, writhed with tiny worms that had just hatched. These were the caterpillars of the domesticated silkmoth, *Bombyx mori*.

'Each year we allow a few of the worms to spin their cocoons and grow into moths, mate and lay eggs. These are eggs I've kept in the fridge since last year, and warmed them up to hatch them,' he whispered. 'We need to be quiet because the worms are very sensitive during this first week of life.'

'Sensitive to what?' I whispered back.

'To many things,' he replied. 'Loud noises and music, perfume, menstruating women. Also the temperature must be just right, not too hot and not too cold, with no draughts, and it must be humid.' He pointed to the plant-sprayer on top of the fridge.

I looked down at the tiny little silkworms. 'They're so small!'

'Not for long!' he explained, as we tiptoed out. 'At this stage they can eat only the very new leaves and these must be finely chopped for them. It is not too much work yet, but soon they will grow and so will their appetites. When they are around ten days old, I distribute them to the village. Come, our neighbour has begun the process.'

We walked down the street, Nuraddin enjoying the kudos of whispered speculation that I produced, and were ushered inside a house by a toothless old woman who tried a few words of Russian on me.

'Grandmother, he doesn't speak Russian, he's from England,' explained Koranbeg. 'You can speak to him in Uzbek. He even understands our dialect!'

She looked unconvinced and led us into the guestroom. Instead of corpuches and carpets, trestle-tables were set up, on top of which were fresh mulberry branches. Dotted all over the leaves were slightly larger silkworms.

'We keep them indoors to protect them from birds and also, in spring, who knows? – maybe today it will be hot or maybe tomorrow it will be cold,' explained a daughter-in-law, summoned to act as hostess.

The room felt humid and had a mingled scent of bird-droppings and freshly cut lawns. The worms slowly and methodically ate away the sides of each leaf.

'Now, the work is easy,' we were told. 'But in a week's time the worms will get bigger and want feeding all the time. They won't eat dried leaves so we must give them fresh leaves five times a day. We're up and in the fields before six in the morning and give them their last new branches at eleven at night. All they do is eat and sleep and all we do is work. I don't even have time for the Kino.'

I smiled at this last reference to the nine o'clock showing of the wildly popular Mexican or Brazilian serialised telenovela, known generically among most Uzbeks as 'the Kino'. If a village woman didn't have time for the Kino then she really was overworked.

I asked her how much they were paid for all this work and she looked enquiringly at Nuraddin. He nodded back: 'You can speak openly with him.'

'Well,' she began, 'during the Soviet times, of course it was much better. Then the collective farm leaders weren't allowed to keep everything for themselves. Now though, many of us don't want to grow the worms. It's such hard work and sometimes we don't get paid. I told Nuraddin that we wouldn't do worms this year, but so did lots of others and soon the collective farm directors were down here making a noise, so we had to do it. *Boshka iloyja yoke* – there is no other way.'

The state had a monopoly on silk and no one was allowed to sell privately. Although it was possible to sell silk surreptitiously on the black market, this was risky and incurred large fines. Nuraddin explained how many cocoons per gram of worms had to be returned by the villagers to the collective farm. For the two months of solid work it would take each extended family to grow the worms, they were meant to receive around $80 or goods in kind, such as flour or oil. Instead, the collective farm bosses would often not make any payments or, if they gave goods in kind, would give far less than had been agreed.

'Last year, do you know what we got for all our efforts?' asked the grandmother angrily. 'A couple of crates of vodka. Do I want my sons to turn into drunkards? We tried to sell them but everyone got vodka that year so no one wanted to buy.'

Nor were these two months of forced labour all that was required of the villagers. They joined the urban population each autumn out in the fields, harvesting cotton. Doctors, nurses, government workers, schoolteachers and their children spent two months of the year cotton-picking. I remember talking with a bitter surgeon who showed me his calloused hands at the end of harvest. 'How am I supposed to operate when my hands look like a peasant's?' he asked.

There had been a big drama in our house when Malika, Koranbeg's daughter, had joined her classmates in the cotton fields. Zulhamar was concerned for her daughter's health in the primitive conditions, and Koranbeg for her honour. Schoolchildren often enjoyed the adventure of being away from their parents, and for some of the girls the work was no greater than the burden of household chores that fell on them at home. Surrounded by classmates, including boys, there were opportunities to flirt and joke away from watchful eyes, with even the occasional *diskoteka* in the evenings. Many a scandal had erupted over illicit liaisons in the cotton fields at night.

Malika and her classmates had arrived at a distant village school which was to be their accommodation, camping in classrooms and cooking in the playground. Early in the morning, the whole class would head for the fields and work there all day. They were supposed to be paid, but the amount was so low that once charges for food (however unpalatable) and accommodation (however basic) had been deducted, many students ended up owing money for the privilege of two months' forced labour. This had been the case with Malika.

Only a doctor's certificate provided exemption, and obtaining one required a large bribe. There was one case I heard of where a disabled girl with no hands had been sent to the fields because her parents had refused to pay a bribe for the doctor's certificate.

Koranbeg had fretted while Malika was away in the fields and eventually decided to drive out and check up on her. I joined him. She was fine, but grateful for the piles of food that Zulhamar had baked. We were given a tour of their fields and I tried tugging a fluffy cotton lump from its stem. Malika's classmates taught me some of the tricks of the trade. It was important to pick as much as possible before seven in the morning while the cotton was still damp with dew. If this was then covered over, the damp cotton would weigh more, making it easier to meet the daily quota. Peeing on it helped for the same reason.

A week later, I returned to Nuraddin's village with Koranbeg to see how the silkworms were progressing. We knew their appetites had greatly increased before we even arrived. The roadside mulberry branches were cut and stacked on donkey carts, brightly coloured village women heaving huge bales of branches on their backs. Nuraddin took us back to the same house and we could hardly squeeze in past the front door. The entire hallway was filled with trestles heaped with mulberry branches over which a sea of thick, white silkworms slowly churned. They had doubled in size and the sound of their munching reminded me of Rice Krispies floating in milk. I tried to pick up a worm but it reared up at me before attacking a leaf. A couple of lethargic worms had fallen from the tables. They moved sluggishly on my hand until I placed them back on the branches, at which point they began decimating leaves at a frantic pace.

'So, now you know why it's such a lot of work for us,' Nuraddin said.

I had read that during their six weeks as caterpillars, they would grow from two millimetres to twelve centimetres in length and become 10,000 times heavier in the process.

'What happened to the worms that you had before in that room over there?' I asked.

'These are the ones,' replied the old granny, who was watching my face with amusement as I surveyed her worm empire. 'They have filled up all the space in that room and in here, and next week we will have to keep them in the stable as well.'

Sure enough, the following week the worms were overflowing even the stable, like a domesticated plague of Egypt. Nuraddin pointed out the different markings for male and female and the spinneret behind each head. Everyone in the village looked worn out, especially as all the nearby mulberry trees had been denuded and they were having to travel further afield to collect branches.

Uzbekistan, the third-largest producer of silk after India and China, often made claims to be 'The Heart of the Silk Road' in tourist brochures. Watching the activity before me, this title seemed well-deserved. Alongside my village visits I was researching more about the Silk Road and the network of routes between China and the West that had given rise to the name.

The secret of silk – according to tradition – was discovered accidentally by the Yellow Empress of China around 4,500 years ago. She was reputedly enjoying a bowl of green tea in her garden when a cocoon plopped into her cup from the overhanging mulberry tree. She tried to fish it out and it began to unravel – changing the fortune of her empire in the process. Not only did silk provide a warm, comfortable fibre for making into cloth, it also possessed a unique luminescence and lustre that made it the queen of fabrics.

The secret of silk's origin was known only in China, and the Chinese little imagined that it would eventually be traded with the far-flung empires of Greece, Persia and Rome. In fact, no one in China was sure that these empires even existed. China was hemmed in by a barbaric tribe they called Shiongu (possibly the Huns) who barred all exploration westwards. It was only a century before Christ, after enduring one raid too many, that the Han Emperor went on the offensive.

Aware that his army was no match for the guerrilla warfare of the horseriding barbarians, the Emperor desired more information about potential Western allies. In 138 BC, General Chang Chien was dispatched with over 100 men to seek out kingdoms beyond the barbarians – should rumours of their existence prove founded – and enlist these Western allies in a fight against the Shiongu.

His quest took him through hostile barbarian territory, and he was captured twice by the barbarians, spending eleven years in slavery. Eventually Chang Chien managed to escape with a few of his men and, undeterred, continued westwards. He made contact with the kingdom of Bactria, and arrived eventually at the capital of Khorezm, the largest kingdom of Middle Asia. The Khorezm Shah demurred at the suggestion of a unified battle. He had no intention of unleashing the fury of the barbarians upon his own empire.

Actually, the Shah and his courts were far more interested in General Chang Chien's wardrobe than in any plans for battle. They had never seen such dazzling material, shimmering with a bewitching iridescent sheen. Chang Chien made a mental note that silk was an unknown and highly tradeable commodity. Having, presumably, sold his clothes to finance the journey home, Chang Chien returned to China via the fertile valley of Fergana. Here he made a second important find. Not only did the people of the West eagerly covet silk, they also possessed horses vastly superior, not only to the feeble horses of China, but also to the warhorses of the barbarians. These heavenly horses were said to sweat blood and run like the wind. His discovery of fine horses and a market for silk would prove more useful than any potential allies.

Arriving home after thirteen years of adventures and with just a handful of his original entourage, Chang Chien was given a hero's welcome by the Emperor, who had given him up for dead. The Emperor obtained Fergana horses to build up his cavalry and the first trading parties were sent out, laden with bales of carefully wrapped silk. Their Middle Asian clients were mystified at the origin of silk and what 'heavenly vegetable' might have produced such a fabric. The Chinese, quite sensibly, refused to share their secret with anyone. Silk eventually made its way to Rome, where it scandalised society. Wealthy noblewomen wore silken 'glass' togas that left nothing to the imagination. Unsurprisingly, demand went through the roof and soon silk was worth more than its weight in gold.

Caravans of a thousand camels braved their way across Middle Asia. It could take as little as 200 days to traverse the entire route, but most traders chose instead to ply just one leg of the numerous routes available. As a result, caravanserais sprang up in the many desert oases, offering both accommodation and the opportunity for goods to change hands. Before long, these caravan stops had mushroomed into fully-fledged cities.

Silk was by no means the only merchandise to make its way from China along the Silk Road. Porcelain, paper, gunpowder, mulberries, rhubarb and spices were just a few of the products taken westwards, with horses, coral, ivory, glass, asbestos, onions, peas, cucumbers and even ostriches returning via the Silk Road to the Celestial Empire.

As merchandise changed hands across the caravanserais of Central Asia, so new religions, philosophies and inventions passed to and fro. Buddhism, on the decline in India, was brought eastwards and continues to dominate many Eastern countries to this day. Nestorian Christianity – a persecuted heresy in the West, led by Bishop Nestor who fell out of favour for opposing icons – found fertile soil in Central Asia, and soon cathedrals dotted the Silk Road, including the Cathedral of St George, built where the Registan stands today in Samarkand.

Eventually the secret of sericulture escaped the Jade Gates, travelling westwards along the Silk Road, hidden in the elaborate hairstyle of a Chinese princess. Marrying a barbarian she was prepared to do, but living without silk was an impossible deprivation. Later, a single cocoon was smuggled to the West in the hollowed-out staff of a Nestorian monk and silk production was established in southern Europe and the Mediterranean. China still produced vast quantities of silk, but alternative sea routes meant that the long, arduous overland journey was no longer necessary and the Silk Road declined in importance. Today, few could name the countries found en route, except that most of them end in –*stan*.

By the 20th century there were few places where silk was still worth its weight in gold, but Khiva was one of them – the Khorezm oasis hadn't ended its love affair with silk, and wove it into money. Until 1924 the Khanate of Khiva was the only country outside China to use silk money, each note hand-woven and then printed in the mint located in the Kunya Ark. When the money got dirty, it was quite literally laundered. After 1924 the short-lived Khorezm Socialist Republic was absorbed into the USSR and silk money was no longer legal tender. Instead it became fashionable, stitched together to make robes or patchwork quilts. They made popular wedding gifts as a wish for new couples to be prosperous together.

And all this started with voracious little monsters like those happily munching on their mulberry leaves before me. I picked up a leaf with a worm hanging upside down from it, determined to let nothing interrupt its guzzling. The life-cycle of these worms was also a silk road of sorts, and they were nearing the end of theirs.

'It feels really good to be …' I paused, trying to find the right expression, '… here in the middle of it all,' I said, still pondering the impact of the Silk Road.

'Yes, you can be,' replied Nuraddin, misunderstanding me and pointing to a hole in the middle of the seething mass of worms and branches. The hole had been strategically placed to allow access to the worms in the middle of the trestles and ensure an even spread of fresh branches. Realising that I was expected to emerge from the hole, I crawled through worm droppings, getting my hair caught in the mulberry branches above and feeling the odd worm bounce softly down my neck, before standing up and brushing myself off. I was surrounded by the undulating ripples of thousands and thousands of worms.

The following week Nuraddin called to say that there was no need to come. 'The worms are bigger than the last time, but otherwise the only change is that they've stopped eating. They'll be like this for another four or five days.'

'Oh,' I replied, trying to imagine what a silkworm would do with its time when no longer doubling its bodyweight as fast as possible. 'Aren't they hungry any more?'

'No, they will never eat again. Now they must prepare themselves for spinning their cocoons. We're happy, we can have a rest. Come next week and it will be very interesting. You can watch them spinning.'

This worked well with my own schedule, as our official opening loomed. I was keen to use the occasion as a signal to any greedy officials eyeing the workshop that we had powerful friends in Tashkent and the blessing of the Mayor in Khiva.

Fatoulah the Bukharan was adamant that we should buy a sheep and slaughter it in the courtyard. The blood-letting would protect our workshop from the evil eye, and the meat could then be eaten at the official opening. I was equally adamant that there would be no sheep coming anywhere near the workshop. Fatoulah, exasperated by my ignorance of the evil eye and its dangers, was willing to compromise with a cockerel, which I also refused to include in the budget. It was only when I gave him the opportunity to buy a cockerel with his own wages, if blood-letting was so important, that he desisted.

Barry, the Mayor and an entourage of local journalists, officials and hangers-on arrived on the day of the opening and the ribbon was cut. We gave everyone a tour, with just a few centimetres of woven carpet to show off, and finished with speeches.

Keen to make our opening something that the apprentices would also enjoy, I'd invited my friend Rustam, the pastor in Urgench and also one of the best *surnai* players in the oasis. He lifted his oboe-like instrument and began a long, wailing note distinctive of the *lazgi* dance. Every wedding, circumcision or cradle party ends with this dance, and as the music began the effects were immediate. The weavers, silent and demure up to this point, began to smile flirtatiously at each other, swaying their shoulders and shimmying suggestively. They were all wearing their shiniest and most glittery dresses for the occasion and even the dyers looked smart.

Rustam had once explained to me that the lazgi dance was the song of creation. God had commanded the angel Gabriel to play the surnai, and out of the music God had created Adam and Eve. This story was reflected in the dance, as man and woman were brought to life through the music. Catriona and Seitske – a Dutch nurse – had abandoned their health education programme to join us for the day, and dragged the weavers into the centre of the courtyard to dance. Each girl lifted one hand, letting the wrist hang limp, and swayed her body like a weeping willow as the surnai continued its long, haunting melody. They froze as the music stopped and then abruptly shifted to staccato rhythms, the hand-held drum joining in.

The music increased in speed and volume and soon Rustam was sweating. His instrument was the hardest to master and, like the oboe, required circular breathing. Toychi the dyer, an excellent dancer, joined the fray and I suddenly found myself dragged by him into the middle. Unlike the women's swaying motion, the men danced in a series of jerks with lots of snapping of the fingers and exaggerated facial expressions. The music increased in pace and inhibitions were cast aside as Andrea was dragged in by one of the weavers. Even Madrim – not without protest – joined us. The music stopped, followed by polite applause from the Mayor's entourage who had considered it undignified to join in. Sweaty and dishevelled, we made our way to a neighbouring hotel where a banquet of plov had been prepared.

The Mayor presented Barry with a gold-embroidered robe of honour – insisting on personally tying the belt on. I wondered how many of these robes Barry had accumulated over the years at similar functions. I was presented with a humbler, stripey robe and a black *dupe*, a skull-cap embroidered with four white chilli-pepper motifs to ward off the evil eye. My robe fastened, I was given a crushing Mayor-hug. Now that I looked like a proper Uzbek, the Mayor said, it was time to find me a proper Uzbek wife, and he began pointing out different weavers and their womanly attributes. I also received a fantastically vulgar brown vase with brown roses all over it and snake handles. This was not the first and, sadly, not the last of these vases given to me: we reserved a shelf in the Operation Mercy office for our collection as no one wanted to keep them in their homes, which probably only encouraged the giving of more.

After lunch, the Mayor departed and Barry returned to his hotel for a rest. The weavers and Operation Mercy girls, however, were in high spirits and returned to the workshop where dancing resumed to a mixture of Uzbek, Turkish, Arabic and Russian pop and even, at one point, the Macarena.

The following week, I set off with Koranbeg and Madrim for one final visit to the worms. We drove past row upon row of bald mulberry stumps and saw a couple of lorries full of spindly, dry bushes that grew in the desert.

'What are they for? Firewood?' I asked Koranbeg.

'You'll see,' he replied, smiling conspiratorially .

Nuraddin met us with bad news. 'You missed the worms weaving; they started a bit earlier than we expected and finished yesterday. But don't worry, we'll look at the cocoons and then visit another of the villagers whose worms hatched a bit later. They should be spinning today.'

Inside, the first thing I noticed was the quiet absence of munching. Where previously there had been a seething blanket of leaves and worms, there was now a winter landscape of fine silver branches laden with snowy white gossamer silk threads. Now I understood the purpose of the desert bushes, which made excellent spinning sites. Embedded among the threads were hundreds of white cocoons. Nuraddin picked one up and rattled it in my ear.

'Can you hear the pupa inside? Now it's getting ready to become a moth. Here, take it. A souvenir.'

It was an incredible sight, the stillness belying the transformation taking place inside each cocoon. I watched as an old woman sat ripping the cocoons from the strands that anchored them in place, removing any snagged twigs before popping them into a cotton sack that she held between her knees.

'Granny, I think you deserve a well-earned rest after the last months of labour,' I said. 'Are you looking forward to getting your house back?'

'Let's just hope we actually get paid this time,' she replied grimly.

After taking some photos, we moved on to another house up the road where thousands of worms were at work. There was still the snowy effect of silver bushes covered in silky gossamer threads, but this room was a hive of activity.

'Look at this worm here,' said Nuraddin. 'You can see it is looking for a good place to begin weaving, a place where there are lots of twigs around and no other worms too close. This one here has started. First it makes these general sweeping motions with its spinneret to create a carpet of threads around it. Then it starts to weave its cocoon; see that one there, the cocoon has already taken shape, but you can still see it inside going around and around.'

We watched, transfixed by the industry around us, concentrating on the efforts of one worm, then getting distracted by the progress of its neighbours. The silk was liquid in secretion and then hardened in the air, coated with sericin, a gum that enabled the cocoon to stick together.

'An interesting thing about the cocoons is that the shape varies depending on the weather,' Nuraddin explained. 'If it's been a cold spring then the cocoons are longer and thinner, and if it's been a hot spring then they're shorter and fatter.'

'Which shape gives better silk?' I asked.

Nuraddin shrugged. It didn't make much difference.

I watched the shadow of a working worm, visible inside its translucent cocoon. Nuraddin described how the cocoons, once collected, were steamed to kill the pupae. After that they could be stored in dry conditions indefinitely, until needed. If the moths were allowed to emerge they would destroy the cocoon in the process, secreting a brown acid that dissolved the fibres. A small proportion were allowed to hatch and lay eggs for the following year. Silkmoths, after 4,500 years of pampering, had lost their ability to fly, so now it was only the sericulture process that kept the species going. An equally large number of worms were probably eaten in the wild before ever reaching pupa stage. This partnership of sericulture allowed one species free food and the other to look more beautiful.

Just before we left, Nuraddin presented me with a bouquet: a couple of bushes bound together, covered in gossamer silk and studded with cocoons.

'So you can show the foreign guests our hard work,' he explained.

Back at the workshop, I perched the bouquet in my office cell and a few weeks later watched as the first cocoon grew brown at one end. A plump, flightless moth emerged, and then another. They mated, laid clusters of bright yellow eggs that darkened, and then died. All those weeks of frenetic feeding and spinning for such a short lifespan seemed a bit of an anti-climax.

Wanting to chart the whole process of sericulture, I was keen to see the next step in silk production. Madrim straight away ruled out a visit to the main Urgench silk factory, notorious for being both inept and corrupt. Instead we arranged to see a smaller silk factory run by deaf people, also in Urgench. Having negotiated our way past a suspicious gate-keeper we headed for a large factory building. Inside were rows of vats full of steaming water and bobbing cocoons that were unwinding onto spindles. The humid air had a sharp, sour smell, distinctive of all silk-reeling factories.

The assistant director arrived, introducing himself above the din of machinery, and took us over to a nearby vat where a woman signed a greeting to us. We watched as she dropped a handful of cocoons into the hot water and massaged them, deftly locating the ends and hooking them onto spindles. They then bobbed around in the water unravelling until the remains of the steamed larvae could be seen. The larvae were fed to chickens, although I'd heard that in China they were popular with young women for aiding breast development.

'How many silk fibres get woven together to make up one thread?' I asked.

'Eight to ten,' the assistant director explained. ' And you can see that the fibres are quite strong. Over here is where the silk threads are wound together.'

I recognised the familiar skeins of silk that we used in the workshop. Madrim asked about prices, as this could be a useful source of pile-thread silk. Unfortunately they hadn't got the machinery to wind these tiny threads together to make the thicker threads we needed for the warp and weft of our carpets. For these, we would have to look elsewhere.

Skeins of silk when they first arrived at our workshop looked slightly yellow and had the consistency of horse-hair. This always surprised visiting groups of tourists, as the silk was totally lacking in the lustre and sheen they expected. This was because it was still coated in sericin – the natural gum released to hold the cocoons together. In order to strip this sericin away we needed *ishkor*. A scrubby bush in the desert with small catkins was our main ingredient for this, and Madrim, the dyers and I collected a large pile of this, covered it in earth and then burnt it. The resulting ash, ishkor, looked like pumice. Once powdered and heated with water it gave a strong alkaline solution that stripped away the sericin as we dunked the skeins up and down in it. Each skein was then dropped into a steaming cauldron of grated soap solution and left there overnight.

Next day the skeins were hung to dry, sparkling white with all the lustre and luminescence expected of silk. They were now ready for weaving if we wanted white, or for dyeing if we wanted indigo blue or walnut husk silver, as these dyes required no mordants. For the other natural dyes, though, the silk needed to be mordanted in a bath of alum solution.

The term 'mordant' comes from the Latin *mordere*, 'to bite', and most natural dyes need the mordanting process in order for their colour to penetrate the fibre and hold there. We used only one type of mordant, called *achik tosh* or 'spicy stone', tasting bitter on the tongue. Reputed to cure most ailments, alum, as it's known in English, was never hard to come by in the bazaar. The translucent crystals were crushed and then added to hot water, in which the skeins of silk were left overnight.

Madrim and Fatoulah talked me through our colour palette. Hoshnaut the dyer was pounding dried pomegranate skins which yielded a deep gold that looked great on silk. Barry had obtained natural indigo from India which we were already using. The blue bricks of this dye were made from crushed and fermented leaves of the indigo plant. I hoped that we would one day grow our own indigo, undeterred by the complicated process required to turn the leaves into a useable dye or the significant role that stale urine played in this. Toychi was already mastering the art of dyeing with indigo. He removed skeins from a murky cauldron, squeezing them out and shaking them in the air. As the indigo oxidised it transformed the skeins from peacock green to a vivid blue. Seeing as there was no natural source of vivid greens, we would first dye silk pomegranate yellow and then indigo, giving us mottled and variegated shades of turquoise and green.

Dried walnut husks yielded a delicate shade of silver, leaving the dyers with stained hands. A blend of onion skins, quince, apple, vine and mulberry leaves gave us a cheerful buttercup yellow, the bits of dried leaves and onion skins beaten out of each skein against the courtyard wall.

We were satisfied with our yellows, blues, greens and greys, but the other colours were proving more problematic. The shades of colour varied wildly from bath to bath, and we weren't sure why. I wasn't too worried about this, knowing that we would master the art in time and that the varying shades produced a pleasing mottled effect known as *abrash*, typical of natural dyes.

More worrying was our inability to achieve some shades at all. I peered into a bath of what appeared to be diluted ox blood where skeins of silk gleamed a coral pink, like skinned salmon. This was a bath of madder root and was giving us delicate shades of coral and salmon but not the vivid reds that we needed.

'I thought that when you added oak gall to the crushed madder root it would change the dye bath from pink to red,' I said as Fatoulah removed the dripping skeins and wrung them out. 'You're sure you used the right quantities, aren't you?'

'Maybe it's this madder root that you brought from Tashkent,' mused Fatoulah. 'I haven't used madder in these big chunks before. The stuff we bought from the Afghan merchant was a fine powder, like red clay.'

'Maybe we should try to grind it up,' I suggested.

We spent the rest of the day visiting flour mills, but no one was willing to try grinding our chunky roots. We were also struggling to find a colour dark enough to use as a contrast. I thought that walnut husks would give us a chocolatey brown colour instead of the light silver. There were dyes like Brazil wood which yield a strong black, but we were in a desert oasis thousands of miles from the nearest rainforest. If it was any consolation, I knew that black was a challenge for wool-dyers too. Despite the profusion of black sheep, their natural black colouring isn't light-resistant and quickly fades, leaving black sheep looking grey by the end of a sunny summer. In the 19th century Turks used an iron sulphate compound to make black, but this corroded the wool, leaving surviving carpets from that period with bare snaking lines where once there was black.

Increasing the quantity of walnut husks in each dye-bath made little difference. Jim had mentioned a mysterious substance called *zok*, found in Afghanistan, which when mixed with oak gall and pomegranate skins produced a strong black colour. I also knew that Fatoulah's superior powdered madder root had come from Afghanistan. If we were going to complete our colour palette, it looked as if I'd need to make a trip there.

Andrea had taken over as Operation Mercy director and wasn't happy with the idea of me travelling alone to Afghanistan, particularly as the Taliban had only just been defeated. Nor was it possible for Madrim to come, as Uzbeks were still not allowed across the border for fear that they might become radicalised in the process. I was also meant to be orientating Matthias, a new volunteer from Germany who had just arrived and was completing his language course in Tashkent. We decided that Matthias would travel with me, receiving basic orientation on the way. He was thrilled at the prospect, keen for adventure.

A week later at the Afghan embassy I received my passport with a new visa stamped in upside down. I asked if this would be a problem, and the official grinned, apologised, and stuck in another one. I watched him writing backwards in swirling Dari, like Arabic, and asked him to write down the name of our workshop and Khiva, as we wanted to repeat this on graph paper, producing a signature that could be woven into each of our carpets. Happy to help, he wished me a safe journey.

'It is safe to travel there now, isn't it?' I asked, getting up to leave.

'Safe? Of course it is safe!' he assured me. 'Afghanistan has always been safe!'

6

Madder from Mazar

Synthetic dyes contain just one colour. But in madder there is red,
of course, but also blue and yellow are in there as well. It makes it
softer and at the same time more interesting.
—Natural dye specialist Harald Boehmer

Everything was organised. We'd asked the UN to put our names on the list of personnel allowed across the border and flew to Termez, the southernmost city in Uzbekistan, just a few miles from the Afghan frontier.

Termez had a typically Soviet feel to it, with large, spacious roads, ordered flower beds, parks, ugly high-rise blocks of flats and an unattractive, modernist clock tower – mandatory for all aspirational Soviet cities. Despite the innate shabbiness of Soviet-era cities, Termez was prosperous and the infrastructure laid down during the Soviet/Afghan war was still largely intact. During the war, convoys of tanks and lorries trundled across the ironically-named 'Bridge of Friendship' into northern Afghanistan. The war had dragged on, and more and more Soviet top brass were relocated to Termez from Moscow, ensuring that the city rose above the average standard of Uzbek provincial towns and provided amenities for the swelling number of Russian skilled workers and army personnel.

While the upper echelons of the Soviet army were largely Russian, many of the soldiers were Muslim Tajiks, Turkmens and Uzbeks. Despite their common ethnicity and religion with the people of northern Afghanistan, most cultivated a passionate hatred for Afghans, having experienced the terror of guerrilla warfare. I met a veteran once in a shared taxi from Urgench to Khiva and hoped he might regale me with stories from the war. Instead his eyes welled with unspoken pain. 'I will not talk of these things. I cannot,' he said.

Driving through the streets of Termez, we noticed how much hotter it was than Tashkent.

'I don't understand,' said Matthias. 'You said that wearing shorts would be culturally insensitive, but everyone's wearing them.'

We passed three burly European men in shorts and then another a bit further along, hand clamped to his Russian girl-friend's bottom. They were Germans and the city was full of them.

'All soldiers, here for Afghanistan,' the taxi driver explained, pointing out the hotel where they stayed. Each morning, a squadron of planes took off for northern Afghanistan, leav-ing off-duty soldiers to hang around, bored, in the tea houses and brothels. Their business had caused some prostitutes from Tashkent to relocate.

We left the wide streets of Termez behind us for the Bridge of Friendship, twenty minutes' drive from the city centre. At the first checkpoint we could see the Amu River a mile or so ahead of us. It was much larger here than in Khorezm, where its waters had already been leeched by the Turkmen canal and wasteful irrigation. This was the mighty Oxus immortalised in the poetry of Matthew Arnold. The lush irrigated fields on the Uzbek side contrasted with the barren desert just over the river – our first view of Afghanistan. Although it was only ten o'clock, the sun was already beating down and Matthias was turning pink.

'You did remember to bring a hat with you?' I asked. 'I know I reminded you.'

Matthias contradicted all German stereotypes; he was disorganised, laid-back and always happy to stop for a chat with whoever he happened to meet. Having forgotten to bring a hat, he improvised with a paper one made from a newspaper, before approaching the first checkpoint, smiling. The guard looked dubiously at Matthias and his paper hat. Clearly we had not made a professional first impression.

'Your visas are in order, but you are not on the list. You cannot come further,' was the guard's clipped response.

'But we must be on the list,' I replied. 'We spoke to Anvar from the UN earlier this week and informed him of our trip. He said that he would put us on the list.'

'You are not on the list.'

'So, what does that mean? Who do we need to speak to about this? Where is Anvar? Can you call him?'

He shook his head.

'OK, how do we get to Anvar's office? Where does he work?' I asked.

The guard gestured vaguely back in the direction of Termez and then turned his attention to a large convoy of SUVs speeding across the Bridge of Friendship in the distance and rapidly approaching the checkpoint. The windows were all reflective glass and the vehicles had no number plates. The guard waved them on as we leapt out of their way. They hadn't been stopped once on their way into the country; rumours abounded of the Uzbek government's involvement with the warlord General Dostum's sideline in heroin-trafficking. It seemed typical of

Uzbekistan that a large convoy of mafia-like vehicles could be waved through unchecked while two NGO workers – one of them sporting a paper hat – were treated as a potentially menacing threat.

An hour or so later we found the UN office and Anvar. He was dealing with a Danish cyclist who had assumed that he could cross the Bridge of Friendship, having obtained an Afghan visa. The crestfallen cyclist was gradually accepting that he would have to change his route, as only journalists and NGO workers on the UN list were allowed across the bridge at that point. Anvar had forgotten to add our names to his list and called through to the checkpoint informing them.

We returned, delayed but triumphant, and presented our passports. This time the problem was with a different list.

'Operation Mercy, Operation Mercy,' murmured the guard as he scanned down the list. 'No, it is not here.'

'But we must be. We're part of the NGO consortium.'

The guard was losing patience. 'Here,' he said, 'Mercy Corps.'

'But we're not with Mercy Corps, we're with Operation Mercy.'

'Do you want to go to Afghanistan?' he asked irritably and wrote us down as Mercy Corps.

We continued to the next checkpoint, passing two Western women coming in the other direction who were removing their headscarves with an air of newly acquired freedom. Here we were accosted by a large, Soviet-looking matriarch in a lab coat: 'Do you have AIDS? No? Do you have a temperature? No? Do you feel sick? No? Then you may proceed.'

We finally arrived at the bridge itself, hot and hungry. There was a slight breeze from the river, taking the edge off the heat, and under the bridge was a large expanse of emerald-green reeds filled with bee-eaters and other birds. There were no vehicles crossing, and in the tranquillity it was hard to believe the role this bridge had played in the horrors of the Soviet/Afghan war. We ate some sandwiches, walked across the bridge and surreptitiously took photos in the middle.

On the Afghan side there was no one around, but after some meandering through empty customs rooms we found a customs officer enjoying a lunchtime nap. We coughed politely, announcing ourselves. He woke, sized me up, and without a word took my water bottle and started to drink from it. We handed him our passports, which he stamped, and we were ushered out. After three hours of bureaucracy on the Uzbek side, the Afghan side took us less than ten minutes. My water bottle, kept by the guard, seemed a small price to pay.

Leaving the customs office, we found ourselves in the sleepy little town of Hairatan. Matthias watched our luggage while I went in search of taxis. Passing men of varying ages wore long beards, turbans and *shelwar kamiz*, baggy cotton pants covered with a knee-length top; and a woman – I presumed – walked by, shrouded in a dirty blue burka. A mere river and checkpoints separated two very different worlds.

Above me was a large, hand-painted poster of Ahmed Shah Massoud, the famous Tajik warlord who had organised resistance to the Soviet occupation. Revered by the people of northern Afghanistan, his assassination by Al Qaeda operatives posing as journalists had made him into a modern-day martyr. Underneath, written in English: 'Masud was the unique man that we cannot find him anymore.'

A little further on was a group of taxi drivers and we soon set off, passing a long caravan of camels – our Turkmen driver bemused at our excitement. The town gave way to huge swirling dunes that engulfed the road in places, forcing us off. An elderly man in a ragged shelwar kamiz, painfully thin, dug half-heartedly at one of the larger dunes with a tiny spade.

The taxi driver offered to take us to a nearby hot spring, perhaps noting our generally dishevelled appearance, and veered sharply off the road and down a dust track. A bubbling pool of chemical-green, sulphurous water was siphoned in rusting pipes to mud-brick cubicles. The water was a little too hot, but we stripped off and washed ourselves and our clothes, the arid air sure to dry them quickly. We continued refreshed and smelling powerfully of bad eggs, the driver explaining that this had once been a popular spot with a larger pool nearby that was now booby-trapped and in ruins.

A checkpoint bristling with weapons gave way to a vast tent city. Refugees ran to the road pleading for alms, but our driver sped up. I asked him to stop but he said we would be mobbed if we did. Matthias opened the window and threw out the remains of our food bag. It was fought over in the cloud of dust we left behind. A year later, the same site was completely empty and I wondered if I'd imagined the endless rows of UNHCR tents that had stood there before.

We stopped for a pee next to a large sand dune which Matthias began to climb until the driver made a sweeping gesture over the area and mimed mines exploding. Half an hour later we reached the outskirts of Mazar. Each passing vehicle was part of a daring competition to fit as many passengers in, on, or around it as possible. We passed a car, the same make as ours, with a group of men huddled on the roof rack, the boot open, filled with more men and two sheep, and the inside a mass of burkas pressed up against the windows. I looked guiltily at our back seat, empty apart from Matthias and a small bag.

A van drove by blaring music, something banned during Taliban rule. Its roof was crammed with men in their shelwar kamiz, singing, clapping and shimmying their shoulders. Two of them played along to the music with round, hand-held drums and the women below smiled and sang, gazing out of the window, their burkas thrown back. They were on their way to or from a wedding. I smiled and they waved at me, singing more raucously. They didn't seem to notice or resent our near-empty back-seat.

The pot-holed roads of Uzbekistan felt silken compared to the craters we juddered around and occasionally through in Mazar. Horses and traps, covered in pompoms and bells, managed to negotiate the craters with ease. SUVs muscled past them, property of drug barons and foreign NGOs. Open sewers swarming with flies ran down each road, flanked by concrete walls, pock-marked with battle scars. The air was thick with dust, muting the colours, until a shaft of evening sun through the pines transformed everything to shimmering bronze.

Most of the foreign staff at the NGO compound we were staying in were away, although Helga – a German who'd lived in Samarkand previously – was waiting to welcome us. We were greeted at the gate by a *chowkidor* – ubiquitous in Afghanistan and Pakistan and acting as a watchman, caretaker and general dogsbody. I knew three of the foreign staff who had previously worked in Uzbekistan. Helga came to the door, adjusting her veil, and welcomed us inside.

'I shouldn't really entertain you by myself as you're men, but Rob and the others are away, so our chowkidors will just have to understand!' she said.

Helga was thrilled to have another German staying and happily welcomed me as a non-American, feeling the cultural strain within their operations as the only European. The foreign staff spent a lot of time together and all had to live in compounds, which Helga was finding a challenge.

'Of course, I knew about the restriction of freedom for women here, even Western women, so I was expecting that. But you know, what I really miss is being part of the community. Why do I have to have a driver, and these chowkidors, and live and work in this compound which is like a prison for me now? Before, in Samarkand, I lived with an Uzbek family and I felt as if I was really living in Uzbekistan and not in this foreigner bubble. You know what I really miss too? It's just sitting outside under the persimmon tree in our garden in Samarkand, maybe reading a book or watching television with my host-family. Here, we are in Afghanistan, but at the same time we are not in Afghanistan at all. We live in our own gated little world!'

There were few foreigners who managed to escape their compounds and integrate with the community, though families with children found compounds particularly claustrophobic and often became more relaxed about security risks. One family who'd lived in Kabul during the civil war allowed their teenage children to play in the walled garden if shooting and shelling could be heard, but they had to come inside when bullets actually whizzed overhead. I expect they had other house rules as well, such as whose turn it was to help with the washing-up.

That night we enjoyed a delicious Afghan meal cooked by one of the chowkidors and eaten sitting on the floor around a plastic picnic cloth. The lights were on, but as dim as candle-light as the wattage all over the city was low. We were to sleep in the compound basement, which was the coolest part of the building. No one had ever really used their basements for any-thing other than storage until heavy gunfire made them the saf-est part of the house to sleep. Soon people realised how much cooler they were, and often moved their bedrooms down. We fell asleep to the sound of distant gunfire.

The next day at breakfast, Helga introduced us to one of their Uzbek chowkidors. A small, sprightly man with a well-groomed toothbrush moustache, he proved invaluable as we set off on our dye quest. I was concerned that our whole trip might turn into a wild-goose chase. I had never seen decent madder root – only powdered madder and the large chunks we were using in Khiva. I also had no idea about zok – what it looked like, whether it was available or, indeed, what it actually was.

The chowkidor seemed confident, though, and we drove to the bazaar in the centre of Mazar. Passing nondescript, bullet-holed buildings, we were suddenly confronted by a dazzling display of tiles, domes and cupolas. This was the tomb of Ali (or one of several sites making this claim). We walked over to it, enjoying the fabulous green, blue and yellow tiles, the turquoise domes and cupolas and the azure blue doorways. An array of small spires pointed from the corners of each building. The complex stood in a lake of gleaming marble, impervious to the general squalor surrounding it. Large bundles of rags scat-tered around the marble turned out, on closer inspection, to be women in burkas sitting on the ground begging. Near them, a gaggle of filthy men and children, many missing a limb or an eye, also begged for alms.

The white pigeons that lived in a nearby bunker provided a stark contrast: fat and sleek and fed by pilgrims who came to the tomb. The pigeons were said to be souls of the martyrs, perhaps explaining their profusion, and even black pigeons that came to roost near the tomb were reputed to turn white. Around the pool of marble were dusty gardens where a few families picnicked, the women ferrying handfuls of food up inside their burkas for consumption. The gardens were encircled by a busy road from which the different sections of the bazaar radiated. We wove our way past the cloth market, around the fruit-sellers (joyfully noting that they sold mangos, unavailable in Uzbekistan) towards the money-changers. We exchanged dollars for Afghanis, counting up the greasy, crumbling notes. The chowkidor checked each note to make sure it was the right type of Afghani, as different factions had printed their own currencies.

We passed the copperware section and entered a small alleyway full of kite-sellers to reach the dye bazaar. Here a row of open-fronted shops brimmed with sacks of things exotic-looking but unidentifiable and lined with jars whose mysterious contents would satisfy the most demanding subject on the Hogwarts curriculum.

One large jar caught my eye and I pointed it out to the chowkidor. 'That jar there, what do you call the contents in Dari?' It was oak gall, which was a good start. We'd need more than the fourteen kilos which was all I'd managed to find in Uzbekistan, and the price here was less than half what I had previously paid. As a concentrated source of tannin, oak galls dramatically affected the shades of colour available from madder, transforming dusky pinks to vibrant reds. There were two different types available, both spherical with knobbly surfaces. All had tell-tale holes in them, drilled by the emerging wasp larvae which had caused the oak trees to produce these growths in the first place. We bought their entire stock and did the same at neighbouring stalls.

'Do you have this thing, er, it's a dye and it's called something like zok?' I asked our chowkidor to translate into Dari. The turbaned merchant reached into a nearby sack and pulled out a small piece of what looked like crumbly white chalk. 'This is zok,' he said, as I looked at it unconvinced.

'Are you sure?' I asked. 'Zok is meant to give a black colour, but this is white.'

He looked at me and grinned before spitting onto a piece of scrap leather, smearing some zok into the spittle. As he rubbed it into the leather, a black stain emerged. I found myself grinning back. This must be it. We now had an important dye to add to our palette.

We bought enough zok and oak gall to last us for at least a year. The merchants were surprised that we would want to use natural dyes, beckoning us to lurid heaps of chemical powders. On a later trip to buy dyes in Mazar, we were delayed because no one sold zok any more. It just wasn't used, and they had to send someone on a two-day journey to a mountain where zok – possibly a sulphuric chalk or iron ore – could be dug up.

Flushed with our success, I started to relax, taking more notice of the open sacks around me. One was filled with yellow roots. 'Is this also a dye?' I asked.

The merchant shook his head and pointed at his mouth. Another sack, full of dried rose petals, released a wonderful scent. I bought some for Zulhamar. Next to this was a sack filled with what at first glance looked like small, dried grey pomegranates. They would make an attractive potpourri with the rose petals and I was about to buy some when I noticed the lines of razor-slash markings and realised that this was a sack of opium poppy-heads. They had been milked for opiates already and were now openly on sale for anyone who fancied growing their own.

'Are these really opium poppy heads?' I asked, just to make sure. The merchant, amused at my expression of shock, grinned back and nodded.

'But how can you just sell them in the open like this?' I asked incredulously. 'How much is a kilo?' The price was less than a dollar, and the merchant playfully cracked one open, offering me some seeds, before pouring them into his mouth and crunching contentedly.

We continued our search for madder root, finding only one shop with a small sack of the spindly dried roots. I still hadn't seen a live madder plant, although later we found some growing wild in Khiva – a scraggy weed with tiny hooks on its stem and leaves that made it cling to passing traffic. I knew that madder roots yielded colour only if they were at least two or three years old, and broke a few of these ones open, pleased to see a strong salmon-pink inner root. However, the asking price for this small sack seemed exorbitant. I thought about the merchants I had encountered in Samarkand, offering naive tourists boxes of cheap safflower stamens that looked vaguely like saffron, with cries of 'Pure saffron from Silk Road!' With no sample of what good madder looked like in root form, I could easily be cheated.

'If you want buy madder you must go Abdullah Hoja cara-vanserai,' explained one of the merchants in broken English.

'He has too much of madder root.' Our chowkidor asked for directions and we worked our way back to the central *maidan* or square, heading up a different street to the small caravanserai belonging to Abdullah Hoja.

Khiva, too, boasted a beautiful caravanserai. It was built by Allah Kuli Khan in the 1840s with two storeys, the upper acting as an inn and the lower as storage for goods. Caravans of camels would arrive from Orenburg or Bukhara and leave for Isfahan, Merv or Tashkent, laden with bales of silks, melons, and Karakul lamb pelts. Sadly, the Khiva caravanserai was roofed over by the Soviets and transformed into a drab, sanitised indoor department store, selling rows of pickled vegetables and sweets and with the best selection of candy-pink polyester wedding dresses in town.

Yet here in Mazar was a real caravanserai, tiny by comparison, but full of sacks of produce, with dusty carpets strewn on the floors and mini stalls containing sleeping merchants, their sons arriving with stacked trays of home-cooked lunch. Although there were no camels, a donkey and cart gave a vague sense of the bustle of the Silk Road.

The Hoja had been napping in his cubby-hole that doubled as a shop. He leapt to his feet on our arrival, calling for a grandson to fetch tea and beckoning us to sit beside him. He looked like an Old Testament patriarch in his flowing robe, sporting a long beard and a large turban. We explained our mission and another grandson was swiftly dispatched, tottering back with a huge bale of madder root on his back.

'Tell us about the quality of your madder,' I said, trying to sound authoritative. 'We need to be sure it will yield a good colour.'

The Hoja explained that the madder had been harvested the previous October. Recent droughts meant that madder was hard to come by. This came from the north-eastern region, which still had good supplies of water from the nearby mountains.

We discussed the price and I asked where we could have the roots ground. The Hoja offered to take us to the mill he used. We purchased 60 kilos in impossibly long sacks and, having loaded these onto the donkey cart, pitched our way towards the mill.

The miller flicked a switch and the air filled with red dust, smelling of custard. Lacking turbans to adjust over nose and mouth, Matthias and I left them to it. Passing a listing balcony housing two cramped-looking urban cows, we discovered an alleyway where anything from sickles to cattle bells could be purchased. The third stall down sold a large bundle of comb-beaters that we would need for banging down the weft thread after each horizontal row of carpet knots. They were impressively heavy with large wooden handles and simple engravings on the metal body. I bought ten. A stall down I discovered rows of hook-knives hanging on strings and purchased several.

As we returned to the mill, a sandstorm broke out. Dust that had been shat on and spat on was whipped into the air and into our eyes, hair and mouths. We hauled sacks onto the donkey cart as fast as possible and lurched our way back to the compound, desperate for showers and keen to buy turbans as soon as possible.

The following morning we drove to the outskirts of the city, where the chowkidor lived in a squat mud-brick house. We were left outside while he alerted his wife; she hid herself around a corner and, though we could sense her presence, we politely ignored it. His daughter sat on top of a horizontal loom laid out on the floor, weaving in the Turkmen style. The colours were darker than rugs made in Turkmenistan, but many of the designs were similar and reds still predominated.

'The wool, do you know where it is from?' asked the chowkidor proudly. We had no idea, but I hazarded a guess.

'Is it from Kandahar or Ghazni?' I asked.

'No, it is from Belgium,' he replied, savouring the sound of this exotic place where flocks of sheep roamed every hill. 'Because of the drought there is no good wool now in Afghanistan. Before, we had such good wool but now we must buy from elsewhere.'

We thanked the chowkidor for his hospitality and set out to explore the bazaar by ourselves. We had been in the country less than a week but already referred to passing women as burkas, their contents de-humanised in our minds. They looked more like birds than anything else, arching and craning their necks to see oncoming traffic or to look around, lacking all peripheral vision.

Interacting with a burka-clad woman felt strange, hearing a voice but unable to see even a pair of eyes. At one stall I stopped to buy some woven reed fans, which made excellent presents. I had tried English and Uzbek to no avail, when a well-spoken voice behind me enquired whether I needed help. I turned to a white burka and thanked the woman within, speculating as she turned, with a flash of ankle, about what she might look like.

Heading for the carpet section of the bazaar, we passed a group of Swedish UN soldiers at one shop and some other foreigners at another. 'Business is really good, thanks be to God,' declared one of the shopkeepers in broken English. 'My brother in Peshawar sends me his stock. So many foreigners here now. They like to buying too much carpets!'

There were lots of carpets depicting maps of Afghanistan or portraits of Massoud. A number of the more tribal rugs featured tank, helicopter and bomb motifs, and there was even one with exploding aeroplanes slamming into the World Trade Center.

Matthias wanted to know more about the rugs piled up in each shop. I pointed out the ones from Turkmenistan in fire-engine red, and how the designs varied according to tribal preference. Some guls or motifs had clear meaning, like the flotilla of boat pendants, bristling with anchors, found in the Yomut rugs woven near the shores of the Caspian Sea. Others incorporated symbols such as rams' horns to ward off the evil eye. I unrolled some Tekke rugs which looked, at first glance, to be all the same, pointing out the minor cruciform guls in each, which were all different.

'Ah, you like to buying Bukhara rug, sir,' chimed in the stallholder. Like Astrakhan wool, Bukhara rugs referred to their main trading outlet and not to their place of origin. The octagonal lozenges contained three cross-like figures in each corner, symbolic (depending on who you asked) of three men on horseback or a Nestorian Christian symbol of Calvary.

Carpet-weaving among the Turkmen was done exclusively by women, who also wove camel bags, storage bags to hang on their yurt walls and decorative door coverings. As the Turkmens were absorbed into the Soviet Union, a few clever weavers, realising that their art was under threat from mass-producing textile factories, began to include woven homilies to Father Lenin at the end of each rug. This transformed them into artistic and ethnic acts of devotion to the Communist cause, and soon huge portrait carpets of Lenin, Stalin and other Soviet leaders were commissioned, woven on traditional horizontal looms and keeping the art alive. In the carpet museum in Ashkhabad there was even a fetching rendition of Castro, complete with cigar.

Rummaging through the piles of rugs, I found a Turkmen one that perfectly illustrated why we were in Mazar looking for madder. The weave was excellent, as was the knot count, and the rug was around 50 years old. Most of the synthetic colours used had faded but there was one orange dye which stubbornly and garishly refused to do so, ruining the whole rug as a result.

Other rugs in the stack were beautifully woven with tiny knots in a blend of wool with patches of silk. The designs were Turkmen but the palette pastel to appeal to Westerners. They were let down by the silk warps, which had not been de-gummed and crinkled like new grey hairs, refusing to lie and jarring with the overall fluidity. These rugs were woven in Afghanistan and were largely the product of child labour. I felt ambivalent towards this issue. On the one hand, the cries of Westerners calling for children to play and study seemed naively removed from the harsh realities of families making ends meet, and smacked rather of a 'Let them eat cake' mind-set. On the other hand, many of the children were not simply learning the craft within the home but being exploited in work-shops where their nimble fingers were barely recompensed. They worked long hours in appalling conditions and earned almost nothing. I had set the minimum age in our workshop at seventeen.

We prepared to leave the following day. I had enjoyed myself immensely despite the heat and dust, but was worried about getting back. As I had discovered at the bazaar, Afghanistan was still the largest exporter of opium in the world, and I knew a lot of it was trafficked across the Bridge of Friendship. Quite what would be made of two young men with more than their combined body weight in sacks of powdered substances remained to be seen. I was particularly concerned about the zok, a crumbly white substance that even I knew looked suspiciously like heroin.

We said goodbye to Helga and the chowkidor and drove back through the desert to Hairatan, our vehicle thoroughly overloaded with sacks and looking considerably more Afghan than when we'd arrived. At the customs office I spotted a trolley we might use to cart the sacks over the bridge – no vehicles were allowed across without special permission.

An impressively moustached border official circled our stack of sacks, asking in textbook English about their contents. I produced letters of explanation from UNESCO and Operation Mercy in English and Russian. He read them through and looked at the sacks again.

'You must know, sir,' he began, 'that this border has been used on many occasions for the smuggling of opiates. These letters are very good, but look at these sacks, they are full of so much powder. I will need to have them analysed.'

'Of course, I quite understand,' I replied. 'Which sack would you like to take samples from? Do you need samples from each sack? Where is your lab, and how long will it take to make the analysis?'

'We do not have any laboratories here. We must take the samples back to Mazar,' explained the official.

'Really?' I asked wearily, imagining the two-hour journey back through the desert. 'We've just come all the way from

Mazar this morning and we need to be back in Uzbekistan today. Is there no alternative?'

The official thought for a moment, and I was seized by a rare flash of inspiration. 'Sir,' I continued, 'I understand your position and the job that you must do. I am glad to meet such excellent guards at this border who search carefully for narcotics, which bring nothing but misery to so many. However, I am a good man here to buy dyes to help poor people gain employment. I am not a drug smuggler, I am a man of honour.'

'A man of honour?' mused the official. He thought for another moment and then said, 'Well, if you are a man of honour then you may proceed.'

Momentarily stunned, I thanked him profusely and left before he changed his mind. I felt both humbled and gratified that I had been given something quite rare in Central Asia: trust.

We repeated our ritual search for someone to stamp our passports and then loaded as many sacks as possible on the trolley and pushed it towards the bridge. The powdered madder seeped out of some of the woven plastic sacks, mixing with our sweat and covering us both in a brick-red sheen. I wasn't sure if we would be allowed to pull the trolley across the bridge, or whether we would have more problems on the Uzbek side and find ourselves refused entry. Just as I was offering up a quick prayer, a UNICEF jeep turned up. After discussion with the occupants and a flourish of the UNESCO letter, they agreed to take the dyes over in the back of their jeep and we trotted behind them.

We unloaded on the other side, the customs officials assuming we were UNICEF personnel and giving us no problems. The sacks of dyes were put through an X-ray machine and a sniffer dog unleashed to check them. I watched, imagining what might have happened had I brought even one opium poppy head with me as a souvenir. Everything ran smoothly and within an hour and a half we were through. Full of gratitude, we parted from the UNICEF staff and found a truck to take us into the city centre. This was to prove the easiest of all my returns. Each year the border became more of a challenge.

Back in Termez, it felt as if a magical transformation had taken place. Instead of dirt tracks and open sewers here were long, straight streets and even flower beds! The drab Soviet architecture exuded a reassuring aura of order. Gone were the three standard types of Afghan women – blue burkas, white burkas and the occasional olive green burka. In their place were women of every age, shape and size, roaming freely.

A van driver at the Termez bus station was willing to take us to Tashkent and we settled down, tired, smelly and red. An hour or so later, in the foothills of the Pamir mountains, we stopped at a large, clear stream near the road for a wash and swim. The water was far too cold for the driver who watched in horror as we jumped in with a bar of soap, convinced we'd be dead by morning.

From Tashkent we'd take a bus with all the dyes back up to Khiva. I was relieved at how well the trip had gone, but there was still the question: Would the dyes be any good, giving us the black and reds we needed?

7

Bukharan cunning

It is a pity that this people, in spite of the high antiquity of their origin, and their grandeur in time gone by, should have attained the very highest stage of vice and profligacy.

—Arminius Vambery on Bukharans,
Travels in Central Asia, 1864

I entered the madrassah with the sacks of dyes feeling heroic, having braved borders and bureaucracy. The weavers were soon squabbling over hook-knives and comb-beaters and the dyers set to work unpacking the sacks and putting them into storage. Keen to see if the dyes would actually yield colour, we soon had cauldrons on the boil. The madder bath was much redder than anything we'd achieved before, and next to it a cauldron of inky black zok brewed.

The following day, Madrim fished out the skeins, rinsed them and hung them up to dry. The colours were strong and we deemed our trip a success.

In my absence, a carpet we'd dubbed 'Benaki' (inspired by the Benaki fragment of a Timurid design) had been completed up to the edge of the border that would frame the field design, and the girls were now waiting for a decent madder-red before starting the central field. The other carpets were also progressing nicely, although something had gone wrong with the colour scheme of the Rustam carpet. Instead of a pomegranate gold border, the apprentices were weaving with a murky olive – not quite green or yellow. It didn't look right, but the apprentices beamed at their hard work. I took the two ustas aside for a telling off.

'It wasn't our fault!' Ulugbibi explained, reverting to a stage whisper. 'Of course we knew the right colours. You made us write them down on the design and everything. It was Ulugbeg. He misled us. There have been other things as well.'

Ulugbibi shut the door, adamant that the cunning Bukharans were attempting to oust the competition. Could I not see that they were worried at our rapid progress? Allegations of sabotage were not to be taken lightly and we summoned Madrim, who confirmed Ulugbibi's suspicions.

'Fatoulah will tell me to write down quantities for making red with madder-root and oak gall,' Madrim began. 'I write everything down but check these figures against the notes I made at Jim's training last year. Then I say to him, "Usta, these quantities that you've given me are different from Jim's. Why is that?" He looks at my notes and excuses himself, and says that he has made a mistake, but it keeps happening. The first time he told me I must have written down the quantities incorrectly, and one time he told me that Jim was wrong. I asked him whether he or Jim were the usta.

'Then there was the fermentation pots. Jim explained that the pH level will only change if there is no oxygen in the pots, but each day Fatoulah stirs them vigorously and they bubble.'

I took this more seriously, as the first skeins to emerge from the pots had been foul-smelling and a dull yellowy-brown in colour – not the stunning reds and blues we'd been promised by Fatoulah. We'd endured the stench of these pots for a month and the few skeins of silk resulting were all an unattractive puce. Abandoning fermentation dyeing altogether, the dyers had filled each pot with earth and seeds, the weavers no longer scurrying past holding handkerchiefs to their noses.

'Aslan, you don't know what Bukharans are like, but we do,' Ulugbibi whispered. 'They're all cunning. They don't want to work if they can steal someone else's work, and they always lie. You can never trust them.'

Just then Fatoulah walked in and our discussion came to an abrupt halt. I wasn't sure how seriously to take these allegations, and whether this was just the age-old enmity between Khivans and Bukharans. I knew that if I spoke to the Bukharans about this, they would simply adopt a wounded tone and deny all knowledge of a conspiracy. We needed a trap of some kind, and while reading a book on natural dyes, I came across one that might work. According to the book, black mulberries produced a vibrant purple dye that fades quickly in sunlight and is therefore unsuitable. I nonchalantly asked Fatoulah what he knew about dyeing with mulberries.

'Ah yes, mulberries,' he began ingratiatingly. 'Aslan agha, you are so clever to discover the secret of these berries. I, myself, have used mulberries for years and the colour they give is the most beautiful purple.'

'So, this purple colour, does it fade at all in the sun?' I asked.

'That is a very good question. No, the colour is very permanent. Why, I still have a *suzani* embroidered with mulberry-dyed silk hanging outside in my garden. After all these years the colour is still strong.'

My trap was working.

'That's good to know,' I said. 'Why didn't you tell us about this extraordinary dye before? You're supposed to be teaching us all you know about dyeing.'

Fatoulah assumed an expression of abject penitence. 'We have been so busy and there is all this work for us to do. It slipped my mind, but now we must use it in one of the carpet designs. What about the Mehmon design you want to start? It would look so nice with mulberry purple in the field design.'

I asked Toychi to collect a bucketful of black mulberries that had fallen from the tree next to the Friday mosque. We made a dye-bath, but dyed only two skeins of silk as an experiment. The skeins emerged a rich purple colour, but after two weeks in the sun had faded to a dull grey lilac. Convinced that a plot was afoot, I called Barry in Tashkent. He wasn't interested and told me not to get involved in petty, clannish suspicion. He further complicated the matter by inviting Davron, a dye-master from Marghilan in eastern Uzbekistan, to join the training in Khiva.

Davron's workshop in the Fergana valley made traditional *atlas* silk – the national fabric of Uzbekistan. Most atlas silk was made on machines, but in Marghilan they had retained the traditional approach, making their workshop a mecca for textile enthusiasts. I visited his workshop a couple of months later and watched the complicated process of dyeing atlas silk using *ikat* dyeing, in which warp threads are bound according to a pattern and then immersed in dye-baths, building up a colour pattern through resist-dyeing, a kind of tie-dyeing. The reassembled warp threads are then woven with just one weft colour, creating a vertical blur of colours subtly bleeding into each other.

A young weaver in love is credited with the invention of atlas silk. The object of his affections was the daughter of a wealthy landowner who showed no interest in the humble weaver. His only hope, she told him, was to dazzle her with the most beautiful fabric ever created. The besotted weaver set to work, but nothing he produced received more than a scornful glance.

Finally – his hands worn to shreds – he gave up. Dejected, he went to a stream that ran near his workshop, dipping his bleeding hands in the waters. Blood-red blended with the shimmering yellow of the reflected sun and dashes of green from the overhanging trees and the patches of blue sky. Inspired, he rushed back to his loom and wove atlas silk. His shallow sweetheart fell passionately and predictably in love with both the design and the designer.

Interesting though the origins of atlas silk were, I was more concerned with the dynamics of another rival usta joining our already strained relations with the Bukharans. I had my own prejudices towards people from the Fergana valley, who styled themselves 'real' Uzbeks and despised anyone from Khorezm.

'They are so uncivilised up there! Almost like animals … no, like Turkmen!' I'd overheard a woman on a bus in the valley exclaim. 'Who can understand their strange dialect? It sounds so horrible, so mangled!'

'And what about their treatment of guests?' began her neighbour. 'You sit down and maybe they say a blessing, maybe not and then what? There's no "*oling, oling*", no insistence that you eat. They just seem to think that if you feel like it you'll eat and if you don't, it makes no difference to them. What kind of custom is that?'

'And the tea!' interrupted the first. 'Always green and impossible to drink with their salty desert water. And do you know what?' She turned to a third woman who was sitting in rapt silence. 'They give you your own teapot.' This elicited an audible gasp. 'Yes, they just leave the teapot beside you and expect you to pour yourself. The host doesn't even say "*iching, iching*", just leaves it for you to pour yourself.'

'Or,' interrupted the second woman, 'if they do pour tea for you, they pour it all the way up to here in the tea bowl – almost halfway! It's as if they just want you to drink up and leave! That's what happens when you live in the desert; you become primitive. Yes, they can dance and sing well enough, but I shall not be going there again.'

My own experience of being a guest in the Fergana valley had been stifling, with overwhelming barrages of 'take, take' or 'drink, drink' when my tea bowl was already at my lips. Each time I drank, my bowl was replenished with a few drops more, forcing the host to continually service my cup. Instead I felt inhibited, leaving thirsty and keen to return to the scandalously casual traditions of Khiva.

Davron, on arrival, immediately allayed my fears.

'Nechiqsiz, Jorim?' he asked in fluent Khorezm dialect, laughing at my surprise. 'Look, my best friend at university was from Khorezm,' he explained. 'We shared a room and he taught me lots of words in the dialect. I really like it!'

Madrim joined us at my house for a meal. After supper – during which I harangued him to eat and drink, hoping he'd feel at home – Davron excused himself and went to ritually wash. He returned and unfurled his cloth belt which doubled as a prayer mat. Few people under the age of 60 prayed like this in Khiva. Afterwards we talked about the situation in the valley for pious Muslims and the restrictions and persecution they faced.

The following morning Davron joined Madrim and the dyers around the cauldrons and was soon correcting much of what he heard, explaining the importance of the pH scale and which products sold in the bazaar could alter it. Fatoulah scowled as Davron revealed other tricks of the trade withheld from us so far. Did we know about *bikh*, for example? Used to

1. The best view of Khiva's walled city, or Ichan Kala, is from the rickety ferris wheel opposite the park. The watchtower embedded into the wall on the right looks over the rest of the Kunya Ark, or old fortress. Left of it is the squat beginnings of what would have been the tallest minaret in Asia, known as the Kaltor Minor or short minaret. The tall minaret in the centre is next to the Islom Hoja madrassah, and to its left is the Friday mosque minaret, from which adulterous women were once hurled.

2. Dawn on my roof. In the foreground are the walls of the Kunya Ark fortress. Behind these are the Feruz Khan madrassah, the distinctive dome of the Pakhlavan Mahmoud mausoleum, and the Islom Hoja and Friday mosque minarets.

3. Sometimes our embroiderers would work up on the roof of the madrassah, usually at dusk when the perils of getting darker in the sun were less. Most of their suzanis look white, but this is the papery cloth we would draw designs on and then cut away at the end. In the background you can just make out the carpet workshop, in front of the Pakhlavan Mahmoud mausoleum on the left and the Islom Hoja minaret on the right.

4. My home, viewed from the city walls. Koranbeg's red Lada is parked on the street. My room and secluded balcony are on the top floor to the right. I would sleep outside next to the ladder leading to the roof in the summer months.

5. A typical day in the carpet workshop. Carpets for sale are on display, the latest batch of dyed silk skeins either drying on racks or flung against the madrassah walls (a method that worked equally well). In the foreground are some of the dyeing vats, and the dyers are preparing a blend of leaves and onion skins to yield a bright yellow. My office is in the right corner cell.

6. A side-door to the Friday mosque in the Ichan Kala, carved with a design we called 'Tolkin'. This has nothing to do with Middle-earth, but means 'wave' in Uzbek …

7. *(below)* … and the resulting 'Tolkin' carpet in Majolica colours, being clipped by Sanajan the widow (far right) and her apprentices. Next to Sanajan is one of the original fermentation dye-vats that we redeemed as plant pots.

8. *(far left)*
A Timurid
miniature from a
Persian *Shahnameh*
(Book of Kings),
1493–94, showing
Husrov (left) seated
inside an arched
iwan.

9. *(left)* Me, outside
the entrance to the
workshop, holding
the resulting carpet.
The 'Husrov' design
was one of my
favourites, and two
years after I left
the workshop some
friends brought back
a carpet from Khiva
with this design, a
gift to me from the
weavers and dyers.

10. A miniature from the Persian poet Nizami's *Khamsa*, depicting Shirin receiving a portrait of Husrov (1494–95), described at the beginning of Chapter 4.

11. *(below)* We used the carpet design in the Shirin miniature as inspiration for both a carpet and suzanis. Here's a close-up of a suzani cushion cover. We called the design 'Alti Buchek', which means hexagon.

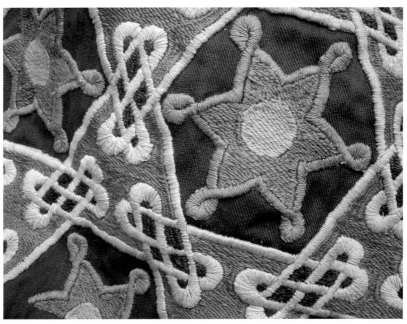

12. *(above)* Three of the suzani embroiderers, including Madrim's wife Mehribon (centre), working outside on suzanis that would become cushion covers. The kilim they're sitting on was made in Miriam's workshop.

13. *(left)* Madrim washing the silk in our nicest copper vat. Behind him, skeins of walnut-husk brown are drying.

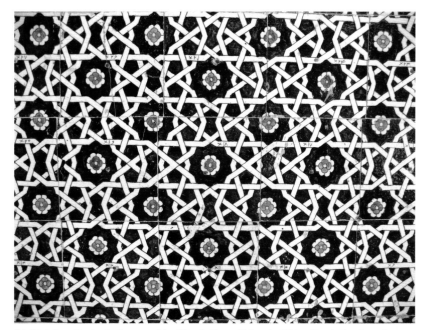

14. Majolica tiles in the harem of the Khan's Stone Palace in Khiva. Look closely and you can see the Arabic numerals on each tile, crucial for assembling them in the right order. You can also see holes in the centre of each tile where they were originally nailed, rather than cemented, in place.

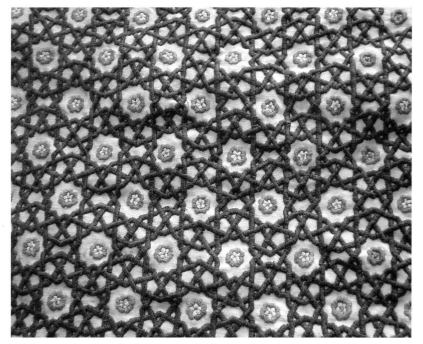

15. Our suzani version of this design with the blue and white colours inverted. Safargul the usta christened the design 'Olma Gul', which means apple flower.

16. Our natural-dye palette. The blue brick at the top is a block of indigo from India. Next to it is the onion skin, vine, apple and mulberry leaf mix used for buttercup yellow. On the left is a bag of dried pomegranate skins which yield a rich gold colour, and underneath are dried walnut husks for brown. In the basket are madder root (bottom) for pinks, combined with oak gall (top) to create

red. The white chalky-looking powder on the left is zok, which when combined with oak galls and pomegranate skins produces dark blue. On the right are lumps of alum which are diluted to create a bath needed for dyes to penetrate into the silk.

17. One of our larger looms, set up in the madrassah courtyard during the summer months. At the back is Nazokat, considered dark and far too flirtatious. The girls are working on the 'Tolkin' design.

make a sticky meringue-like syrup with beaten egg-whites and sugar, Davron explained that bikh – cream of tartar – washed over a finished carpet, brought out silk's lustre and sheen. He was with us for only two days, but left us with a wealth of information.

We were still stuck with the Bukharans. I debated the wisdom of a head-on confrontation with them, deciding that it really wasn't worth the effort. A few days later they left – taking with them, we discovered later, many of our original designs.

'UNESCO pays them to come here and train us, but who did the training?' asked Ulugbibi in disgust. 'Zamireh teaches them a better way of knotting, and Davron teaches them how to dye properly. What did they teach us? Lies, nothing else – and how to steal.'

With the Bukharans gone, we settled into a routine. My day began with a tour of the looms – the two weaving ustas in tow. Sometimes the weavers used mismatched colours and would need to undo a line or two, or had made obvious mistakes that needed correcting. The rest of the day was spent working on designs or giving tours of the workshop. We experimented with local plants to see if any of them yielded colours. The weavers showed us how they used *usma*, a nondescript little plant that looked like woad. They ground the leaves into a paste, adding a little water and smearing the resulting kohl over their eyebrows, creating a mono-brow once considered the height of beauty. But as a dye-plant it proved useless. The only successful discovery we made was that the broom plant's seeds yielded an attractive fawn colour, but we could already achieve this with a light madder bath – and a few onion skins tossed in.

Tourists began trickling through, often pausing to photograph the Pakhlavan mausoleum dome framed in our front archway. Only then would they notice the racks of drying silk and the steaming cauldrons. Some were incredibly rude, marching around the workshop uninvited and not even acknowledging my offer of a free tour. Others sat at the looms learning to weave knots and posing for pictures with the weavers. The apprentices chorused 'good morning' regardless of the time of day and learnt that tourists expected them to smile for photos.

A number of tourists, after a lengthy tour and a look through the albums of miniatures and sericulture I'd produced, wanted to buy a carpet and were frustrated that we had nothing for sale. One or two wanted to contribute anyway, insisting that I take money from them, so we set up an ice-cream fund with this extra cash, dipping into it for birthday celebrations.

As the pace of work slowed, I decided to spend more time with the apprentice dyers. We'd started with four boys but one had quit after a week, leaving Toychi, Davlatnaza and Hoshnaut. I invited them for an evening at the Anusha Khan homom. Madrim declined, stating that it would be undignified to disrobe in front of his apprentices. The rest of us set off after work, armed with towels and shampoo. The homom – one of the oldest in Central Asia – was tucked between the Strongman's Gate and the White Mosque. Unfortunately, the interior had been modernised. Inside a domed hallway an ancient television garlanded with plastic flowers spluttered to life, a greasy, threadbare couch in front of it. A home-made bar sold drinks and soap. Next to this was a corridor in which shifty-looking men waited impatiently. Toychi – an authority on the subject

– explained that this was one of the most popular brothels in Khiva. The communal homom, once a stone domed maze, had been partitioned into three separate chambers, each with a grubby Russian-style sauna and shower inside.

We entered one of them and I watched Davlatnaza peel off his filthy trousers, explaining superfluously that this was his first time in a homom. There was no bathroom in his house and I wondered when was the last time – if ever – that he had actually washed. He used the shower first – a thick snake of dirty water pouring down the drain. Once showered, we sat in the sauna and I asked them if they knew how the Anusha Khan homom got its name. They didn't, and – as it was one of my favourite stories garnered from Isak the guide – I decided to tell it to them.

There had once been a young prince called Abdul, who fell madly in love with his distant cousin, Anusha. They talked of a future together, the prince declaring that he would take no other wives, for his heart would always belong to her. Tragically, Anusha suffered from incurable ill health and as she lay on her deathbed, the prince sobbed, clasping her hand. He vowed never to forget her, promising to name his first daughter Anusha in her memory.

The years passed and the grief-stricken prince became Abdul Gazi, Khan of Khiva. Determined that Anusha's memory should live on through a daughter, the Khan was constantly frustrated as his plethora of wives bore him son after son. Finally, in exasperation, he summoned his entire harem and railed against this conspiracy. The next woman to bear him a son, he declared, would be executed along with her baby.

This was particularly bad news for one heavily pregnant wife, and even worse when she gave birth to a son. In desperation, she wrapped the baby in swaddling clothes and – with nothing to lose – presented him to the Khan, saying: 'At last, my master, here is your first daughter, Anusha.'

The Khan, happy to take her word for it, was delighted and Anusha quickly became his favourite – the mother showered with favours.

Anusha grew up freer than other girls, keen to ride and hear stories of battle. The Khan enjoyed her company, secure in the knowledge that a daughter would not be plotting patricide as some of his sons were wont to do. Anusha, pained at the deception, longed to tell her father the truth, but knew that this would condemn both her and her mother to death. The Khan, oblivious to this, could not understand why Anusha, at the ripe age of fourteen, had dissolved into tears at the mention of marriage.

But all plans for Anusha's betrothal were placed on hold as the Khan prepared for war against the Emir of Bukhara. Together with his sons and vast army, the Khan rode off to battle, leaving the city of Khiva largely undefended. This fact had not escaped the attention of a marauding band of Turkmen robbers. They planned a massive raid on Khiva to loot and pillage with impunity. Wisely, the Khan had installed his spies among the Turkmen and one of them sent word to Khiva of an imminent attack.

Pandemonium broke out within the harem, but as the Khan's wives became hysterical, Anusha veiled herself and ordered the Royal Guard to assemble before her. She had a plan, simple and audacious. The remaining soldiers were to call up the entire adult population of the city and have the women dress in men's clothes, bringing with them all horses and donkeys. They would then assemble in battle formation outside the

Grandfather Gate, with the Royal Guard stationed in the front two rows.

This done, Anusha joined the ranks of unlikely soldiers standing before the gate. Soon, a cloud of dust, visible in the distance, announced the arrival of the Turkmens. They drew closer and closer until the captain of the Royal Guard gave the order to charge. The pretend army surged forward on horseback, on donkeys or on foot. The ruse worked. The bandits, assuming that the Khan had discovered their scheme and returned to slaughter them, turned tail and galloped away as fast as they could. Anusha had saved her city from certain destruction.

Hearing of this, the Khan swiftly returned from the battlefield, throwing a lavish banquet in honour of Anusha. As the celebration progressed, the Khan summoned his daughter before him.

'Anusha, my daughter,' he began. 'Today I owe you my Khanate and my honour. What is it that you want? Name it and it shall be yours.'

Anusha thought for a moment and said in a quiet voice: 'If it please my father and master, I ask for only two things: my life and the life of my mother.'

There was a puzzled silence, followed by assent from the Khan. Anusha then took his father aside, revealing his true identity and explaining his mother's subterfuge. The Khan was gracious, and declared: 'Behold, my son Anusha. To him will I give my inheritance and he will become Khan after me.'

And so Anusha became Khan, and he and his father are both entombed in the Pakhlavan Mahmud mausoleum. The Khan bequeathed Anusha the city of Hazerasp, and named Khiva's homom after him.

As the story reached its conclusion, all three dyers gratefully staggered out of the sauna to douse themselves and get some air.

We began scrubbing ourselves, and as the streams of filth slithered off Hoshnaut and Davlatnaza they both became visibly lighter in colour. Toychi – ashamed of nothing – scrutinised me, wanting to know whether British men were usually circumcised, why I didn't shave my pubic hair, which brothels I frequented and who was my favourite. He then explained his own sexual frustrations. Although just seventeen, he'd been engaged and set to marry when his father unexpectedly died. All wedding plans were postponed until a year of official mourning had passed, leaving Toychi's passions untrammelled. This inevitably gave rise to the subject of donkeys.

My first confrontation with this subject had taken place while wedged in the back seat of a shared taxi on my way from the Tajik border to Samarkand. The journey was long and, as I tried to read, my fellow passengers quizzed me on my sexual conquests in Uzbekistan. Disappointed with my answers, they then suggested that, as a wealthy foreigner, the least I could do was to pay for a trip to the brothel. I declined. Would I, they ventured, prefer a stable-stop instead? At first I thought this was a joke, but soon they were regaling each other with amusing anecdotes of their own teenage liaisons with donkeys, agreeing on a preference for foals. Hadn't I heard the proverb, 'An Uzbek man's first wife is his donkey'?

I asked whether any donkey would do, or whether it had to be female, provoking an outraged response. What sort of men did I think they were? Of course they would never touch a male donkey, and nor would any other animal arouse their ardour. I was obviously extremely ignorant, and they helpfully asked a policeman at the next checkpoint where the nearest donkeys were tethered, to initiate their foreign guest. Only a feigned deep sleep changed the topic of conversation.

Eager to avoid more talk of donkeys, I asked the dyers about their family backgrounds. Toychi's was predictably scandalous. His mother had left her husband and eloped with a young musician, despite the fact that she already had three sons. This was unheard of, even among the few Russians living in town. Toychi had been their love-child and had inherited his father's impudence and charm. His older half-brothers had all gone to Russia in search of work and Toychi would have joined them if he hadn't been given a job at the workshop.

Hoshnaut – small and wiry – was born in Turkmenistan but had moved to Khiva as a child. It was from other sources that I learnt he had been placed in the Khiva institute for those with learning difficulties and was considered something of a joke. He strutted around the workshop declaring to no one in particular that he was a dyer now and a man of importance, and the weavers took great delight in baiting him. Toychi and Hoshnaut bickered and fought like cubs, but Toychi leapt to his defence whenever Hoshnaut was picked on.

Hoshnaut and Davlatnaza were good friends and neighbours – Hoshnaut living in an equally tiny and squalid hovel. Davlatnaza was thrilled to have work. He had always been told what he couldn't do because of his disability, but now he wasn't just living on a pension and maybe people would take him seriously.

It was a week after a subsequent trip to the homom with the dyers that I finally decided to investigate the source of constant

itching. Having stripped, I discovered that these were no mosquito bites but colonies of body-lice – one particularly fat louse
in the process of laying eggs. Cursing Davlatnaza – undoubtedly the source of these creatures – I wondered what local or
Soviet cures were available to get rid of them. All I knew was
that I had no intention of being 'radiated' again.

'Radiation' was probably my most bizarre experience of
Soviet-style medical treatment. It took place during an integration camp for the disabled run by Operation Mercy in the
mountains near Tashkent, and began with the discovery that
two deaf brothers from Namangan had scabies. The camp
doctor examined them and – rueing the day she had ever con-
sented to let these disabled vermin into her camp – ordered that
we must all leave at once.

Catriona reasoned with her and we were grudgingly given
permission to stay. There was one condition. All those from
our camp wanting to use the swimming pool must be radiated.
Some of our foreign volunteers, horrified at what this might
entail, refused. I on the other hand had endured a long dusty
summer in Khiva and was unwilling to relinquish my swimming rights for anything.

That afternoon, I found myself in the medical facility monitoring a group of boys from our camp, all of us stripped to our
underwear. The girls had been radiated that morning and had
told us the routine.

'First I must power up ze machine!' explained a mad-scien-
tist Russian matron in a lab-coat. I caught a glimpse of a large
lamp on a stand in the room behind her that emitted ultraviolet
light. Once the radiation lamp was powered up, I had to blind-
fold each boy and march them all into a circle around the lamp.
We all dropped our pants, blindfolded, and stood spread-eagled

as the lamp was switched on. Thoughts of cancer and infertility flitted through my mind, but I focused on the cool pool I would soon be plunging into – a bellow from the nurse outside signalling that it was time for us to turn and radiate our backs.

I brought my embarrassing louse situation to Madrim's attention, miming the word for louse which I'd never needed before. He agreed with my conclusion that Davlatnaza had been the source, and with *anti-bit* written on a scrap of paper, I headed for the chemist section of the bazaar. Dousing myself with half a large bottle, I gathered my clothes and laid them in the sun for a few days, as nits were often laid in the seams. Davlatnaza received the remaining half-bottle and a lengthy homily on hygiene. Regina, an occupational therapist working with Andrea, had recently suffered from an outbreak of fleas after spending the night in one of the village houses, and found them breeding in her own house. I knew of other foreigners who could only visit village houses wearing anti-flea cat-collars on their wrists and ankles, having proved particularly popular with the local parasites.

Although I spent time with the apprentice dyers, they were younger and there was always the barrier of my being their boss. It was with Madrim that I became really close. He would often invite me to his home after work and we'd lounge on corpuches, drinking bowls of green tea and discussing the latest challenges at work. I told him of my original misgivings about employing him, as Koranbeg's brother, but how grateful I was that we had. Never had I come across someone so untiringly scrupulous in their work.

Madrim told me more about his background. He had been painfully shy at school, weight-training to defend himself in the playground. His fine physique stood him in good stead during his service in the Red Army. Like so many Khivans on army service, he was sent to Leningrad speaking almost no Russian, having never travelled further than Tashkent. Suddenly he found himself eating pork, drinking vodka and joining in with the inter-ethnic fighting that made for recreation in the barracks. Uzbek and Azeri recruits were the bitterest opponents unless a squabble broke out with Russians or Ukrainians, at which point they leapt to their fellow Muslims' aid.

I asked him if there had been any romances with Russian girls during his service and he just laughed. On arrival at the barracks they were given a medical which included injections repeated twice a year. They soon realised that these caused impotence for around six months, ensuring that soldiers kept their minds on the job. He had been promoted as an exemplary soldier and had even served briefly in Afghanistan, although had never experienced any fighting.

Madrim returned from the army and his parents began looking for a suitable wife. He mentioned a girl in his class who he'd always liked, and the marriage was arranged. He wanted to train as a doctor but instead applied to the Institute of Restoration, learning the different styles of *naqsh*, or design – both arabesque and geometrical.

Loving his job, Madrim had always worked hard, restoring the Naqshbandi mausoleum in Bukhara and a couple of mosques in Shakrisabz, as well as the Khan's palace in Kokand. Slowly, he had saved enough money to buy land and then build a house. Along with his wife and three children, he had lived a simple but happy existence until the realities of independent Uzbekistan began to sink in.

'When they told me that there was no more work for me, I didn't know what to do. In the Soviet times everyone had work, or the government would help you to find work. Now they just said *bulder*, it's finished, you're on your own. We were still setting up our own home and there was so much work to be done, and three children to feed. I talked with my brother and he told me that I must do what everyone else was doing and go to Russia or Kazakhstan as a builder. I asked around and found a man who knew someone who knew someone and, together with four or five others, we travelled to a place near Chimkent.

'The Kazakhs, they were so hard. You know, we used to make jokes about the Kazakhs. We thought they were simple, and now here we were begging them for work. Everything was more expensive there and people were earning much better wages. We had to build a school, and it was winter and really cold. They showed us an old railway wagon with no heating and told us that we would live there. They gave us such thin blankets and old corpuches to sleep on. We had to work really hard and we kept asking them when they would pay us and they always promised it would be soon. In the end they cheated us out of everything. They didn't even pay for our transport home. Coming back, the border guards stole my jacket – my one decent piece of clothing. I came back to Khiva with no hope. My wife cried when she saw how thin I was, and I had such a fever from the cold.

'Aslan, I prayed to God and asked him why this was happening. Why was he punishing me? What had I done wrong? My wife, she was so worried about me, even more worried than about the children and how we would get money. I did some odd jobs for my brother, but that wasn't enough. Then the workshop started and now I have a job and I'm learning the skills of my forefathers that we have forgotten. Now I can lift up my head again. I will always work as hard as I can for you and for our workshop.'

~

Madrim's story was a common one, and tales of unemployment and desperation repeated themselves around the country. Factory after factory had closed, unable to run on market principles and unsure what to do without orders issued from Tashkent or Moscow. Petty trading with Russia and neighbouring countries took off. Large women, capable of hefting their bodyweight in bazaar bags, were prominent on every train or bus – usually shouting at a guard or policeman angling for a bribe. The 'kiosk economy', as it was known, had kept former Soviet countries afloat during the first rocky years of independence. As the fortunes of Russia and Kazakhstan improved, manual labouring jobs became more popular and now, every spring, convoys of clapped-out buses left for Orenburg, Kazan and Perm.

This changed the whole demographic of Khiva. In winter I would sit for up to two hours waiting my turn at the barbers while being interrogated about the price of meat in England, the price of a loaf of bread, a car, a trip to the brothel, the wage of a teacher or football player. How much did I earn, was I circumcised, had I ever been to Liverpool, Newcastle, Arsenal or Manchester? In summer, the barber greeted me like a long-lost friend, desperate for business. It wasn't long before he too packed up his shop and followed everyone else in search of work.

The annual migration split families, giving little time for newlyweds to get to know each other after an arranged marriage. They were often virtual strangers, and living with extended family, a new bride spent more time with her mother- and sisters-in-law than with her own husband. A friend once called me with the good news that he was getting married in three weeks and that I must come and give a speech at his wedding. I congratulated him and asked him who the bride was, but he still wasn't sure – his parents hadn't told him yet.

Children grew up without their father's discipline, and boredom drinking was becoming a serious problem in the latter winter months. Women had mixed feelings about the forced separation. Many missed their husbands, brothers, sons and fathers but also enjoyed greater freedom and responsibility while their husbands were away. There were stories of teenage boys seduced by desperate housewives, though generally speaking it was the men who kept the brothels of Russia and Kazakhstan in business.

In fact, there was a marked double standard when it came to sexual practices. Young men boasted of their exploits with donkeys or 'bad girls' but expected blood on the sheets after the wedding night as proof of virginity. After marriage many men continued to frequent brothels, using the tenuous argument that the Prophet had more than one wife. When I asked how they would feel if their wives behaved in the same way, they got upset, suggesting that I questioned their wives' honour. Over a bowl of tea, one friend asked me if I would permit my future wife to place my tool in her mouth. I mumbled something non-committal as he expounded on the wickedness of this practice, assuring me that this was something he did only with 'bad girls'. Asked what his wife would say if she knew this, he simply shrugged. She didn't.

Morality, as far as men were concerned, seemed to be a case of not getting caught; but this was certainly not so for women. If there wasn't blood on the wedding sheets, the new bride would be thrown out on the street and returned to her parents, where a thrashing awaited her. Women were expected to endure rather than enjoy sex with their husbands, merely lying back and thinking of the sons they would produce – their character questioned if they exhibited too much pleasure. Bored with their wives, men would seek out prostitutes or, if they could afford it, take a mistress or share one with a few other men. A friend from a village told me how hard it had been for his father, sleeping in the same room as all his children. My friend would lie there, listening to bedclothes rustling and then his mother's whispered hiss: 'You came to me last night. Just give me some peace. How many donkeys do we own? Can't you bother them?' His father would slink out to the stables, my friend ensuring that his own nightly forays never coincided.

The differing expectations of men and women were engendered young in life. Little boys were spoilt and coddled, spending their days swimming naked in the canal or playing football with friends. Their bodies were fawned over – tiny penises tugged affectionately by older relatives. Little girls were taught to feel shame over their bodies, even toddlers expected to cover up. They learnt to sweep and to help their mother and older sisters prepare food for their brothers, ready for when they charged into the house, exhausted by play.

The spectre of AIDS hung over Uzbekistan, with its large population of promiscuous and itinerant men who knew little about sexually transmitted diseases. I asked friends if they used condoms and they usually just shrugged, saying, 'May God save us'; or they explained that they always washed carefully afterwards.

'I only use the good girls' was another common response. My neighbour's son told me about a doctor who, for a bribe, administered injections that gave protection from all sexual illnesses for three months.

To fend off the bombardment of questions on my sex life each time I visited the gym, I asked my companions instead about their own habits. If I raised the issue of marital fidelity, the reply was always the same. 'Aslan, do you like plov?' they would ask, to which there could be only one answer. 'Yes,' they would continue, 'but you wouldn't want to eat it every day, would you?'

I parried with a culinary question of my own. I asked my friends if they enjoyed steamed meat dumplings, fried meat pastries or boiled meat ravioli, pointing out that they were the same dish, just cooked in different ways. Often the root cause of married men visiting brothels was that their wives had been taught that sex was a sinful necessity in order to produce children, and that they should simply accept it as a duty. I found myself dispensing simple bedroom tips – the type found in any women's glossy at home – to spice up married relationships a little.

I felt that the development of the workshop was going well, but my feelings weren't shared by Barry, whose passion for carpets had made him a little too involved in the project, leading him to micro-manage from Tashkent. I baulked at being ordered around and reminded him that we were partners and that he wasn't my boss.

'Yes, but who's paying for this project?' Barry threatened after a fraught discussion over the phone.

'If it's a question of money, Barry, I'm sure Operation Mercy would be happy to provide funding as well. We could go halves,' I countered, and the matter was promptly dropped.

However, phone discussions remained terse and visits were worse. Barry monitored a number of locally-run regional projects and was used to Uzbeks anticipating his arrival, ensuring that everything looked perfect and ran smoothly, at least for the duration of his visit. Whenever the President visited Khorezm, the electricity, gas and water all magically functioned, the roads were swept, buildings – even private houses along important streets – were painted and flowers planted in a grand charade of progress. I saw this as papering over the cracks and wasn't about to do the same with Barry. He was keen to visit the workshop every few months and would usually begin by complaining and nit-picking.

'Why have you drawn this design in two different shades of red?' he demanded once, sitting in the office cell.

'Because they're two different shades in the miniature. Here, look,' I replied, handing him the original picture.

'No they're not!'

'Yes they are.'

'No they're bloody well not!'

'Barry, you can swear at me if you like, but it doesn't change the colour. There are definitely two different shades of red in that miniature. Take the book out into the courtyard and look at it in natural light.'

Barry returned a few minutes later, complaining about our lack of decent office lighting in lieu of an apology.

Our strained relationship was saved a few weeks later by Barry's fall down a flight of stairs. He was rushed to Paris for an operation and six months' recuperation. I felt guiltily over-joyed, hoping for some peace and quiet and space to get on with things.

With Barry gone, I felt more at liberty to pursue an idea which Barry had vetoed. I loved our Timurid carpet designs but also wanted us to weave something unique to Khiva. The beautiful majolica tiled walls of the old city, complete with field and frame, already looked like hanging carpets and the designs were original. There even seemed to be a link between the Timurid designs and the oldest tiles in Khiva, found on the tomb of Sayid Allaudin. The tiles were contemporary with the Timurid miniatures and featured the same stylised Kufic knots found in Timurid carpets. I visited the tomb and asked for permission to climb over the barrier and explore it more thoroughly. The old lady in charge, keen to offend an ageing mullah who had recently installed himself on her turf, happily guided me through.

The tiles were raised in a subtle relief and of a higher qual-ity than the more commonplace 19th-century ones. The design and colour palette of deep blue, turquoise and white worked well, and a repeating octagonal pattern found on top of the tomb would make an excellent field.

Madrim was keen on the design but nervous of Barry's response. Still, Barry was in Paris and would stay there for some time, so I put plans for our 'rebel rug' into action as we prepared for our first wage day.

8

The dawn sweepers

*'You would never believe it,' he said, 'how our women are spoilt
among us Sarts (Uzbeks). You can often see Kirghiz women
working in the fields, or Russian women too, but you'll never see
a Sart woman doing so. Even in the house they do not do much;
they can't even cook a decent plov, they only spoil the rice.'*
—Paul Nazaroff, *Hunted Through Central Asia*, 1932

Money-changing was part of my initial orientation in Tashkent.
On my arrival in 1998, a dollar was worth around 240 som in
the bank and around 280 som in the bazaar. Changing in the
bazaar was easier (the service was much better) but illegal.
Over subsequent years, the gap between the bank and bazaar
rates widened considerably until there was 700 som difference.
Key government ministers amassed a personal fortune from
this two-tier system despite the financial ruin it was causing
the country. International businesses despaired and left. The
private sector dwindled and the police enjoyed the bribes they
collected each day from the money-changers in return for turning a blind eye to their practices.

I was introduced to a shop selling underwear and perfume in
Mirobod bazaar next to the Operation Mercy flat in Tashkent.
The majority of other customers also came for illicit monetary
exchanges. We would hand over our dollar notes and linger
until a stout woman returned with a carrier bag bearing the
equivalent in som. The system worked well until a policeman

drew close, at which point we immediately feigned interest in displays of thongs or a mannequin leg festooned with garters.

The Khiva bazaar – keen to exploit unwary tourists – was not a good place to change money. My policy was to count the bundles of greasy som notes before handing over my dollars, ignoring the impatient assurances that the money was 'with guarantee'. As the dollar devalued, changing money surreptitiously became less simple. The handing over of a dollar bill was no problem, but the bundles of som given in return were a little more conspicuous. The largest denomination was 500 som – around half a dollar – and suitcases full of money were needed to make transactions for cars or to buy plane tickets.

Early on the morning of our first wage day in the spring of 2002, I went down to the bazaar with Madrim. We passed the fish-sellers, stalls of stationery and toiletries, reams of bright polyester material for dresses, and crates of vodka, arriving at a group of men loitering next to a clothing stall. We were immediately solicited with calls of 'Dollar, Rusiski!' announcing the two currencies used alongside the som. I wanted nothing smaller than 100-som bills and we found someone willing to change, assuring us that we could bring back any bundles missing a note or two. Filling a sturdy bazaar bag, we heaved the contents back to the workshop, where there was a general air of festivity. Weavers sat in gaggles outside, discussing an especially glittery pair of shoes they had in mind, or the material they'd seen in the caravanserai which was expensive but particularly shiny. Work had ground to a halt.

Ulugbibi and Safargul, the weaving ustas, joined us in the office cell as we tipped out the bundles of som onto the table and began counting. The smaller notes were held together with nothing but grease, sweat and dirt. Women tended to keep their money in their bras; and in summer, returned change was moist to the touch, especially after a plump matriarch selling cherries had rooted around in her cavernous bra for the correct notes.

The weavers filed in, loom by loom, to receive their wages. Outside, they fanned their bundles of notes at those still waiting, laughing, joking and keen to hit the bazaar as soon as possible. The dyers swaggered in like khans, ignoring heckling from the weavers, and strutted out waving their wages in the air to mock applause. The actual wage was pitiful, but for many in the workshop it was the first time they had ever received such a thing, and they were relishing every moment. I hoped that we could increase these basic apprentice wages to something more substantial once we began selling carpets.

I wasn't being paid a penny to run the workshop, but I received more than enough payment watching the younger weavers discuss what gifts they would buy family members, or seeing women like Sanajan the widow quietly fold her bundle of notes into her bra, knowing that she would be putting food on the table for her children.

After our first wage day there was a deluge of women wanting to work with us. We started a list on a first-come, first-served basis, undeterred by applicants who attempted sobbing or seduction in order to jump the queue. The weavers, feeling flush, bought enough material to make into a kind of uniform, returning with reams of black polyester fabric covered in large neon-green and yellow bow motifs. Wasn't this the most beautiful fabric? I was asked, lying in reply.

Shirin invited everyone to her house for her birthday and we enjoyed the first of many social gatherings outside the workshop. Friendships were forming, along with a corporate sense of identity. I was limited in how much time I could spend, as a man, with the weavers. Most were deferential, at least at the beginning, although there were some definite exceptions. Dark Nazokat was one of them. A continual source of worry to her mother, her dark skin colour reduced her chances of ever finding a husband, further dampened by her loud, boisterous character. She was usually at the centre of workshop gossip or scandal and developed a worrying crush on Madrim, who dreaded every encounter with her.

'The darkness of the heart shows itself in the skin,' tutted one of the older weavers, quoting an Uzbek proverb, as Nazokat began a slanging match with Toychi the dyer, with whom she either flirted or sparred.

I spent more time with the weaving ustas and, as we worked together, Ulugbibi liked to complain about her mother-in-law, who kept a tight rein on her. Ulugbibi herself was a striking woman and had been quite a head-turner in her youth – promptly married off to keep her out of trouble. She lived with her husband, his mother and her two sisters-in-law who had never married and enjoyed picking on her. Ulugbibi longed to move out, but her husband struggled to find work and they couldn't afford their own place. I asked her if she loved her husband, which she considered a strange question and one to which she hadn't given much thought. Safargul the usta was in a similar predicament as the main breadwinner in their house. Her husband, according to Madrim, was a good-for-nothing. Safargul was careful to keep her earnings away from him, knowing how quickly they could be turned into a wild bout of drinking or frittered away on 'bad girls'.

Although women were undoubtedly second-class citizens in Khiva, their lot had improved dramatically. In fact, the impact of Communism on women's rights all over Central Asia was nothing short of revolutionary. Previously they had been veiled, largely house-bound and the property of their husbands – who could divorce them by merely repeating 'I divorce thee' three times. Suddenly they were presented with a bewildering level of status. Under Soviet law, women could divorce their husbands and gain employment, and were provided with unlimited access to birth control and abortion.

As the Bolsheviks gained control over Turkestan (later carved up into the current –stans) in the early 1920s, they called on women to emancipate themselves, to throw off the veil and discard domestic servitude for equal rights as factory workers.

Gustav Krist, an Austrian POW interned in Turkestan during the First World War, escaped to Persia but returned in the mid-1920s to witness the transformation taking place under the Communist regime. Previously veiled women now wore Soviet skirts and jackets. He met a young proletariat leader of one village who had, a few years previously, been an illiterate slave, third wife to a rice merchant. Now she was the most powerful person in the village, learning how to read and to speak Russian.

Schools of ballet were set up to better the toiling masses, and Uzbek girls, previously scolded for exposing too much wrist, now paraded on stage in tights and tutus. Liberated bare-faced Uzbek women braved the old city in Tashkent, going from house to house and preaching emancipation. The first batch had their throats promptly slit and their successors were provided with revolvers. Mass veil-burnings were conducted in public squares, the air acrid with the smell of burning horse-hair. The scratchy black horse-hair veil was worn under the *paranja* – a long cape with extended ornamental sleeves, sewn together at the wrist like handcuffs to symbolise that this wearer was the property of her husband. The veil could be flicked back, exposing the face and allowing free conversation with other women, then flipped over again if men passed by. They were stifling in summer, made breathing difficult, and with regular use left scabs on the nose and chin where the rough horse-hair continually rubbed. The overall effect was best described by a Swiss traveller to Central Asia in the 1930s, Ella Maillart, who referred to passing women veiled in this way as walking upright coffins.

In order to liberate women, not only from the veil but from motherhood, huge crèches were set up in the factories. Neat rows of beshiks were rocked by nurses, their contents tightly swaddled inside. Most Uzbek babies spent the first year of their life strapped tightly into one of these cradles, which flattened the back of their skull. They proved essential in traditional families, in which women produced large numbers of children and were unable to watch over them all at once. Dummies dipped in sugar and opium kept babies happy and quiet, their mothers lifting a breast over the rocking wooden structure to feed.

The beshiks were designed to keep mess to a minimum, each floored with a mattress with a hole strategically positioned halfway down to collect piped urine. Strings of cloves and chilli peppers adorned each beshik, bread and a knife were placed under the mattress, and triangular amulets stuffed with Koranic verses hung from the wooden rocking handle that ran the length of the cradle. These were all *achik*, and kept the evil eye at bay. European cradles were introduced in the

Soviet factories but met with stiff opposition from the workers and were soon replaced with beshiks. These were, after all, a practical way of caring for large numbers of infants, and the time-honoured tradition of dipping dummies in sugar and opium also proved popular with Soviet nurses, quietening the unhappiest of squalls.

Another Soviet concession regarded the use of *isfan*. This dried yellow plant – the equivalent of garlic in medieval Europe – was said to cleanse the air of evil spirits, particularly those causing disease. Anyone taking to their bed with flu needed nothing more than a thorough smoking – a pan of acrid isfan smoke wafted around them. The Soviets, attempting to ban such superstitious nonsense, soon realised the futility of this and instead secularised the practice. Soviet doctors declared that isfan rid the air of microbes. Even today, each time there's a flu epidemic, school nurses wander the classrooms in their white coats and surgical masks, smoking each child with a belching pan of isfan.

Despite gains for women made under Communism, traditional values remained strong, as I witnessed during my seven years in Uzbekistan. In the Khorezm oasis women had a particularly hard time, as brides were sold for a hefty bride-price – the groom's family then expecting value for money.

Grooms were expected to provide a chest full of new dresses, a set of corpuches and heavy gold-hooped earrings. Most families, struggling to make ends meet, could hardly afford this or the huge quantities of food and vodka consumed by hundreds of wedding guests.

Weddings took an entire day, beginning with a tour of the Ichan Kala's holy sites for the bridal couple and their friends. A madrassah converted into a wonderfully kitsch confection of plasterwork, zodiac signs, stained-glass windows of bride and groom, and even a stork with a baby-sized parcel in its beak, made for the 'house of happiness' where a register was signed and the couple were legally married.

The wedding party, enjoying the absence of older relatives, then raced in their cars to one of the war memorials where they would lay flowers in a nod to Soviet tradition – the cars festooned with ribbons and balloons and LOVE written in English on the back window. The groom's car sported a large tiger or teddy-bear strapped to the front, while the bride's had a plastic doll attached to its bonnet, the driver speeding to make her skirts fly up.

The groom retired to a friend's house with his mates for a feast, while the bride returned home to begin her farewells. Old grandmothers sang '*Kelin*, don't cry' as the young girl wept, knowing that she was no longer a member of this household. She was torn from her parents and driven to the groom's house, her parents remaining alone and taking no further part in the celebrations, for they had just lost their daughter. The young girl, shrouded in a blanket, had to bow low before each of her in-laws. She was beginning her new life as a *kelin* – meaning literally 'come in' – and taking her place at the bottom of the family food-chain.

The kelin's female relatives took her to the bedroom she would share with her new husband and covered her in a silk blanket, standing guard outside the door. The groom, return-ing with his mates, had to fight his way into the room, offering gifts on the way, before picking up the bride and throwing her onto the bed. His robe, hat, shoes and belt were removed and everyone watched as he joined her in bed – grannies laying charms around and under it as a baby boy was passed through the sheets in hope of a first-born son.

As the day drew to a close, the wedding feast began. Plastic chairs and tables were set up outside the groom's house and lighting was rigged. A large factory-made carpet hung as a backdrop, the names of the couple written on it in cotton-wool. Live music blasted, distorted, through speakers and made conversation almost impossible; for there should be no distraction from the main entertainment provided by the professional dancer. Dancers were usually considered 'bad girls' and were often available for other services after the celebration. Men leered as the dancer swayed her voluptuous hips – her plump figure almost bursting out of a sequinned costume, tiny braids flying as she spun.

It was the dancer's job to collect money from the male relatives, who were expected to finance the musicians. She danced up to their table and one by one they staggered drunkenly to their feet, bank notes in hand, offering a token few. These were glanced at disparagingly, and with a toss of her head and shimmy of her shoulders, the dancer looked enquiringly for more. This continued until the dancer was satisfied with the sum or the drunk relative stuffed it down her bra and stalked off.

A few times I had been called upon to present money in this fashion, and – hoping for more lucrative business after the wedding – the dancers exceeded themselves in flirtation. Despite the hoots of laughter my embarrassment produced, this was still preferable to making speeches. I rarely escaped without a microphone being thrust into my face by the roving master of ceremonies, with demands that 'our guest from afar' say a few words. My first speech had been a rough translation of what I might have said in English and was a complete disaster. It was far too short, lacking in superlatives, and with no deluge of extravagant wishes.

People I scarcely knew invited me to their weddings, hoping the exotic garnishing of a foreign guest would improve their status within the community. I avoided these if possible, but always enjoyed workshop weddings. The entire group was usually invited, and the uninhibited weavers could be relied on to get the dancing started. I enjoyed the astonishment produced when, as a foreigner, I danced the traditional lazgi. I learnt to make better speeches, parroting the same formulaic blessings as everyone else. Toychi the dyer disgraced himself, getting violently drunk on numerous occasions and trying to start fights with the groom's relatives. Each time he would appear hungover and penitent the next day, vowing never to touch another drop.

My most memorable wedding was Shoira's. She was a small, pale orphan who lived with her brother and his wife who mistreated her. Quiet, and self-conscious about her speech impediment, she was both damaged and vulnerable. She wasn't a particularly good weaver, although she improved dramatically under Fatima-the-twin's tyranny. Once she tried to kill herself, drinking a bottle of powerful vinegar but thankfully vomiting. Her throat was damaged and she was unable to speak or eat solids for two weeks.

As an orphan from a poor family, unable to defend herself, she was picked on at first by one or two of the weavers who were swiftly castigated by the others. They became quite protective of her, knowing the beatings and other hardships she endured at home. One day Shoira entered the workshop, eyes shining, and invited us all to her wedding. She was marrying a poor village boy but that didn't matter, because he had told her that he liked her and no one had ever said that to her before.

She looked stunning at the wedding, wearing a particularly lavish wedding dress. It was only afterwards that I heard the story behind this. Her in-laws, happy with their bargain bride, had presented her with a stained and dirty old wedding dress to wear for the occasion. Devastated, she'd wept with shame until the outraged weavers had taken the matter in hand. They pooled their wages and presented her with a brand-new outfit. Speechless with gratitude, she wore the dress with pride. At that moment our workshop became more than just a collection of weavers and dyers; we became family.

I had attended enough weddings to know that the bride and groom weren't expected to look happy. Both were unused to all the attention and still tired from the preceding days of preparation. The couples, usually in their late teens or early twenties, often felt awkward with each other, having met only a few times previously. The bride, at least, was allowed to look miserable, her eyes downcast and unsmiling. She had, after all, just left her family; and there was also the ordeal of the wedding night looming.

Young men discussed just how much blood should be spilt on the wedding sheets to really prove a girl's virginity, and were unrestrained on the first night. Despite a female relative discreetly monitoring proceedings, new kelins' first sexual experience was invariably painful, many unable to sit down properly for days afterwards.

A newly married kelin's life wasn't a happy one – a system perpetuated by miserable young women who eventually became mothers-in-law, keen to inflict cruelty on the next generation. In Khorezm, kelins were expected to wake at five in the morning and sweep the street outside the house. This was followed by preparation of breakfast and domestic drudgery to keep her busy until late at night. She mustn't look at her mother-in-law but keep her eyes downcast, and must speak only when spoken to. Her lowly status gradually eased as she bore sons, or as her younger brothers-in-law married, bringing a new, lowlier kelin to the household.

Right from the start there was pressure to produce children, kelins experiencing regular interrogation from their mothers-in-law as to why they were still menstruating. They were expected to greet all in-laws with three slow bows, rubbing their hands against their knees at the same time. Kelins often lost weight, feeling ashamed to eat more than a few silent bites at the table. Insubordination led to beatings, often administered by mothers-in-law, or by husbands at their mother's command. The first birth was always a big occasion, demanding another large feast and further debt. While everyone wanted their firstborn to be male, daughters were a pragmatic consolation as they would soon be doing the cooking and cleaning around the house.

Why any woman would want to marry at all, I wasn't sure, but it was still the most important aspiration for the younger weavers at the workshop. I assumed that once our weavers got married, this would be the last we would see of them. After all, they had streets to sweep, dinners to cook and drudgery to do. Thankfully, the economic realities of independence meant that no one could afford to give up a good job, and even the most controlling mother-in-law returned her new cash-cow to the workshop, eager for the extra income. Most newly married kelins were given two weeks off to begin a honeymoon of silent servitude, before gratefully returning to the workshop.

At the workshop, silent and demure kelins reconstituted themselves into the vibrant young women they were. Free from the tyrannies of mothers-in-law, they could talk and laugh, eat as much as they liked and enjoy their freedom. They could show off their new wardrobe and their gold-hooped earrings fitted with turquoise stones, while gaining marital advice from the older weavers. Each new kelin wore a gold-embroidered square skull-cap with tassels for the first month or so, and a headscarf after that to show her married status.

Earning a wage brought all the women in the workshop more status within their families. Kelins gained more freedom and were less likely to receive severe beatings, and older women were able to save money their husbands might otherwise have drunk, to buy clothes and food for their children.

Although the workshop increased status, it didn't stop domestic abuse. A number of the married women arrived at work purple and bruised, having 'fallen over' – an excuse that would be met with knowing glances from the other women. Of all the workshop girls, Kamolat suffered the most. She was a stunning young woman with huge dark eyes, full lips and porcelain skin. On one of my morning rounds, the girls in her cell announced that Kamolat had just got engaged. I congratulated her and asked her what her fiancé was like. There was an awkward silence which provided a clear answer.

I asked her why she was getting married to someone she didn't like. He was the son of her father's good friend and everything was already arranged, so why make a fuss?

Toychi knew her fiancé, who was a notorious drunk and good-for-nothing.

After the wedding, Kamolat took the usual couple of weeks off. She returned having aged at least a decade in the process, her skin pallid, large rings under her eyes and a vacant, dead expression where once there had been such animation and life. Everyone noticed but said nothing. Soon she came to work bruised. Of course, the weavers agreed, it was permissible for a man to beat his wife occasionally, but Kamolat was being thrashed on a regular basis.

I insisted that we do something but was told quite clearly that my interference would only make the problem worse. Her loom-mates wove more on her behalf and tried to lift her spirits. She developed a steely streak that had not been there before, declaring that she would attend a birthday party despite the fact that her husband had forbidden it.

'What can he do? He can only beat me. If he does a good enough job then I won't be able to work and then we'll see what his mother has to say.'

I was away when Kamolat's husband turned up at the workshop in a drunken rage. He began shouting at her to come home and she refused. He hit her, dragging her screaming by the hair. Madrim had been at the bazaar with Toychi at the time, and the other dyers hadn't known what to do. I hoped that the husband would try something similar again on workshop property when we were around, so we could press charges – wife-beating being unacceptable if done in public.

Kamolat's main aim was to get pregnant, which she managed within eight months of marriage.

'Of course, he doesn't care about me,' she explained, 'but he's not going to risk hurting the baby. It might be a son.'

Kamolat begged us to keep a place for her at the workshop, her refuge, after she had the baby, and so we gave her six months' maternity leave. A few years later, she finally divorced her husband, able to provide for herself with her weaving wages.

Women also endured the unspoken reality of their husbands' infidelities. Most were more angry at the money wasted than heartbroken that their husbands would seek another woman's arms, or so they said. At least they had the status and security of being the official wife. Women who had lost their reputation often became 'second wives' and were kept as mistresses. They had no rights, relying on enticement to keep their man, and were shared with other men if their lover hadn't the means to keep them.

Most women accepted their husband's passions, but were unwilling to endure anything more whimsical. Jeanette's house-help complained over a cup of tea that her husband wanted her to try 'positions'.

'There was none of this nonsense during the Soviet times,' she declared. 'Now they have all these films that give them silly ideas. I told my husband, "If you want to try acrobatics, then go and pay some young girl. I'm too old for it."'

Spring turned to summer and Khiva quietly simmered. Streets were deserted from midday until late afternoon as a white heat pervaded everything, hurting the eyes and sapping energy. Those unbound by office hours woke well before sunrise, retiring to a darkened room after lunch for a siesta. In the evenings we didn't eat until eight or nine, enjoying an after-dinner melon outside with our neighbours, trading gossip.

Baking bread in this weather was an unpleasant task, to be attempted only in the cool of the evening. Malika was responsible for stamping circular patterns onto the dough; Zulhamar then slapped them against the inner walls of the mud-brick oven, a headscarf low on her forehead to keep her eyebrows from singeing, Koranbeg's old army jacket protecting her arms. The walls of the oven rippled with heat as the dough puffed and baked, and Zulhamar deftly peeled each piece off, placing them in a large steaming stack. I tried my hand at this once, succeeding only in burning myself and dropping the dough into the flames.

A carpet-seller had given me a ginger kitten as a gift, which was now fully grown. He flopped dramatically anywhere shaded, rousing himself only at mealtimes to beg for food. The family taught me that cats in Khiva were fed on mouthfuls of masticated bread, which the cat would bolt down hungrily. What mine really wanted was meat, and I fed him surreptitiously with chunks of mutton until caught by Koranbeg's mother who had come to live with us for the summer. She hated the cat, who seemed completely oblivious, approaching her for food only to scamper away yelping as she doused him with a bowlful of scalding tea. When the cat wasn't available, she did as all Khorezm grannies still do, and lifted the corner of a carpet to deposit the dregs of her tea beneath it.

There were other animal encounters. The roof of our madrassah was the perfect place for snakes to bask peacefully in the summer sun. A snake once managed to slip through the ventilation hole in the centre of the domed ceiling, bounce off my head and drop into my lap. I shrieked in surprise, as did Safargul, who hadn't seen the snake but was startled by my sudden outburst. The snake – also startled – shot into a corner looking for a place to hide. Toychi grabbed it, ignoring the bites, and threw it outside, waving it in the faces of a few weavers en route. I was concerned that he might swell up and die, but Toychi assured me that this one wasn't poisonous, giving the neat puncture holes on his wrist a cursory rub and spit before returning to work.

Summer was proving a trying time for most of the weavers. They were used to a domestic routine that allowed for siestas in summer, and would often nod off during lunch breaks, which became more and more extended. We discussed the possibility of having proper breaks after lunch and working later into the evening, but most women were expected home promptly to prepare the evening meal. Some of the girls were still industrious but some were getting downright lazy. Ulugbibi the usta also decided that summer was a time to put one's feet up and snooze. She was careful not to do this in my presence, but on mornings when I was at the Operation Mercy office she would intersperse napping with tirades at the weavers to work harder. I heard about this from dark Nazokat – never far from trouble – who had challenged Ulugbibi to do some work herself. Now they were no longer on speaking terms. Clearly there needed to be some kind of working incentive for the weavers, and the obvious one was financial.

I discussed the matter with Madrim, inviting Matthias to join us. We worked out a new wage system that paid by the length of carpet woven each month. This would provide an incentive to weave more, and also meant that the wages could increase above the measly apprentice rate we had started with. I wanted the wages to be fair but our carpets to be competitively priced.

It was difficult to know what a fair wage was. We were paying more than a teacher or nurse received, but then their wages weren't enough to live on and they supplemented their income with bribes. Hospital workers simply filched medicine and equipment, while teachers arranged a more elaborate system. Each class elected a go-between, and this student then haggled with the teacher over how much the class needed to pay communally to receive favourable marks. It removed the teacher from the unsavoury business of extorting money, leaving this for the students themselves to work out.

Our new wage system proved an effective motivator, and soon a race was on as two of the looms neared completion of their first carpets. Whenever I talked about the carpets being cut from the loom, I unconsciously sliced at the tip of my forefinger, the way Khivans did when referring to circumcision. Soon the weavers were joking about our first *surnat toy* or circumcision party, wondering which loom would be given the honour. I asked Madrim how we should celebrate our first carpet circumcision, but he was preoccupied with his own preparation for the real circumcision of his youngest son, Husnaddin.

I'd been made to watch the video of Jalaladdin's circumcision along with that of his two cousins. The young boys first paraded around the walled city wearing mini-robes and polyester turbans. Back at the house, a jester entertained them, presenting each boy with a *chiman* – a mobile of sorts, hung with sweets and small toys. Once these were removed, the chiman hung outside for all to know that a circumcision had taken place. I had assumed that the video would tail off at this point, but no. Each boy was shown being brought into a room and held down on a corpuche, writhing as the barber approached. The camera lens narrowly avoided a spattering of blood, the whole procedure filmed from close range. I blanched at the howls of each of the boys as my Uzbek family guffawed at my squeamishness. 'This is the best bit! Jalaladdin cries like a girl. Look at him wailing!' yelled Malika as Jalaladdin launched himself at her. Madrim asked if I would come and take photos of Husnaddin's circumcision and to give him moral support. He had struggled to hold back the tears watching his first son under the knife.

The following Saturday I arrived at Madrim's house to find corpuches laid out against every available wall space. I was ushered into a room of male relatives, where the status of my own foreskin became the chief topic of discussion until I managed to extricate myself and help serving tea.

Husnaddin seemed a little shy at all the attention he was receiving, wandering around in his little robe and turban. The barber arrived and Madrim looked nervously at me. Mehribon retired to a different room with the women, where she was given a bowl of oil in which she immersed her forefinger to assuage her son's pain. Meanwhile, Husnaddin's trousers were removed and Madrim's relatives pinned him down as he began to sob. The barber prepared his kit, clamping the penis with a bamboo peg, leaving only the foreskin exposed. Husnaddin wailed loudly and with a lightning guillotine motion the barber swooped his knife across the bamboo peg, cleanly severing the foreskin.

Husnaddin shrieked, Madrim left the room, and I took photos. Men waved banknotes in Husnaddin's face, congratulating him on becoming a man as he sobbed inconsolably. A toy tractor appeared, and a new school bag. The barber propped cushions around the mattress and draped a large blanket over them, careful not to touch the freshly tinctured wound. Mehribon was allowed in, prompting a fresh bout of sobbing, and relatives filed past, congratulating Husnaddin and depositing banknotes around his pillow. It was Mehribon who paid the barber and, in return, was given a seeping red piece of cloth containing her son's foreskin. She would let the foreskin dry and keep it until Husnaddin was grown up, one day sewing it into the stuffing of his wedding mattress.

A week or so later we celebrated our first carpet circumcision. After a race between the Benaki and Shirin weavers, the Benaki design was finished just a few days earlier. Fatima finished weaving the last few lines of the kilim fringe as we piled into her cell to watch. 'Jacob Bai Hoja workshop, Khiva', helpfully written out in Dari Persian script by the Afghan embassy in Tashkent, had been woven in as our signature. Later we were told that we'd written 'beaver' or 'weaver' instead of 'Khiva'.

Safargul pointed to the place where Fatima should make the first cut, leaving enough of the warps to make a generous fringe. The severed warp threads pinged, shooting into the air and sending up plumes of dust as we cheered and applauded. Dragging the completed carpet outside, we were able to examine it in greater detail. It was lumpy and dirty and needed a good wash, but the colours were good and the design stunning. It wasn't perfect, being wider at one end, and there were a number of mistakes running down the side where Sharafat had worked. For a first attempt, though, I was really pleased. We dipped into our ice-cream fund as Fatima and her fellow weavers knotted the fringe.

Madrim flipped the rug over and lit a nozzle attached to a rubber hose and the nearest gas outlet. Running the flame over the underside, he scorched away the excess fluff to leave a clean, smooth finish. During the warmer months we were able to wash the rugs in the nearest canal, issuing a strict ration of shampoo and conditioner, as the girls used it to wash their hair on the sly. In winter, the washing process was more unpleasant, pouring buckets of icy water over each rug and then scrubbing on top of it.

Our first rug was now ready for trimming, just as the second rug was cut from the loom. It was a horrible job, leaving blistered fingers no matter how many rags were wrapped around them. The girls sat on top of the rug with a pole underneath one segment, trimming the excess pile and working their way steadily from one end to the other. The rug needed a final wash in cream of tartar and, once dry, lay glossy and lustrous in the courtyard. I circled it, watching the colours darken. As with all hand-woven carpets, the pile stood at an angle, reflecting light on one side and absorbing it on the other. Picking it up and shaking a corner, I sent shimmering ripples down the rug, relishing the luxuriant, supple feel of the silk. It was beautiful – but could we sell it?

9

A carpet called Shirin

When you see with the eyes of your head, you are no different from an animal. When you see with the eyes of your heart, all spaces are open to you.

—Rumi, 13th-century Persian poet

Our third carpet, named Shirin, lay washed and gleaming in the sun. Shirin told many stories, not all of them revealed at a glance or even on closer inspection. Admiring tourists could know little of Shirin's complex journey: its silk warp and weft produced by villagers paid a pittance for their labours under the oppressive state monopoly; the warm brown of its border created from walnut husks, collected by farm children in a village near Shakrisabz; the yellow scrolling vines dyed with dried pomegranate skins; the bright red diamonds at its centre coloured from the roots of the scrawny-looking madder plant grown in Afghanistan; and the rich indigo of the field design, produced from crushed and fermented leaves harvested in southern India.

Even the name Shirin held secrets of its own. Some might have thought we dedicated the carpet to the tall, fiercely loyal weaver who had laboured for more than four months with her sister Zamireh and her deaf friend Iroda – squabbling, gossiping and joking as nimble fingers flew. They wouldn't know that the name referred to a different Shirin, a tragic heroine of Persian literature, pictured in an exquisitely detailed miniature as she sat on a richly coloured carpet, awaiting her beloved

Husrov. The design gave no indication that it had lain dormant for half a millennium on a sheet of burnished vellum, painstakingly painted in ground lapis, white lead and minium; nor the changing hands through which the book had passed on its journey from Herat to London. A simple glance revealed little of the efforts that Zamireh had made to transcribe the Tumurid design onto graph paper, or her sense of outrage when she discovered it stolen by Ulugbeg, our rival from the Bukharan workshop.

None of these stories, woven into the very fabric of the carpet, was evident to a casual observer. Yet there was one story that played itself out quite clearly: row by row the florets became increasingly elongated, distorting the original design. It was this story I was most concerned with.

Shirin and her sister Zamireh squatted beside the carpet with Iroda as I scrabbled over it with a tape measure.

'Here' – I pointed to a place in the second row of florets – 'this is where everything starts going wrong. Exactly when we introduced the new wage system.'

It was my fault. Originally we had intended to count the number of vertical knots on the carpet each month and then subtract last month's total, multiplying this by the number of horizontal knots to arrive at an accurate total from which we could work out a fair wage. I had crawled under one of the looms, trying to count each knot, which appeared on the reverse of the carpet as a rough square. Emerging dusty and with a crick in my neck, I had decided that maybe we could cut corners and simply measure the length of the carpet and multiply this by the number of horizontal knots.

The crafty weavers soon realised that larger twists of silk woven into chunky rectangular knots beefed up the length of the carpet, increasing their wages and stretching the design in the process.

Zamireh protested that the problem was with the graph paper, but was silenced once the carpet was flipped over and the rectangular knots were plain to see. Other carpets still on the loom were similarly stretched; the only solution was to squeeze under the looms each month, counting the total of vertical knots and working out wages from there.

I planned to introduce the concept of a fixed price for our rugs, knowing how trying many uninitiated tourists found the process of haggling. Zafar the wood-carver offered wildly differing prices to tourists, which I felt was unfair until he pointed out how easy it was to distinguish between a backpacker on a tight budget and a member of a tour group with all the latest camera paraphernalia. Surely it was fairer, he argued, to fix the price according to the affluence of the buyer?

As news of our finished rugs spread, the attitude of local guides changed considerably. Before, they'd been happy to sit and smoke while I gave their group a free tour of the workshop; now that there was the potential for money to be made, they were keen for us to make a sale – expecting a 10 per cent cut.

Ulugbeg told me how the system worked in Bukhara. Guides released their groups for an afternoon of shopping, gathering again before dinner. At this point the guides feigned interest in everyone's purchases, noting prices and where each item had been bought, before surreptitiously doing the rounds, demanding 20 per cent from each stallholder. The woodwork shop installed in the madrassah next to ours paid hefty commission to the guides and received all the tour groups as a result, which left the better artisans struggling, the tourists with mediocre products and the guides making a small fortune.

Considering we were adding only 25 per cent profit, I had no intention of giving 10 per cent away. Nor was I stuck behind the language barrier like most sellers – a point not lost on many of the guides, who often resented my presence. After making it clear that there would be no commissions, we received such vitriol from the guides, with threats of boycott, that we capitulated, giving $10 to $20 commission, depending on the carpet size. This worked well with the Khiva guides, but those from Bukhara and Samarkand were used to their 10 or 20 per cent cut. They would still bring their groups to our workshop for a free tour, but would inform them that carpets in Samarkand were much better and cheaper. Catching a French-speaking guide in the act, I butted in, explaining to his group that the Afghan factory in Samarkand paid all guides 10 per cent for every purchase. He never returned.

A group of Belgians arrived at the workshop, without a guide, and decided to buy the carpet called Shirin. They were the first of many customers who desperately wanted a rug without ready cash to pay for it. I explained that we couldn't take credit cards, as this would entail a time-consuming attempt to extract our money from the bank – impossible without paying a hefty bribe. Instead, we asked customers to pay what they could and take the carpet on trust, completing their payment in Tashkent – where larger hotels had cashpoints – by leaving the money at the Operation Mercy office. It wasn't a very professional way of doing things, but no one ever abused the honour system – extended only to those we deemed trustworthy.

Toychi bundled the carpet into a bazaar bag while Madrim wrote out export documents. I handed the rug over with a sudden rush of mixed emotions. This was our first sale and a cause for celebration, but I felt as if I were giving away one of my babies, thinking of all it had taken to bring this carpet into existence.

'You will take good care of it, won't you?' I implored. 'Remember, silk doesn't have the bounce that wool does, so make sure you don't leave furniture on it. You should walk on it, though, as the friction of your feet polishes it and fluffs open the knots.'

I was sure there was more I could have said, but the Belgians just nodded indulgently and assured me that the carpet was in good hands. They took photos of themselves with the weavers and promised to send back a picture of the rug in its new home. The whole workshop came out to see them go. Madrim gave my shoulder a squeeze and I felt stupid for getting emotional.

September and October were the most popular months for tourism, and a time when small hills of melons were on sale in the bazaar. The days were warm and the nights crisp. This pleasant weather ended abruptly in late October when a few days of rain and cloud sent the temperature plummeting. The flimsy wooden doors of each madrassah cell were no match for the icy draughts, and we needed some form of insulation. I set off with Madrim to enlist the help of Khiva's last felt-maker.

We were greeted by the felt-maker himself – a diminutive old man with a flowing white beard, stooping heavily. I shook his extended hand and he yanked mine sharply, knocking me off balance.

'You see!' he cackled, 'I may be 80 but I'm still strong as an ox! Just you ask my wife. Every night I'm ready and she doesn't have the strength to fight me off anymore!'

We smiled weakly at this revelation as he beckoned us in. His wife had positioned herself over a beshik cradle and was breast-feeding her grandchild. Many village grandmothers still lactated, and grandchildren as old as ten or eleven often came for a cuddle and comfort feed.

'I'm the last felt usta, you know,' the old man explained. 'My sons, they're all lazy. None of them want to make felt when they can run off to Russia every summer. What will happen when God takes me? Who will you go to then?'

In his workshop behind the house, tufts of wool were laid out on the floor on top of a large sheet. Most of the wool was a natural cream or dark grey, but some had been dyed a lurid magenta, to which the usta proudly drew our attention. He explained that the clumps of raw wool, laid out in a rough pattern, were rolled up in the sheet and covered in boiling water. The sheet, folded into a reed mat, was then rolled continually for a couple of hours as the shrinking wool fibre matted, creating felt. This would keep the draughts out nicely, and we ordered enough mats to cover each cell door.

Once nailed in place, the felt insulated the cells effectively but left a pervading odour of sheep. Now I understood why felt alone was enough to wall the yurts used by nomads in winter, keeping out the sharpest wind and cold. According to Gustav Krist, the infamous *kara kurt* or black widow spider never ventured onto felt, making it the ideal ground-sheet for camping.

It was now the end of 2002, and Barry emailed announcing his return to Uzbekistan and plans to visit the workshop. I wondered how he'd react to our 'rebel rug', now one third complete. We would just have to let him rant and then get on with life as normal.

On his arrival he wanted a tour of the premises, and surprised us all by complimenting us on our progress and admiring the finished carpets. Assuming that his approval would be short-lived, I reluctantly led him into the weaving cell where the 'rebel rug' was taking shape.

'Please, ask the girls to leave,' said Barry, his eyes glued to the rebel rug.

Galvanising myself for a huge row, I asked the weavers, who were nervously exchanging glances, to step outside.

'That's better,' Barry continued. 'I just needed some space and quiet to really enjoy this magnificent design.'

I wasn't sure what to say. Barry was transfixed, examining the borders and then the field and comparing it with the laminated graph-paper pattern. He asked me to inform the workers how pleased he was with our progress, so much better than the Bukhara workshop. This last comment was particularly well received, marking a turning point in my relationship with Barry. We still had occasional disagreements, but a little praise had gone a long way to improving our working relationship.

A few weeks later the first really cold snap arrived, with temperatures down to −15°C at night. In timely fashion, there was also a gas cut for the whole town. Uzbekistan curiously managed to export gas but never seemed to have enough for its own population, who shivered as the fat cats running the state gas company disappeared to Thailand for some winter sun. My Uzbek family colonised one room, where two electric heaters took the edge off the cold. Here, they ate, slept, bickered and watched TV. I was invited to join them, but opted for peace over warmth. Sleep was possible only if I wore a woolly hat and snuggled under two duvets with a hot-water bottle. Each morning I began my winter routine, lifting weights to warm up a bit before jumping under the freezing cold shower just enough to lather up. As I'd discovered, most Uzbeks were unwilling to brave the perils of cold water – fearing immediate death – which meant the sickly-sweet smell of unwashed bodies pervaded every crowded bus, train or building.

Our house wasn't equipped for the cold at all, having been built in the Soviet heyday of cheap and plentiful gas supplies when women would leave their stoves on all day in order to economise on matches. Before the arrival of gas pipes in the 1960s, charcoal – scarce and expensive – was the main source of fuel. Houses were built with a small living room in which everyone huddled together in winter. A small pile of burning charcoal kept the samovar brewing for hot bowls of green tea. In the centre of the floor was a depression in which a brazier of coals was placed. A low table stood over it, covered by a large quilt. Family members sat around the table wearing layers of robes, their nether regions covered by the quilt and warmed by the brazier's heat. At night, during particularly cold winters, it wasn't unknown for whole families to freeze to death in their beds.

The gas cut meant that progress at the workshop ground to a halt. Madrim tried to coax a tiny flame under one of the cauldrons, but after a brief flicker there was nothing. The price of firewood rocketed. We had no choice but to buy a donkey-cart's-worth. While the weavers sat huddled at their looms, bundled in woollen shawls, gloves and headscarves, fogging the air with their breath, the expensive gas heaters that Barry had insisted on stood cold and redundant. We bought some simple electric heaters and promptly overloaded the electric circuits.

Power cuts were a fixture of life, although the walled city was generally spared – tourism requiring a facade of development. Too many people trying to use electricity to heat rooms and cook, however, meant long cuts even in the walled city, so we gave everyone a week off while we looked for alternatives. The weavers were grateful, as Ramazan – the Uzbek pronunciation of Ramadan – was approaching, and they would be expected to cook huge evening banquets for their extended families.

The imminent arrival of Ramazan was heralded each evening by gangs of small boys who roamed the streets knocking on doors, expecting payment in coins or sweets, shouting a traditional poem that announced the month of fasting. By the third evening of incessant knocking, rewards were usually replaced with scolding, the boys running away jeering and undeterred to the next house. In Khiva few people actually fasted, but it was still considered the done thing. Invariably, whenever I asked someone if they would do the fast this year, their faces assumed pained expressions followed by explanations that, if only their kidneys, or heart, or some other body part were functioning properly, they would gladly, with God's help, observe Ramazan.

Much to everyone's surprise, Abdullah, Koranbeg's wayward brother, had decided to fast this year. Koranbeg, in solidarity, opted to join him. They spent the first day miserably in front of the television, switching channels whenever vodka or Maggi instant noodles were advertised. That evening, our family hosted a special banquet for the faithful to break their fast in style. On television, a mullah announced when nightfall was official (when it was too dark to distinguish between a white and black piece of string) and cupped his hands in prayer.

Koranbeg's mother prayed for our own gathering in a pained whisper that left us guessing when it was time to echo the 'Amin' and wash our cupped hands over our faces in blessing. The prayer over, Koranbeg and Abdullah immediately slung back bowls of cold tea and pounced on the bread, scooping up trailing white strands of gooey *nashallah* and bolting the whole lot down. This treacle-like mixture made with beaten egg-whites and sugar appeared only during the month of fasting, as did boxes of dates from Iran. Bowls of thick laghman noodle broth were brought through by Malika, who was also fasting but still expected to serve. These were followed by large platters of plov. Koranbeg's friends, having heard about his fast, came by for a free meal and were soon lolling on the corpuches, replete but keen to keep eating. A bottle of vodka appeared and was opened, but Koranbeg and Abdullah piously declined – a first as far as I could remember.

The following day they continued to fast, waiting impatiently for the announcement of nightfall before attacking the evening banquet. Koranbeg's friends returned for another free meal and again a bottle of vodka made its way to the table. The novelty of piety was wearing thin, and this time both Koranbeg and Abdullah were soon knocking back shots, breaking the fast Uzbek-style. Koranbeg surfaced the following day at the breakfast table unshaven and hungover.

'I thought you were fasting,' I said, as he poured a bowl of green tea for himself.

'How can I fast now after getting drunk last night?' he asked ruefully. 'Maybe next year, if God wills.'

While the men in our household had fasted ostentatiously, Shirin – the only weaver fasting at the workshop – displayed none of Koranbeg or Abdullah's theatrics. Although the biting cold dampened her thirst, the lack of food or hot drinks made staying warm even harder for her. Another friend working in the Mayor's office also kept quiet about his own piety. A devout Muslim, he'd stopped attending the one working mosque and prayed only at home. He was still thought to be a little too religious and lost his job soon after – the state wary of devotion to anything other than the Motherland.

Khiva may have been 'the most homogeneous example of Islamic architecture in the world', but it now had a curious 'pick and mix' approach towards Islam. Once the Khan had ruled that all drinkers of alcohol – along with smokers – were to have their mouths slit from ear to ear, which proved particularly unfortunate for Captain Muraviev who had brought the Khan an embellished hookah pipe as a gift. Hearing of the Khan's edict, he hurriedly explained that it was, in fact, a vinegar bottle. Much had changed after 70 years of Communism, and today the faithful in Khiva weren't averse to breaking fast with a round of pork shashlik and a tipple of vodka.

Before the Bolsheviks, madrassahs built by the wealthy and the pious attracted students from as far away as Kashgar in China. They came to study the Koran, some memorising it entirely, spending their days in the shade of a black elm debating the finer points of their religion. Sufi pilgrims heavily influenced the Sunni Islam of Khiva, curing the sick with holy breath or with dust from Mecca and collecting alms in return. Sufism proved popular with Khivans; a more spiritual approach to Islam, it was redolent of their pre-Islamic Nestorian Christian and Zoroastrian roots. Khorezm had been populated by Nestorian Christians up until the arrival of Amir Timur, who wiped out all but a few isolated communities. Their religion was propagated by itinerant monks whose woollen robes and deep spirituality gave rise to the term *suf,* which means wool in Arabic and was a slang word to describe Muslims wanting to emulate the spirituality they saw in Nestorians. Khorezm was also once a centre for the Zoroastrian faith. Popular Sufism, or folk Islam, was influenced by these earlier faiths, and focused on traditional folk beliefs coated lightly with Muslim rhetoric.

Under Soviet rule, popular Sufism proved far more resilient than orthodox Islam. Mosques and madrassahs could be closed, and the faithful forced to fast in secret in order to keep their jobs; but home life was harder to control, and in this women's domain popular Sufism thrived. As I'd witnessed, babies and cradles were covered in stuffed triangular amulets with verses from the Koran placed inside them. Bracelets of 'eye beads' fooled the evil eye into believing it already possessed the wearer, and strings of dried chilli peppers and bundles of the dried isfan herb hung outside, protecting houses from spiritual attack.

Zafar exhibited some of the seemingly contradictory ideas that many Khivans believed in. He was an atheist, he said, clearly evolved from a monkey. I asked him why, if this was the case, he still cupped his hands in prayer at the end of each meal. He paused for thought, explaining that he did believe in some kind of God but wasn't interested in going to the mosque, fasting or praying. His belief in the evil eye, however, was unwavering.

'Did you know that my wife had a twin sister?' he asked me once. 'She was a healthy and happy baby, while my wife was sickly. One day her parents were invited to their neighbours' and an old woman there kept playing with her and giving her compliments. The baby became sick an hour after they returned home, and they knew that the evil eye had struck. They took her to the hospital, but everyone knew that she would die and, of course, she did.'

Old women – often with the best intentions – were particularly capable of inflicting the evil eye if they'd never had children of their own. Babies were especially vulnerable and complimenting them was a dangerous provocation, unleashing the evil eye's jealousy. Instead, if any compliments were given, they were either exaggeratedly inverted – 'Never have I seen such an ugly baby' – and stated loudly for the eye to hear, or were followed with two spits and the incantation: 'May the eye not strike!'

During a power cut, as the weavers squatted outside, I asked some of them what they thought of fasting. Dark Nazokat, hoping to shock, declared that she didn't believe in fasting or Islam. 'Father Lenin will save us!' she declared jokingly. The majority of the weavers took a more pragmatic approach towards religion – more interested in what God could do for them than in what they could do for God. If they needed something badly, then they would pray or, better still, cook offerings of borsok, fried diamonds of dough, taking them to the tomb of a saint who might intercede for them.

The most important saint in Khiva was Pakhlavan Mahmud. Some of the weavers told me that he had come to them in dreams, demanding their allegiance and promising good fortune in return. Barren women, often from far away, made pilgrimages to his tomb, weeping as they touched the exquisite elm door inlaid with coral, ivory and pearl, and then transferring blessing from the lintel over their faces. Bridal couples came to the mausoleum on their wedding day, the groom drawing water from the courtyard well and offering it to his bride in the hope of ensuring many children. Removing shoes, the bridal entourage entered the interior, cool in summer and icy in winter. A mullah sat on corpuches next to an electric radiator, intoning prayers in sing-song Arabic, while the bridal couple offered fresh bread, money and borsok, watched with distinct lack of interest by an enormous white cat who lived there.

Another popular pilgrimage site was Sultan's Garden, an inaptly named wilderness of rocky hills littered with tombs, located halfway to Nukus. A trip to Sultan's Garden, about 30 miles away, was the furthest most of the weavers had ever travelled in their lives, and it was one of the few places permissible for groups of women to visit. Red and white votive rags were attached to the few bushes that clung to the hillsides near carefully piled stones, symbolising wishes, placed next to the tombs of saints.

Where saints failed to respond, *tabibs* could be consulted. Some of these traditional healers were herbalists, but most were akin to shamans, administering curses and love-potions, consulting mystical books in Arabic and writing out talismans. Zamireh told me she had once approached a local tabib when her wayward fiancé was led astray by another girl.

'He was entranced by her,' Zamireh explained, 'and I realised that she'd given him a love potion or pinned a love amulet on him. I knew this spell needed to be broken, so I went to the tabib who wrote something in Arabic on old paper and then burnt it. After that my fiancé was fine and stopped seeing that other girl.'

It seemed a convenient way of avoiding personal responsibility to me. Safargul the usta told me about her visit to a *palmin*, a local fortune-teller, who had read her palm and her tea-leaves. Safargul wasn't sure if she believed it all, but had been curious. Most of the weavers, while not particularly religious, maintained a wary respect for the evil eye. As well as black and white eye-beads, or chilli amulets, they wore wisps of camel wool – a powerful talisman – wrapped around the buttons of their long cardigans to keep the eye at bay. Most of the looms now had triangular amulets hanging beside stickers of Bollywood film stars, providing spiritual protection. One of the younger weavers had removed an amulet from her loom and the heavy wooden crossbeam snapped a few days later. This had caused all to spit on their hearts twice and intone 'May the eye not strike' on hearing the news, and the amulet was hurriedly returned.

By December, plastic green New Year trees, sparsely covered strings of tinsel and bright turquoise baubles were on sale at the bazaar. The Soviets, compromising on Christmas, had taken its non-religious imagery and tacked it onto New Year celebrations. There was also Grandfather Snow – a generic Santa – and a snow bunny who had, perhaps, hopped in from the Easter narrative. With just a few weeks to go, I was looking forward to a Christmas back home in Cambridge and three months staying at my parents' house. It was the end of my fourth year in Khiva.

Before that, however, I was keen to prepare for workshop expansion, planning to invite more weavers to join us on my return. With new looms in mind, Madrim introduced me to the metal bazaar in Urgench. Situated on the edge of the city and battered by relentless winds, the metal bazaar was a graveyard for products of Soviet industry. Derelict factories, stripped of anything metal, kept the bazaar in business. We found thick, hollow steel pipes for the crossbeams of each loom and iron girders for the sides, but needed a welder to assemble them.

Welders in Khiva proved a fearless bunch, happy to weld in sewers up to their knees in water, oblivious to the risk of electrocution. One welder, in response to my concerns for his safety, proudly revealed a pronounced scar on one buttock where a huge electrical charge had exited. Foolishly we hired Hoshnaut the dyer's father, who made a terrible job of the new looms, which later required re-welding by someone more competent.

The first beneficiaries of a new loom were to be the two weaving ustas. Ulugbibi, in particular, had become quite lazy, shouting at the weavers to work faster while doing very little herself. But my plans for new equipment were put on hold after a phone call from Barry in Tashkent informing us of Hatice's imminent arrival. Hatice, pronounced 'Hatijey', was a Turk from Ankara and a carpet specialist whom Barry had invited to provide us with some much-needed advice. We were particularly hoping for more help with the dyeing, as Fatoulah had taught us virtually nothing of use. Unfortunately, Hatice's timing couldn't have been worse. I was leaving for the UK halfway through her proposed visit and we had no gas in the workshop, making any dyeing extremely time-consuming as the boys spent half their time chopping wood.

Barry was outraged when I explained the situation.

'But why don't you have gas? How can the whole of Khiva be without gas in the middle of winter, and how is this woman meant to teach you anything if there's no gas?! I shall speak to the Mayor about this immediately!'

Barry's wrath provoked a swift response, and a few hours later three men from the Mayor's office appeared. I asked them angrily why – if Uzbekistan was able to export gas to Russia – there was not enough for its own people? They looked uneasy, assuring me that the Mayor would personally provide us with gas canisters, enough to warm each cell and fuel the cauldrons.

'And would these canisters be available all winter?' I asked, to which the answer was, of course, no. Unfortunately they could provide them only for the duration of our guest's visit.

It was the usual cosmetic approach: the more important the visitor, the more impressive this illusion of progress became. During one presidential visit, the Mayor of Urgench had once even arranged for the dwindling canals to be filled with water during a summer of drought – as if the realities of life might prove too much for the President to bear. These little fictions served no purpose – a game of charades with no winners.

Barry called to confirm Hatice's arrival in Tashkent.

'Chris, I think I'll come up with her and stay for the first day or so, just to make sure that she's OK. She doesn't speak much English and obviously my Russian is useless on her. She seems a little … overwhelmed.'

They arrived at lunchtime, Hatice looking around warily, obviously ill at ease. I greeted her in Turkish and managed to explain that I was born in Ankara and that she could call me Aslan. She was tired, so we postponed a workshop tour until after lunch and took her to the Arkanchi Hotel, just across the orchard from our workshop.

The hotel interior boasted kitsch on a lavish scale. Fussy net curtains, festooned with rainbow garlands of plastic flowers, competed with gilt-framed pictures of tigers and deer reclining beside waterfalls, and an iridescent picture of Mecca that flashed when switched on. As if this wasn't enough, the rooms were warm, and a good spread was prepared for us. Hatice looked around in dismay.

'I don't understand,' she began. 'Why have you put me here? Where are the good hotels?'

Barry gave me a look.

'This is the best hotel in Khiva,' I explained, 'and you'll be really close to the workshop!'

Hatice was not impressed.

'I'm sure you'll be well looked after,' Barry added with false jollity.

'What is this?' Hatice asked in disgust as I poured green tea from a round teapot emblazoned with cotton motifs.

'It's tea,' Barry replied.

'Tea?! But it has no colour' – she took a judicial sip – 'and no taste.'

'It's green tea. That's what people drink here. Would you prefer black tea? I can ask them if they have any,' I replied civilly.

'And what's this?' Hatice continued, pointing at the bowl I was filling.

'It's called a *piola* in Uzbek or a *kassa* in Khorezm dialect. It's what everyone drinks tea from,' I explained.

'But it has no handle and it isn't a glass! How can you drink from it?' Hatice swept it aside, dismissing the whole primitive concept of drinking from a bowl.

The soup was too oily (a fair point, in fact), the plov passable – although Hatice blanched as I began to eat with my fingers. Her bedroom was not acceptable and nor was Barry's, which he offered in exchange. I tried to make much of the beautiful view, but we weren't off to a good start.

After lunch we gave Hatice a tour. She enjoyed looking at the looms, and Zamireh seemed particularly adept at catching the meaning of her Turkish. She asked Hatice to teach her a few Turkish words, at which point our visitor began to cheer up.

We, however, weren't feeling quite so cheerful, having discovered that Hatice knew almost nothing about natural dyes and didn't have a great deal to teach about carpets, preferring her favourite subject: the innate superiority of Turkish culture over anything Uzbek.

I put Ulugbibi in charge of Hatice as penance for not working harder, and she was soon picking up Turkish words – Hatice refusing to learn Uzbek. Matthias was popular with Hatice because he was German and therefore modern. Ever since my hand-eating episode I was considered suspect, with a few too many 'native' characteristics.

One evening Madrim invited Hatice to his house for some traditional Uzbek hospitality, along with Matthias, Ulugbibi and myself, greeting each of us at the door with a jug and basin of warm water. Madrim's wife, Mehribon, had produced a table heavy with salads, nuts, fruit, cookies and cake.

'But where are we to sit?' asked Hatice. 'There are no chairs. Surely you don't sit on the floor?'

I was getting tired of this routine.

'Chairs are so uncomfortable,' I replied, 'so Uzbeks have modernised and sit on these mattresses called corpuches. They're much better than chairs. Don't you have them in Turkey?'

We sat down and Madrim uncorked a bottle of wine as Hatice toyed with some Korean salad on her plate, explaining to Ulugbibi how much better the salads were in Turkey. I had asked Mehribon to cook an egg ravioli dish unique to

Khorezm, and Hatice managed to eat this without complaint. We relaxed until Hatice whispered to Ulugbibi that she needed to 'rest'. Madrim became visibly tense as Ulugbibi escorted Hatice out of the back door and down to the toilet at the bottom of the garden.

Returning, Hatice was clearly shaken. She had barely sat down before she turned to Matthias. 'Germany, modern,' she said, and then to me: 'England, modern. Turkey modern!' Then turning on Madrim: 'Uzbekistan, why?! Why?!'

Madrim, turning crimson, apologised that there was no sewer system in this part of town and that flush toilets were not permissible. I cut him off and told Hatice not to be so rude, and that, should she ever step outside of Ankara, there were plenty of toilets far less modern then the one she had just used. After an awkward pause I suggested that now might be a good time to leave, and asked Madrim if he would give us permission, praying a closing blessing on the food. We cupped our hands but Hatice protested.

'You cannot pray! Look! We have been drinking wine. It is a sin for Muslims to drink. How can you pray after we have sinned?'

When I pointed out that Madrim hadn't drunk anything other than tea, she gave her grudging approval.

The evening with Madrim was also a farewell dinner of sorts. My bags were laden with knitted slippers, carved cutting-boards, Koran-stands and even an impressively carved Scrabble set – beautifully executed by Erkin the wood-carver after a lengthy explanation on my part. Zulhamar had baked flat pastries to give to my mother, and I had visions of the unlimited hot water, gas and electricity that awaited me.

I made one last round at the workshop, admonishing Ulugbibi the usta to weave more and Madrim to work less. The weavers and dyers saw me to the door and passed on greetings to my family and friends whom they'd never met.

Three months was a long time for things to go wrong, and I wondered how they would cope on their own. My aim was for the workshop to become self-sustaining, and this would provide an excellent trial run.

But what state would I find things in on my return?

10

Navruz and new beginnings

*The accommodation here is three tiers high – that is to say
three layers of shelves, and all of them packed with humanity,
its bundles, its bedding, its kettles, its stinking dried fish
and garlic sausage.*

—Ethel Mannin on Central Asian trains,
South to Samarkand, 1936

I arrived back at Tashkent airport in March 2002 after ten days
hiking in the Canary Islands with my family. Feeling tanned
and trim, I hoped to avoid the usual exclamations of 'How
beautifully fat you've become.' My bags bulged with books on
miniatures and I had brought with me the article on Timurid
carpets by Amy Briggs. My head was full of new ideas for the
workshop.

After paying Barry a visit and showing off my finds, I
made for the northern train station. The recent completion
of a new rail track meant that the train no longer meandered
into Turkmenistan. Turkmen border guards were notorious for
demanding imaginary documents and extracting large 'fines'
for all manner of fictitious infractions. The worst incident I
knew about concerned a luckless Peace Corps volunteer on
his way from Urgench to Tashkent. Forced off the train in
Turkmenistan, his passport was confiscated and the train left
without him. The guards returned his passport in exchange for
all his money and belongings, leaving him with no other option
but to walk back to the border and then swim across the Amu

River – fearful of patrolling guards – into Uzbek territory. He then hitched back to Urgench, relying on Uzbek sympathy, and their unifying dislike of Turkmens, for the remainder of his journey.

This new train track followed the old one as far as Navoi before veering northward, cutting through the Red Desert as far as the Three Wells oasis before bending to the left towards the oasis of Khorezm. I loved this trip, despite the twenty hours it took. No longer was I enduring bus journeys of blaring Uzbek pop in a foetal position for eighteen hours, with constant checkpoints. It was always me, the foreigner, who held up the bus and created extra paperwork, redeeming myself only by submitting my passport to the scrutiny and pawing of every single passenger. No longer would summer bus travel incur the wrath of aged matriarchs, bundled up in 45°C heat and com-plaining loudly if a window was opened. Nor would I arrive in Bukhara after eight or nine hours, sweaty, cramped and aching – the bus submerged in a detritus of sunflower seed shells – knowing that we were merely halfway.

Instead, I arrived at the train station, found my berth and ensured that the unscrupulous *wagonchi* put no one without a valid ticket in the other three berths. Despite stringent security, there were always traders preferring to bribe their way on to the train, usually carrying several times their body weight in cloth bundles of merchandise and squalling babies.

All train stations in the former Soviet Union were known as *vaksal* – a result of two Russian 19th-century engineers who had visited London. They emerged, blinking, from their first ride on the London Underground at Vauxhall station, and assumed its name to be the generic term for all train stations.

As we pulled out of the vaksal, I was joined by a young Karakalpak student on his way home for Navruz, disappointed by my lack of porn. Within minutes the train bazaar was under way. Women lurched up and down the aisles selling bottled water and vodka, bread and sausages, hair-dryers, assortments of underwear, magazines and – occasionally – themselves. At each stop, the on-board traders vied with village women in a riot of colourful headscarves and house-dresses, who ran to the slowing train bearing steaming rounds of bread and salami. Passengers shoved dirty notes through the windows in exchange for these, or for boiled eggs with paper twists of salt.

Train etiquette dictated that food was shared, and I swapped a packet of instant noodles for some stale rolls. None of the lights worked in our cabin, so I turned in early, woken up in Samarkand by an old man entering the carriage. He fumbled in the dark, stripping down to his underwear – a strengthening odour informing us of his progress.

I woke at dawn as the train passed through the undulating Red Desert. It was the beginning of spring and the desert was in bloom. Tiny bright pink flowers decorated nondescript scrub, delicate crocus-like bulbs emerged from barren sand dunes and venom-green plants with waxy leaves erupted everywhere. The old man and the student were both asleep and I savoured the tranquillity, the rocking rhythm of the train as we passed the occasional desert yurt. The wagon toilet – best not described – was a trial, but the berths were comfortable and a communal wagon samovar was kept constantly on the boil. Some of the windows could even be opened, and a plastic bottle wedged in the gap kept them that way.

By lunchtime the train had reached the edge of the Khorezm oasis and fields of spring green abruptly replaced the desert.

We passed flat-roofed mud-brick houses, young shepherd boys with sticks leading cattle, women in the fields pinching the first shoots of spring clover for making *gok burek* (delicious parcels of pastry that tasted like spinach ravioli), and cheerfully ragged village children waving – excited when a passenger waved back. I was coming home.

The following day I was given a warm welcome at the workshop and inevitably congratulated on how beautifully fat I'd become. Most of the weavers, by contrast, looked wan and pallid. It was the time of year when fresh fruit or vegetables weren't available in the bazaar, except for those who could afford greenhouse tomatoes, and home-made stocks of jarred and pickled produce would be running short.

I wandered through each madrassah cell with Madrim. Four new rugs had been cut from the loom in my absence, one of which in particular, a large one with a medallion design, looked spectacular. Less impressive were the three centimetres of carpet woven by Ulugbibi the usta, which was all she'd managed during the three months. That night, over gok pastry parcels, Madrim explained how lazy Ulugbibi had become, and how strained relationships were as a result.

I became well aware of this myself, wondering how to fire Ulugbibi in a way that wouldn't leave her with a huge beating from her husband. I decided to blame the budget, announcing that we could employ only one weaving usta now that the weavers were trained.

The workshop atmosphere rapidly improved with Ulugbibi's departure, and we focused on the more enjoyable task of celebrating Navruz. The spring festival – literally 'new day' in

Persian – was celebrated on 21 March and the workshop had decided to make sumalek.

Early that morning we drove out to an uncle of one of the weavers and bought huge amounts of wheat sprouts, mincing them into pulp. This was mixed with water and then the pulp squeezed and set aside for Davlatnaza's sheep. The remaining liquid was mixed with a little flour and was now ready for cooking. A wizened sumalek usta – brought out of retirement for the occasion – barked orders as a fire was lit beneath each cauldron. She gave a prayer of blessing and then poured in oil and beaten eggs, which spluttered and sizzled. These were removed and kept for lunch. The buckets of raw sumalek mixture – the colour and consistency of single cream – were then emptied into the cauldrons, followed by a tossed handful of walnuts still in their shells.

Now began the eighteen-hour job of stirring, ensuring that the sumalek didn't stick to the bottom, burn or become lumpy. Over time this process transformed the starch in the flour and wheat-shoots into sugar. For the first few hours stirring was easy but later, as the mixture boiled to a paste, it would require a lot more muscle. There were two stirring paddles for each cauldron and we took turns at the pot. I would lose myself in the swirling, mesmerising currents until a billow of wood-smoke left me choking and brought me back to my senses. Our sumalek usta periodically worked her knife around the rim of each cauldron, scraping off the dried paste and popping it back in the bubbling mixture. We hoped to produce a thick malty paste, sweet and rich in vitamins.

Sumalek, I was told, was first created by Fatima – daughter of the Prophet Mohammed. One early spring day, she searched her kitchen in vain for something to cook for her two young sons. The cupboards were bare, and her small vegetable patch outside seemed devoid of anything green after a long cold winter. On closer inspection she discovered shoots of wheat beginning to sprout, which she collected and minced, throwing them into a pot with her last handful of flour. She stirred the mixture but, weak with hunger, soon dozed off beside it.

The next day she woke up, remonstrating with herself for not feeding her sons. And yet a rich, sweet aroma pervaded the air; the wheat-shoots had transformed into a thick, nutritious paste. On top of the thickening mixture she saw the imprint of her own hand. Trembling, she offered up a prayer to God, for who else could have performed such a miracle? Our sumalek usta explained that, God willing, our caldrons of sumalek would also be imprinted by the hand of Fatima as they cooled.

As some stirred and others went for their first watery ice-cream of the year, we prepared for an open-air lunch, laying down plastic tablecloths and corpuches. Friends and casual passers-by dropped by to observe our progress and to take a turn stirring.

After lunch most of us were free to enjoy the festivities going on outside the workshop. In the Ichan Kala, streets teemed, everyone in their best clothes, and gaggles of teenagers preened and flirted. Photographers equipped with large stuffed toys and plastic thrones offered their services, and there was a sense of spring in the air, everyone determined to enjoy the most important festival of the year.

I headed for the stadium – the roaring crowd audible from far off. It was crammed with men watching wrestling. A few strapping youths in bright red spandex outfits flexed before sparring, but all eyes were on an older, bare-chested and burly challenger wearing a traditional tunic and heckling the crowd for a worthy opponent. A teenage boy pushed forward by his mates scrabbled back to the safety of the crowd, and groups of friends challenged the strongest among them to compete. Wrestling, along with football, was the most popular sport in Uzbekistan, with some excellent champions. Bizarrely, the President had decreed tennis – a game little known before independence – as the official sport of Uzbekistan. Tennis courts were duly built and instructors trained.

The wrestler remained unchallenged and was given a prize. The field was then cleared of all but two men, each tugging a rope with an enormous ram attached. I'd always been against blood sports, but ram-butting, more concussive than bloody, proved extremely entertaining. The two rams, with huge over-hanging bottoms, were lined up by their owners; one was shorn, making recognition easy. With a slap on their wobbling rumps, the two rams charged each other, colliding in mid-air and rebounding with a loud 'tock'. Dazed, they went back to chewing grass until lined up for a second charge, their fat bottoms rippling as they clashed, accompanied by a lusty cheer from the crowd. On the third charge the shorn ram veered away to the derisive yells of his owner and the crowd. He was led away in disgrace, and the woolly ram – still a little unsure on his feet – pronounced the winner.

I left after the ram-butting with no intention of watching dog- or cock-fighting, and took a short cut through the park, where the sap had risen in the trees and the first new buds were bursting open. Back at the workshop, the sumalek had dark-ened in colour and had steamed down considerably. Shadows lengthened and a nip in the air drove the weavers inside to fetch extra layers. The workshop had arranged for a traditional singer, known as a *halpa*, to entertain us. She arrived sporting an entire set of gold teeth, her mono-brow painted with kohl. Two other musicians came with her, one playing the *doyra* – a round drum held at the heart – the other a small six-stringed instrument known as a *tar*.

As the sun set, the older, married weavers busied themselves with food preparations, leaving the dancing to the younger girls. At first shy, pushing each other into the circle and squealing before returning to clap at the rim, it didn't take long before inhibitions were shed and they wove between each other, wriggling their shoulders suggestively. A gaggle of drunk youths wandered in and made a nuisance of themselves until accosted by our knife-waving sumalek usta. Three local policemen, enjoying a break from bribe-taking, came to stir the cauldrons for a while – the mixture thickening nicely. A few curious tourists drifted by and were beckoned in and invited to dance. The older weavers had brought their children, and I rolled out a large plastic 'Snakes and Ladders' board which kept them entertained.

In the dark, songs of love, loss and passion mingled with woodsmoke and the fragrant steam of sumalek, the hypnotic beat of the doyra and the crackle of logs burning. Older women circled the cauldrons stirring, while the younger women danced in two large circles. The evening took on a dreamlike quality: a meeting of *Macbeth* and *A Midsummer Night's Dream*. I struggled to keep my eyes open and eventually left quietly, hoping no one would notice and that someone would save a jar of thick brown sumalek for me.

∼

After Navruz we began increasing our staff with four new weaver apprentices. This required a complex re-shuffling of the best weavers to ensure that each apprentice was flanked by two experienced women. Braced for a storm of protest, we knew that none of our existing weavers would want to leave their loom-mates and train up new girls – the time taken resulting in a loss of earnings. As an incentive, we decided to pay apprentices a mere $10 a month for the first two months, with the additional earnings split between the trainers.

Safargul, the remaining usta, oversaw their induction, while Madrim and I discussed the success of the rebel rug, which was completed while I was away. The majolica tile colours, in vivid turquoise, white and midnight blue had been reproduced to good effect with natural silk-white, indigo and zok. Carpets in this colder palette were unusual and I was sure they would sell well.

We visited the Khan's harem in search of more potential designs. This rectangular two-storey courtyard with balconies on one side and five huge iwans on the other was the gilded cage that had once accommodated the Khan's wives and concubines. The walls were covered in tiles, each with a repeating field design bordered by complex arabesque swirls of stalks, tendrils and blossoms. Everywhere were beautiful potential carpet designs.

On one tiled wall, a complex geometrical pattern of white latticework left deep blue spaces where turquoise flowers bloomed. Madrim began tracing this design, which we called 'Olma Gul', meaning apple flower. In some cases the same design could be seen on the tiled walls and also carved into the wooden doors. I hadn't considered doors as a source of carpet designs until now, and began exploring each of the carved doors in the harem.

In the Kunya Ark – the Khan's fortress – we traced more doors and tiles with stunning designs. Entire walls were covered in majolica tiles. These had been so numerous that, when commissioned by Allah Kuli Khan in the 1830s, they were fired in different kilns, each tile with a painted Arab numeral, to be assembled like a giant jigsaw puzzle. There was a small hole in the middle of each, where it could be nailed. Their name came from the island of Majorca where the colour combination of blue, white and turquoise predominated in ceramics. The ceramics were traded, and the cooling colour combination rapidly became popular among the inhabitants of hot, arid North Africa, and later Persia and Central Asia.

The tiles were coloured with white glaze made from lead, and with turquoise (meaning 'colour of the Turks') made from copper sulphate. The vivid midnight blue, however, was a pigment harder to come by.

In the 1960s a team of Russian specialists had been dispatched to Khiva to begin restoration. At the time there was one aged master ceramist left who knew the secret of midnight blue. Thrilled that his city would be restored to its former glory, he sought council with the Russians, offering to reveal his secret.

'I'm the last person alive who can make midnight blue,' he explained. 'Of course, everyone knows that it's made from the ash of the forty-joint desert bush, but do they know what I mix with it, or the exact temperature to fire it? No! But I will share it with you.'

His offer was spurned in favour of modern Soviet scientific methods of colouring the tiles. The secret of midnight blue was lost, and today the replacement tiles can easily be distinguished from the spectacular originals, appearing as if coloured in by a slightly dry marker pen.

～

Madrim spent the next few days in a reverie of design. There was nothing he enjoyed more than losing himself in arabesque swirls, ensuring each stalk and tendril curved and curled exactly where it was meant to. We planned four new designs based on tiles and doors, including that of the Grandfather Gate which I had walked through on my first day in Khiva.

The warmer weather ushered in the tourist season, and my time was consumed with tours. I was keen to make us more sustainable and trained up Aksana, the stunning older sister of Rosa the weaver, as our new workshop guide. Aksana spent a couple of days shadowing me as I gave tours, writing down new words. Soon, dressed in a national costume of atlas silk, she was conducting her own tours, introducing a guestbook for tourists to write comments or specifications for a rug commission. She also taught the weavers some basic phrases, and they were soon chorusing 'What is your name?', 'I am glad to meet you' and 'I made this carpet'.

Tourists enjoyed the tours but didn't seem interested in buying; our carpets were deemed too big and expensive. Numbers were still down after the World Trade Center attacks the previous year, followed by the SARS epidemic. Our UNESCO budget was dwindling as our stock of unsold carpets grew. What we needed was an exhibition of some kind to boost sales.

A perfect event was on the horizon: the European Bank for Reconstruction and Development (EBRD) had chosen Tashkent as the location for its annual conference. Surely some of these rich businessmen could be persuaded to purchase a silk carpet or two? The choice of Uzbekistan for the conference had caused a storm of protest from international human rights groups. How could the EBRD ignore its own charter condemning the use of torture and repressive regimes, by holding their conference in Tashkent – capital of one of the worst-offending regimes? The EBRD's response was that economic engagement provided a better carrot and stick than ostracism. This conference was the perfect opportunity to challenge President Karimov and his regime to embrace democracy and economic progress.

In Tashkent, frantic efforts were made to upgrade the crumbling Soviet hotels. The city was garlanded with flags, welcoming banners and a new series of 'happy worker' posters emblazoned with the President's oft-quoted statement: 'In the future Uzbekistan will be a great nation.' One defiant poster of factory workers declared in Uzbek: 'We are not less than anyone else and we never will be.'

I was curious to see how an autocratic regime like ours would cope, jettisoned into the liberal world of European economics. How would the government react to investigative reporters roving around its capital asking ordinary people to comment on the current economic situation? This was a far cry from the propaganda parroted by Uzbek journalists, and the secret police would be clearly stretched.

I phoned Barry, asking if he could make enquiries about craft stalls in the conference centre. I heard nothing further until two days before the conference, when Barry called having secured us a place on the condition we were ready to set up the following morning.

Uzbeks have a particular talent for making things happen at the last minute, and the workshop galvanised into action. Two of the weavers, Shokhla and Zamireh, were nominated to join Madrim and myself, as both spoke a little English and would be the most useful weavers. The dyers dismantled our smallest loom to use as a demonstration and bundled up the carpets.

A few hours later, we were on our way to the Urgench bus station. The trains and buses had all left, and one lone car remained. Through a complicated series of contortions we managed to wedge the dismantled loom parts into the boot, cramming bags, bundled carpets and ourselves into the car itself. The chassis sat heavy on the road as we set off.

We reached the edge of the oasis an hour or so later, the car buffeted by a sandstorm, and scuttling desert rats and foxes caught in the headlights. For both Zamireh and Shokhla, this was the furthest from Khiva they had ever travelled.

At some point I fell asleep, wedged between carpets, and woke at dawn as we entered Samarkand. This seemed a good place to pause for breakfast. Our driver had already stopped to buy heavy rounds of Samarkand bread from the roadside. Samarkand bread – delicious when fresh, and a formidable bludgeon when stale – was usually purchased by passers-through, and most cars displayed a row of bread in their rear window. We clambered out of the car to the nearest tea-house, which was furnished with generic plastic garden furniture, vinyl tablecloths, chipped blue and white cotton-motif teapots and matching drinking bowls. We ate greasy fried eggs, perking up after some tea, followed by a wander outside to admire the panoramic view.

Samarkand stretched below us, carpeted in trees, the occa-sional flash of sun gleaming on the giant portals of the three madrassahs of the Registan and the ribbed, turquoise dome of Amir Timur's mausoleum. Although we were quite far off, the Bibi Hunum mosque – another crumbling Timurid masterpiece – towered above the surrounding trees, clearly visible. Much of Samarkand's ugly Soviet architecture was masked by the trees, and only its magnificent historical monuments soared, glinting in the sun, above them. This was Samarkand at its best.

I turned to the weavers, about to point out another ancient monument, but they were facing in the opposite direction, transfixed. Silhouetted against the rising sun were the Zerafshan mountains. Growing up in our flat desert oasis, the highest point the weavers knew was the Islom Hoja minaret. They viewed their first mountains with awe, followed by a more pragmatic desire to pose for photos.

We arrived four hours later in Tashkent, the weavers craning their necks out of the car window to watch passing high-rise buildings, scandalised at the plunging necklines and tight jeans worn by Uzbek women as well as Russians. We drew up outside the Intercontinental Hotel, which was acting as the main conference site, and were directed to a disused shopping plaza, spruced up for the occasion with craft boutiques. Madrim and the weavers stopped to admire the reflective glass of its 45 storeys, then negotiated their first-ever revolving doors and marvelled at the gleaming marble interior, their jaws dropping at the indoor fountain cascading from the ceiling.

Our shop, we discovered with mutual vexation, was to be shared with the Bukharans. Fatoulah, our old nemesis, had already hung out his carpets in the best spots, but after some forced pleasantries we negotiated a fairer division of space. He eyed my albums explaining silk production, natural dyes and Timurid carpet designs and I warned Zamireh not to allow them out of her sight.

Once set up, there seemed no point in hanging around, as the conference started the following day. The weavers weren't interested in museums, but wanted to see the Amir Timur statue and Tsum, the largest department store in Tashkent. I decided to follow this with a trip to 'Broadway', a pedestrian street full of candyfloss and ice-cream stalls, fortune-tellers, artists, sellers of trinkets and antiques, and large gazebos that served plov and sticks of piping-hot shashlik kebab.

Zamireh and Shokhla were happy meandering slowly down the busy streets in their bright village dresses, overtaken by bustling Tashkent women with dyed hair and tight leopard-skin leggings. After their first experience on a tram we took the metro – far cleaner and nicer than the London Underground, and a fraction of the cost. On the way out we took an escalator – the girls jumping on and off dramatically, never having been on one before. The weavers would be hosted by a South African couple who were good friends, and I would stay with Madrim at the Operation Mercy guest flat – it being improper for the girls to stay with us.

The following morning Madrim returned to Khiva and I took the weavers back to our shop. The conference had started but all the delegates were at the opening address, leaving us with time on our hands. I joined Zamireh and Shokhla at the loom for a lesson in weaving. Shokhla explained the correct way to hold the hook-knife and how to reach for a warp thread, hook it forward and then twist the silk around it. I tried and failed, then tried again successfully. For each of my knots, Shokhla had woven four or five, tidy and uniform. I completed a few rows. It was my first time.

Absorbed in the work, I didn't notice a couple of smartly dressed businessmen peering through the shop window, no doubt wondering why a casually-dressed delegate might require carpet-weaving tuition. They seemed politely interested in photos of our workshops and explanations of Timurid designs, taking a casual sweep around the shop. Instead of then leaving, as I expected, they both produced credit cards and wanted a carpet each. We directed them to the nearest cashpoint, feeling thrilled.

Once the rugs were bundled up, I asked them how the first day of the conference was going. The EBRD president, they informed me, had lambasted the Uzbek government in his opening speech, condemning the destructive economic policy, the two-tier money-changing system and the appalling human rights abuses. Clare Short, Britain's Secretary of State for International Development, gave a similarly fiery speech naming and shaming President Karimov. He sat at the podium looking completely devastated. This had all been broadcast live on Uzbek TV (a condition imposed by the bank), and the image of Karimov holding his head in his hands later cost the political editor his job.

I questioned the businessmen on the topic of human rights abuse. This had been acknowledged from the podium with specific examples, including a particularly infamous case. I'd first heard about it through a young Norwegian on the staff of Human Rights Watch. Over an evening meal he'd told me about two inmates housed in a new prison in Karakalpakstan, built specifically for suspected Islamists and as far from the Fergana valley – where most of them came from – as possible. Conditions inside were thought to be appalling, but nobody knew for sure.

These inmates died under mysterious circumstances, and their families were summoned to collect the bodies. The caskets were sealed and guarded to ensure they weren't opened. But the guard fell asleep and a bereaved mother opened her son's casket, determined to embrace him one last time, and recoiled in horror. The corpse was bloated and purple. Her son had been boiled alive.

The family photographed the cadaver, knowing that an official autopsy would never take place. Human Rights Watch had taken up the case with the support of the British ambassador, which forced the Uzbek government to provide some kind of statement. The chest-high scalding was explained away by the government as a result of the inmates fighting and tipping over a boiling samovar. How this would result in immersion scalds was not explained.

Although I had no first-hand experience, I was aware that torture was routinely used and that people regularly disappeared. Young men in custody were raped into signing confessions, although this was less common now as a more effective method was to haul in the victim's mother and strip her in front of the accused, threatening to rape her if confessions weren't signed. Sometimes, as I walked down Broadway with an icecream, past the former KGB headquarters, I wondered what was taking place in the basements beneath me.

Often family members of suspected Islamic fundamentalists bore the brunt of government repression. Young, radical men who would willingly give their lives for *jihad* were soon stammering for mercy when their frightened fathers or sisters were hauled in for interrogation and threatened with long prison sentences or worse. Sometimes loved ones of an absconded young man were taken as unofficial hostages. Jihad and paradise suddenly became tradeable commodities for young men anguished at the violent retribution they had brought upon their families.

Nor were Islamic fundamentalists – dubbed wahabis – the only ones to suffer. Many pious Muslims with no violent aspirations were persecuted for their beliefs, expelled from state employment and often imprisoned or used as scapegoats. It seemed baffling that a government proud of its Muslim heritage would persecute the faithful. Many compared the political situation, particularly in the Fergana valley, to the purges under Stalin, as people still disappeared and the general population were kept in check by state terror.

Khiva was not immune from this. A father, emboldened by too much drink at his son's wedding, announced: 'I want to give a toast to Putin because it's Moscow and President Putin who give my son work. He's the one that keeps bread on the table for us here in Uzbekistan!'

Perhaps there was an informer at the wedding, or the secret police obtained a copy of the wedding video. Two days later the man disappeared and was never seen again.

The government persecuted other faiths as well. Bakhtior, my gangster friend turned Christian, was regularly hauled in to the former KGB office for interrogation, and was even offered a lucrative contract as an informer. During one session he was presented with a photo of the two of us drinking tea in an open-air *chaikhana* or tea-house. Who was this foreigner, they wanted to know, and what was the purpose of our meetings? He told them we were simply friends, but they didn't believe him.

Our office phone was tapped by the secret police, as were the phone lines of all foreigners. Unwanted listeners were a silent reminder that certain topics should be avoided, and that calls lasting longer than 40 minutes would be cut off as the recording tape needed changing. I heard from an American who'd lived in Tashkent in the early days after independence. His call had been interrupted by a heavily accented voice requesting: 'Please, speak a little slower.'

The state employed many secret police – a job with the former KGB was considered an aspirational career option – providing them with generous salaries. New enemies of the state were constantly needed to justify their payroll. For now the focus was on pious Muslims, for whom I felt sympathy, little realising that soon they would turn their attentions to foreign development workers.

For the next few days, we arrived at the shop each morning, worked on the loom, and provided tours. We sold the large medallion rug, which I'd been concerned was too large and pricey for a tourist budget. I met Neville, the new director of the British Council, who purchased the rebel rug. Over lunch we discussed the possibility of future collaboration.

Word got out among the delegates that I could offer free and impartial travel advice. For those wanting to visit the fabled Silk Road cities, an official package was offered at an astronomical price. Delegates enquiring about independent travel were told that the road to Samarkand was closed for repairs, with the official tour by plane their only option. Happy to subvert this fiction, I explained where to take a shared taxi to Samarkand and recommended small, family-run hotels there.

Nor was this the only duplicity taking place during the conference. The government had been heavily criticised for its paltry state wages – averaging around $20 a month – clearly not enough to cover even a weekly grocery bill. In response, secret police entered the two bazaars nearest the Intercontinental, ordering stall-holders to write new prices next to their piles of fruit and vegetables – a fraction of their normal cost. Their plans backfired as chaos broke out in the bazaars. Customers demanded the incredible prices displayed, stall-holders refused to sell, and the sham was exposed.

Creating the illusion of progress was something the government was well practised in. All over Tashkent, the shells of gleaming glass buildings exuded a sense of modernity. Entering them, it quickly became apparent from the crumbling concrete and ageing interiors that these were mere facades built over existing Soviet blocks.

The issue of corruption was also raised at the conference and a new term – neo-feudalism – coined to describe the transfer of state property into the hands of an exclusive coterie of oligarchs. Uzbekistan, in the economic sense of the word, was now merely a euphemism for the deep pockets of its oligarchs. Most notorious was President Karimov's daughter Gulnora, who had built up a huge empire of factories, hotels and businesses, buying anything she wanted, whether it was for sale or not. She divorced her husband – director of Coca-Cola Uzbekistan – who had enjoyed government favour, and the fortunes of Coke rapidly soured, government harassment leading to the closure of all their factories.

Nor was corruption restricted to the upper echelons of society. My initial disgust with school teachers expecting bribes from students was tempered when I learnt that they in turn had half their salaries stolen by their directors, and were threatened with the sack if they complained. Doctors and nurses wouldn't operate without a bribe, gas meter-readers were financially induced to ensure low gas bills, and of course the police were the biggest law-breakers, some even renting out their uniforms to friends so they could wave down traffic and collect 'fines'. Factory workers stole produce to sell in the bazaar, and so it went on. Work hours in government jobs were treated with scant regard. The rule of thumb was: 'You pretend to pay me and I'll pretend to work.'

Corruption had created a grey economy with no regulation, recourse to justice or accountability. The reality and danger of this unworkable system was brought home when one considered the latest crop of graduating doctors; the majority being rich kids who had paid their way through study and knew little about medicine.

It was impossible to determine a person's real income merely from their wages, as a badly-paid government job might provide excellent opportunities in the grey economy. The Mayor of Khiva, for example, somehow made his $60 a month stretch to encompass a fleet of cars and drivers, a palatial house studded with satellite dishes, a rampant drinking habit, and lavish banquets on an almost daily basis. A friend whose father was the vice-Mayor explained how much bribe money was needed to attain the position of town, city or regional Mayor. The regional position currently demanded up-front payment of one million dollars.

Seamlessly, the country was returning to the feudalism, nepotism and oppression of the Khans and Emirs, undoing any progress towards meritocracy made under the Soviets.

We finished our last day at the conference, selling all but one of the carpets. Our sales would pay wages for some time to come, and I gave Zamireh and Shokhla money to buy a small gift for each of our workers. We spent a free afternoon back at Broadway, where I browsed the art stalls while the weavers haggled over plastic key-rings full of liquid and glittery hearts.

We returned by train, managing to get a whole cabin to ourselves. It was the weavers' first-ever train journey, but the novelty of all these firsts was wearing off. Soon, tired but happy, they were curled up asleep. The evening sun slanted through the window as we passed village women out in the fields tending cotton seedlings.

11

Warp and weft

'You are a strange and complicated lot of people: why does a person have to waste his time three times a day, washing fifteen plates, and knives and forks, when only one dish is necessary?!'
—Observation of a local boy to the Mennonite Germans of Khiva, Ella Maillart, *Turkestan Solo*, 1933

Back from Tashkent, Zamireh and Shokhla were the centre of attention. Weavers peppered them with questions as they recounted tales of escalators, trams and other wonders of the big city.

Our presence in the capital had raised the workshop profile, and soon orders from the expatriate community trickled in. Our most lucrative initial client was the director of a dodgy-sounding company that had a 'special agreement' with the Uzbek government – whatever that meant – to exclusive uranium mining rights. They ordered a number of huge carpets as gifts for their clients.

New carpets were cut from the loom and most sold quickly. Often buyers connected with a particular design straight away and, despite looking at others, it was clear which one they would purchase. The one left-over rug from Tashkent remained unsold for weeks until a one-legged Englishman fell in love with it, writing twice afterwards to say how much joy it gave him.

I came across an eclectic mix of eccentric travellers, some working their way around the world using conventional means, others cycling or driving antique cars. The passing travel-

lers who stick most firmly in my mind were two middle-aged
German brothers, David and his brother Helmut, and David's
son Willy. They arrived in a large camper van, having driven
overland from Germany to Kyrgyzstan and then on to Khiva.
They hadn't come as tourists, but to deliver aid and to fulfil a
quest – they wanted to discover their roots. Helmut and Willy
were German Mennonites, and Khiva – the birthplace of their
parents and grandparents – was their destination.

The German Mennonites of the 19th century were a
Protestant sect similar to the Anabaptists and Amish and were
staunch pacifists, keen to work the land in peace. Having
refused to involve themselves in military service, they were
exiled from Prussia and made their way east, settling in the
Volga valley in Russia. In 1881 the Tsar made military service
compulsory. The community refused again, and the Tsar was
about to deport them when salvation came from an unlikely
source. The bloodthirsty General Kaufmann, better known
for his exploits on the battlefield subjugating Turkestan to
Tsarist rule, interceded on their behalf. He himself was an
ethnic German and was keen to colonise the newly conquered
Emirates and Khanates of Turkestan.

'Why not send them to the heathen in Turkestan?' he suggested to the Tsar. 'They might have a civilising effect on them.'

And that is what happened.

The Mennonites arrived in Tashkent just as Tsar Alexander
II was assassinated and General Kaufmann suffered a stroke,
leaving them homeless. They travelled to Bukhara, hoping to
claim asylum from the Emir, but, unimpressed with the lack
of hygiene and the oppression they witnessed, they hurried on.
As they followed the Amu River, the decision of where to settle
was made for them. A band of marauding Turkmen stole their

horses and livestock while on Khivan territory, leaving them no option but to claim restitution from the Khan. Feruz Khan knew that the livestock were gone for good but offered instead the village of Okh Mejit (white mosque), a saltmarsh on the edge of the oasis, ten miles from Khiva.

With their strong Protestant work ethic, the Mennonites had soon drained the marshes and built a little community; and the Khan, hearing of their skilled carpenters, employed many of them in his palaces. The result was a fusion of Central Asian and European design that can still be seen today in Khiva's summer palace, the hospital and post office.

These honest Germans found favour with the Khan and some became his most trusted advisors. Safe in the knowledge that they would never plot or scheme behind his back, he was also mystified at their complete lack of sycophantic behaviour. The Khivans also found them a mystery, with their different religious festivals and their austere black and white clothing, in marked contrast to the riotous colours of local robes.

Although the cultures couldn't have been further apart, they co-existed well and the Germans particularly endeared themselves to their neighbours when they provided them with food during a year of famine. They also introduced Khiva to the cucumber, the tomato and the potato, all unheard of before the Germans' arrival. Happy to lead a quiet life, most Mennonites were saving money to buy passages to Canada, where many others of their sect had settled.

In 1899 a British traveller, inspired by Captain Burnaby's horseback adventures 25 years earlier, decided to cycle all the way from England to Khiva. After terrible culture shock and disillusionment with Khiva, he cycled a little further to Okh Mejit and thoroughly enjoyed this unexpected European oasis.

Two decades later, Ella Maillart from Switzerland and Ella Christie from Scotland travelled separately to Khiva before the collapse of the Khanate, spending time in the German village, remembering to chew slowly and not indulge in idle chatter. They noted the impact the Mennonites had on the community around them, introducing photography, glass-blowing and new methods of agriculture.

Helmut and David wanted to drive out to Okh Mejit to see what was left of the German settlement. They told me how their grandmother, Eustina Penner, had been the Khan's flower-girl. Under her care his rose garden bloomed and she was regularly invited to his lavish banquets. Eustina spoke both Platts German and the Khorezm dialect and married one of the Mennonite farm boys. David and Helmut's parents were both born in Okh Mejit but were just a few years old when the whole community was forced to leave.

In the 1930s, the village became a casualty of Soviet policy. The Bolsheviks generally found fomenting discord between the ruling oppressors and the proletariat a fairly easy task. However, in Okh Mejit the villagers already exemplified the Communist virtues of equality and had no oppressed proletariat in need of a revolution. The Mennonites had no interest in changing their ways and, although pacifists, they were still Germans with a strong stubborn streak. The Bolsheviks, unable to change them, decided to exile them instead, shooting those who refused to leave – including David and Helmut's uncle.

They were moved to the newly established Soviet state of Tajikistan and forced to work on collective farms. Those who would not – like Eustina's husband – were promptly shot or sent to gulags in Siberia. During the Second World War the whole community was once more displaced, this time to the Ural mountains where they were forced to work the mines under harrowing conditions. The survivors experienced a revival of their faith after the war but feared the brutal reign of Stalin and his religious persecution. The community elders had heard that in Kyrgyzstan, far from the iron fist of Moscow, there was greater tolerance of religious practice, and the community were given permission to move there – where some are to this day.

Most, like David and Helmut, accepted the invitation of repatriation to Germany. They left Osh – the second-largest city in Kyrgyzstan – in 1981, to make a new life for themselves. Many found the transition difficult, as Germany was more alien than anything they had previously encountered. They were known as 'Russian Germans' and often stuck to their communities – their 19th-century dialect and values jarring with modern, secular Europe.

Arriving in Okh Mejit, David and Helmut surveyed the site of their village, which had been turned into a Soviet youth camp and was now in a state of general decay. A middle-aged Uzbek man came to investigate our presence and was excited to hear who David and Helmut were. He pointed out a gnarled old pear tree in a field.

'Your people planted that!' he explained. 'And it still bears fruit. You see this well here – it still works, after all this time.'

There wasn't much else to see. Most of the houses had fallen down or been razed. It was hard to imagine that this was once a little slice of Europe buried in the heart of Central Asia.

We had our own departing German. Matthias finished his six months in Khiva and the workshop held a farewell party for him. We couldn't afford to give him one of our own carpets but some of the weavers had woven a wool kilim for him. He had rescued my accounting efforts at the workshop from complete disaster and had been a great asset to our Operation Mercy team.

My life took on a steady rhythm. Monday mornings were for Operation Mercy meetings which seemed to go on for ever, regardless of what we had on the agenda. On Wednesdays each team member took a turn cooking a slap-up meal for the rest of us. Saturday mornings were a ritual of sleeping in (except in summer when it was too hot) and reading in bed, followed by a leisurely work-out. I enjoyed the local gym, considered the best in Khiva.

Our office had accumulated a decent collection of DVDs, largely from China and Afghanistan and often of dubious quality, which provided great opportunities for escapism. In winter there wasn't much to do other than visiting friends in their homes or going to the homom. In summer I visited the desert lakes with Bakhtior the wrestler and his mates. They were a fearless lot except when it came to swimming – convinced that man-eating catfish prowled the depths. I also hung out with Zafar and the other souvenir-sellers, discussing passing tourists in Uzbek and enjoying being the gossiper for once rather than the source of endless idle speculation. With my improved language ability I'd often sit on a bus in silent amusement as passengers loudly speculated about me, unaware that I understood.

It was the souvenir-sellers who invited me to join a *tashkil*. At first I wasn't too keen on this specialised collective party, remembering my first experience of revelry with Zafar and his friends during my early months in Khiva. The party had been held in the guestroom of one of the local tourist guides.

The floor was covered with a long plastic tablecloth, plastered with food that had obviously once been laid out in an orderly fashion. Now it was covered in dismembered bones, corks, crumbs and stray pieces of salad. Around the tablecloth, sitting cross-legged on corpuches or lolling on the lap of a friend, were the other guests – about ten of them and all male.

I attempted conversation with my neighbours but this had quickly petered out. Someone poured a large shot of vodka for me that I politely declined; another offered me a cigarette, but I don't smoke. Huge platters of mutton swimming in fat arrived and the crowd attacked them with gusto. 'Oling, oling!' they said, pointing at the food. I smiled weakly, trying to explain that I was vegetarian. Someone made a joke and they all guffawed as I tittered, pretending to understand.

'So, Aslan,' began one of the woolly hat-sellers, leaning towards me and putting a conspiratorial hand on my knee. 'What do you think of the girls in Khiva, eh? Have you been getting any?' At this point he made a fist which he slapped against his other hand. 'What?' he roared. 'You haven't found a "mattress" yet? What's the matter with you?' Jabbing at my crotch, he made a slicing motion at the tip of his forefinger. 'Are you cut?' I looked down at my own finger in confusion. 'No.' He cupped my crotch. 'Are you cut? Circumcised?' All eyes were upon me at this point, as I sat in miserable silence.

'Maybe we've got something that will give you a little help, eh?' The hat-seller bellowed with laughter, spraying my plate with congealing pieces of sheep. 'Hey, have you got a sex kino? A good pornografika?' he asked our host, who began rooting around for a video at the back of his cupboard.

Desperate to extricate myself, I was saved by Zafar, who spotted a video of *Mr Bean* and decided that I would enjoy watching a fellow Englishman. The conversation moved on, with more toasts and another whole course of food. Belts were undone, followed by a round of belching, and the guests reclined against bolsters or a friend's knee. Three of the men roused themselves and, with smirks, disappeared for an hour to a nearby brothel.

A rowdy game of cards ensued. Zafar tried to involve me, but however patiently the rules were explained, I proved inept. Sitting there watching *Mr Bean* in the midst of the bawdiness, I felt complete empathy with my fellow social pariah. After all, I didn't smoke, didn't drink, didn't eat meat, didn't understand jokes, couldn't pick up card-games, didn't want to watch porn. What, in fact, was I doing at this party anyway?

By eleven, the party showed no signs of slowing and I asked Zafar when it would finish.

'Maybe till one, or maybe two, who knows? Maybe we will all sleep here or maybe we won't sleep at all and just play cards until breakfast.'

'What about the women who are making all this food?' I asked.

'What about them? If we stay up all night, then they will cook for us all night. Our women are very good and look after us well.'

I finally begged my leave, making hollow excuses about ill health. The oldest man began a prayer as the guests, blinking drunkenly, cupped their hands, washing them over their faces at the 'Amin'.

My first Uzbek party was a disaster and I had no intention of ever attending another one. So I treated this new invitation with caution, but reminded myself that my language ability had vastly improved and that the tashkil would include my Uzbek host mother and an old lady who knitted socks a few stalls down from Zafar's. If these women were also guests, the party wouldn't get too rowdy; and I still wanted to be part of a tashkil – an ingenious party that doubled as a bank.

Uzbeks are notoriously bad at saving money. Putting money in an Uzbek bank is tantamount to burning it. Stashing savings under a mattress isn't much better, as it soon gets raided for a vodka binge or frittered away on everyday household expenses. For the frugal few, relatives seem equipped with some kind of radar and always know when money is available, arriving with requests for loans.

Instead, a tashkil brings together a group of people who all know each other and have some degree of trust. They might be former classmates or nieghbours or, in our case, an eclectic selection of people working in tourism. This included Zafar, Matiyopka the puppet-maker, Oybek, a young wrestler who made shag-pile hats, Dilmurad, our resident historian and antique-dealer, his friend who also sold antiques, Umid, whose shop was next to Zafar's, Madrim from the workshop, a ceramic master and a knife-seller and, of course, Zulhamar and the old woman. We would meet monthly, taking it in turns to host a banquet. Our banker Umid would collect $20 from each guest and the host would receive this lump sum. There were more than twelve of us, and this represented over a year's savings. The host would swiftly spend this the following day, buying a television, paying off debts or even purchasing one of the new satellite dishes now available, before relatives could come clamouring for it. This continued until each person had taken a turn as host.

Our tashkil followed a strict, unvarying three-course menu starting with salads and cold meats, followed by chicken (and something vegetarian for me), and then fruit and cake. There were always bottles of lurid soft drinks, vodka and wine ready for a rowdy exchange of toasts. Thankfully the watchful presence of our two older women ensured that things never got out of hand.

My turn to host came in August. It was baking hot and I decided to tackle the bazaar early with two of Koranbeg's nephews in tow to help carry bags. We jostled through the crowds and started at the fruit and veg section. I loved haggling in the bazaar, although I was well aware of my lack of anonymity, being a lot taller and blonder than anyone around me.

'Look at the tourist!' cried one young girl, pointing at me.

'Who are you calling a tourist, eh?' Her eyes widened at a tourist who knew how to talk. The old lady I bought tomatoes from wanted to know what I was doing in Khiva.

'Oh, I'm a spy,' I explained casually, which set her cackling.

'A spy! Bless me, I've just had a spy buying my tomatoes,' she crowed to a neighbouring stallholder. This woman, in turn, explained that I was from England, working with Operation Mercy, and that I was still unmarried. I'd never met this woman before, but this was a small town with no secrets.

Heaving plastic bags straining with groceries, we made our way to the caravanserai, savouring its cool, dim interior after the heat and glare outside. I'd managed to buy everything on my list except melons and chicken. Perversely, the only dead chicken available in Khiva was frozen and came from America. Still, I preferred frozen meat to the bazaar's hanging carcasses swarming with flies; and I had no intention of buying live chickens, which tended to be scrawny and bought solely for their egg-laying abilities. I approached my friend who sold imported goods but there was no chicken of any description to be had from him or anyone else in the bazaar.

Unsuccessful, we left the caravanserai and made for the melon bazaar next to the city walls. Huge mounds of melons of all descriptions and sizes were available. Each mountain had a bed next to it where the sellers slept at night, guarding their produce. I'd received much training in the complex art of choosing a good melon, but had proved largely unteachable. As I tapped and patted the melons with a look of feigned expertise, an old bearded man came to my rescue. Satisfied with the dull 'tok' from his taps, he sniffed a particularly huge melon and felt the smooth depression at the opposite end to the stalk. This he pronounced to be the best and I thanked him, explaining that he had saved me from shame as I was hosting a tashkil that evening and only the best would do. Overjoyed that a foreigner even knew what a tashkil was, he helped me buy an enormous water-melon. I heaved the melons home as the two nephews staggered behind me in the sun with groaning bags of produce, dripping a trail of sweat.

The next hour or so was spent on a fruitless quest for chicken in all the import shops of Khiva. Just as I was giving up, I remembered a shop by the stadium which stocked chicken, exorbitantly priced, aware of its monopoly. When I returned home, Zulhamar and Malika were already making a large cake and preparing food for that evening. Being the weekend, I enjoyed an afternoon siesta before arranging corpuches and a plastic picnic cloth up on the roof, where the evening might yield a few cool breezes. Our roof was overlooked by the Khan's watchtower, which provided one of the best views in Khiva. A group of tourists up there were taking photos and obviously interested in this ritual laying of bread rounds in the centre of the *dasturkhan* or picnic cloth, flanked by clusters of bottles and bowls of fruit, with plates of salad, nuts, pastries, and drinking bowls radiating from these.

At around eight, my guests arrived and I enjoyed the role of host, pouring water over their hands and ushering them upstairs. We were soon seated around the dasturkhan and tucking in. A few curious tourists continued to take photos from the watchtower. The skyline of minarets, domes and madrassahs made a wonderful backdrop to our feast as dusk softened their colours and bats and swallows darted through the air.

Our main topic of conversation was unburied treasure. In a village outside Yangi Arik, Zulhamar's home town, a young boy had been planting rice when he noticed something glinting under the water. It turned out to be a gold coin from a pot that contained many more. Soon the whole village was scouring the rice field, with further finds. The gold was good quality and the coins were at least 500 years old. Zulhamar had bought a few from her relatives, who had obtained them extremely cheaply from those keen for a quick sale before someone told them it was illegal. I bought three from Zulhamar, rescuing them from certain destruction, as ancient coins were usually melted down and turned into Khorezm earrings. Few women have wedding rings in Khiva, but a decent groom will always ensure his new bride has a pair of gold hoops filled with filigree gold ball decorations and threaded river-pearls or turquoise.

I offered to take gold coins instead of dollars for my turn as host. Toasts followed, with long speeches expressing hope that God would provide me, very soon, with a wife, and that she would be hard-working so that Zulhamar could relax, and that I would have many sons and that I would live a long and peaceful life and so on. The sky grew dark, moths buzzed around the lamp, and behind me the minarets, domes and madrassahs were black silhouettes as the moon began to rise. Oybek asked me what I would do with the money. I told him I had plans to buy a digital camera. A few tourists clambered up onto the city walls and passed by at eye level with our roof. They waved and we held up our drinking bowls in a toast to them. I received a few curious stares and wished I could tell them that not all foreigners in Khiva were tourists. Some were guests, and some were even hosts.

The carpet workshop flourished. Aksana gained confidence as a guide – a few tourists assuming we were a couple, which was flattering. After gradual expansion we had now reached capacity, with five dyers and just under 50 weavers. Madrim had grown in confidence and ability and managed the day-to-day running of things. It felt as if the warp and weft of the workshop had really meshed together.

The weavers, spurred on by higher wages, had speeded up considerably. A carpet that would have taken three weavers five months now took just three. Some of the weavers were now earning more than $50 a month, almost double a government wage. It still wasn't much to live on, but for many of the women whose men were in Russia for six months of the year, this money was what the whole family relied on.

Word got out that women with cash could be found at the Jacob Bai Hoja madrassah, and entrepreneurial matrons from the bazaar regularly arrived carting anything from cakes and cookies to large bundles of clothing. I would often enter a cell with a group of tourists as a large pile of assorted knickers was hastily stuffed into bags.

Perennial personnel issues still surfaced and had to be dealt with by a committee of elected weavers and dyers we had set up the previous winter. We sacked Hoshnaut the dyer. Some of the weavers became mothers, working until their bulge impeded weaving. Toychi the dyer – charming, able and extremely untrustworthy – almost got the sack. Married at eighteen, his wife had scandalously given birth five months later. Twins followed, as did an infatuation with one of our weavers. I caught them together, arm in arm in Urgench, and brought the matter up with the committee, knowing that this could easily tarnish our reputation, and more importantly, that of the weaver. The committee were of one voice: Toychi had obviously been led astray and was entirely innocent, and the weaver-who-knew-no-shame must be fired immediately. I thought this was unfair and I was adamant that we sack them both or give them both a second chance. They agreed not to see each other again and realised why we took the situation seriously. There were few workplaces in Khiva where unmarried women and men commingled, so our workshop had already raised a few eyebrows. Still, gossip persisted about the weaver-who-knew-no-shame and she was judiciously married off to a boy from a distant village.

I made another dye-buying trip to Afghanistan in late spring, this time taking Madrim with me. He'd been in Afghanistan as a Red Army soldier and, although he'd never been in combat, we both felt that this fact was best left unmentioned. We stayed with an American family who worked for Operation Mercy, and Madrim got friendly with their Uzbek-speaking chowkidor or caretaker. Although they were both ethnically Uzbek, and roughly the same age, their lives were totally different. The chowkidor talked of the Taliban occupation when beards longer than a fist were mandatory and men found outside the mosque during Friday prayers were dragged inside and beaten. Madrim was shocked at the burkas in the bazaar and the squalor, but impressed by the entrepreneurial attitude – something markedly absent or penalised in Uzbekistan. Here in Afghanistan, he too was a foreigner.

We found the dyes we needed and passed through the Afghan side of the border without incident. The Uzbek border guards refused to let me through, angling for a bribe. We asked them to call Anvar from the UN but they smugly refused. I fumed back over to the Afghan side, paying $5 for an international call to Anvar a few miles away, and he called through to the guards. Suddenly they lost their swagger, adopting wounded expressions at the 'misunderstanding' that had taken place. We crossed over the Bridge of Friendship but no further. Another official took one look at our sacks, shook his head and ordered us back.

I had learnt that the only way to deal with officious Uzbek bullies was to create a scene. I barked at the official for his impudence. Didn't he know who I was? Was this the usual discourteous way he treated important people, and was he really so keen to lose his job? Allegations of inhospitality coupled with threats of recrimination from above often did the trick, and the flustered official waved us on to the customs point.

Here, as before, general paranoia ensued at the sight of so many sacks of powdered substances. Sniffer-dogs clambered over the sacks, and we dragged each one through the X-ray machine. I tried to take a photo of a sniffer-dog, which caused an outcry. Only further bluster ensured that my camera wasn't confiscated and the offending photo on my new digital camera deleted.

We finally arrived back in Khiva exhausted. There was no respite. Madrim was immediately summoned by the secret police and interrogated as a suspected terrorist, for why else would he go to Afghanistan?

Zulhamar, my Uzbek mum, ran one of the more successful souvenir stalls. At first she had stocked the same souvenirs that everyone was selling, but seeing the Turkmen cushion covers in my room, and with a little persuading that tourists 'like me' would buy them, she arranged for her sister-in-law in Turkmenistan to stock her up with Turkmen textiles. There was an amazing Sunday bazaar just outside the capital, Ashkhabad, where all manner of cushion covers and other Turkmen handicrafts were sold cheaply. Koranbeg's formidable cousin was duly dispatched to Ashkhabad and returned with a huge bulging bag; Zulhamar's little shop became the envy of all as tourists flocked to it.

Other than the souvenir shop and my rent, there wasn't much other income in our household. Koranbeg was still unsure who to bribe in Tashkent in order to obtain a new restoration contract. I suggested renting out two of our rooms – hardly used, as the family slept together in the main room – as a hostel. Koranbeg did some research and I lent him the $300 bribe money needed before Uzbek Tourism would issue a licence. It took around half a year to finally secure the necessary documents, and most of our initial guests were my contacts.

More tourists came to us thanks to Zainab, who lived near the workshop. Koranbeg had helped her with registration of her

bed and breakfast business, and now that she'd been proactive
and put up a sign, she had more tourists than she could accommodate. Apart from one or two culturally insensitive backpack-
ers, the guests were generally inoffensive and the money good.
Extremely good, in fact, compared with what I was paying for
my room. One evening I took Koranbeg aside and explained
that I would be moving out, as he could earn more money in
two days from my room than I was paying in a whole month.
Incensed, Koranbeg reminded me that the guesthouse would
never have happened without my help, and asked me what sort
of man I thought he was to kick out his son for a few extra dollars. I apologised gratefully. I loved my room and my Uzbek
family and had no desire to leave.

Another summer came, and I escaped the heat for two weeks
trekking in the mountains of Kyrgyzstan with my sister and
some others. September and my 30th birthday loomed, as did
a visit from my Uncle Richard and Grandma. She was 82 but
determined to see what her oldest grandson was up to. Uncle
Richard, as he became known to all in Khiva, had visited before
and loved it so much that he'd come back. I warned Grandma
that most Uzbeks didn't make it to 80 and that she should
expect semi-deity treatment. Sure enough, Koranbeg doted
on her, bolstering the armrest of her chair with extra cushions
and worrying over the steepness of the stairs. The whole family
marvelled that Grandma could ride a bike and drive a car at
82 – and as a woman too! Grandma's every whim was met and
her offers to help with the washing up remained untranslated.

Richard's birthday was close to mine, so we decided on
a joint party. I invited all the workshop staff, the Operation

Mercy team and an assortment of other local friends. Seeing as I was starting a new decade, I decided to splash out and invite some live entertainment. Richard helped me buy everything from the bazaar. Feeling decadent, we hired a trolley-boy who careened wildly through the crowded lanes shouting 'Khosh! Khosh!' and bashing the shins of those slow to leap from his path. A former classmate of Koranbeg agreed to cook plov on an industrial scale for us, proud that it would be sampled by international guests.

Mamiko from Japan was one of them. She had previously ordered a set of five small rugs for an exhibition in Tokyo and was back in Uzbekistan, keen to buy more. I invited her and her English travelling companion to the celebration. Although it was September, summer had not yet abated; and despite the size of our guestroom and the presence of a fan, the air was soon stifling as the room filled with weavers, dyers, Zafar and the souvenir-sellers, other friends and the Operation Mercy team. I stood at the door, offering a jug of warm water to wash each guest's hands and relieving them of newspaper-wrapped gifts. Thankfully, lots of my friends had souvenir shops and knew Western tastes, so there were only a few brown snake-handled vases and plastic lotus lamps that flashed.

Each wall of the guestroom was lined with corpuches and the usual long plastic picnic cloth or dasturkhan. Guests sat on the floor eating nibbles and judiciously sampling the Japanese soup that Mamiko had made. The halpa arrived with her entourage, including a dancer bursting from her blue sequinned dress who flirted shamelessly with Uncle Richard, despite the nearby presence of his mother. Our bawdy halpa had, I was told, been a famous dancer in her youth and was now a large, voluptuous woman. She sang, and soon Toychi the dyer had pulled the more brazen weavers to their feet. As more guests stepped over the plastic dasturkhan and joined the dancing, Richard was dragged to his feet by the halpa, who began dancing with him. Her party piece was to sing while quivering her buttocks and breasts in unison, the rest of her body remaining motionless, causing much hilarity and embarrassment – a few weavers glancing nervously at Grandma to make sure things hadn't gone too far. The evening finished with birthday cake and toasts – their main theme being that at 30 I was really getting old and needed a wife.

Grandma and Richard left – Grandma weeping her farewells, having enjoyed herself thoroughly and been touched by the marked respect given to the elderly.

Perhaps it was turning 30, but I'd been feeling restless for a while and in need of a new challenge. Madrim managed the workshop excellently and I'd noticed on my return from Kyrgyzstan that things had run smoothly in my absence. We had no more room to expand, but still our list of women wanting work grew. I began thinking seriously about a second workshop making *suzanis*.

These bridal embroideries were produced mainly in southern Uzbekistan and Tajikistan, and there was no tradition of them in Khorezm, but they looked wonderful and sold well. Many visitors to the workshop loved our carpets but simply couldn't afford them. With a suzani workshop we could produce low-cost items like cushion covers which everyone could afford. And the flush few who did order a carpet could accessorise with matching cushion covers or tablecloths.

The idea of working with Barry on a new project was far from appealing, and I was keen to find other partners. Neville from the British Council had shown real interest in the carpet workshop and was excited to hear about a potential second workshop, wanting a budget breakdown. I discussed the matter of premises with Madrim and the director of the Ichan Kala. There was a disused madrassah just round the corner from our workshop. It was off the beaten track, and in bad condition, but if we were willing to restore it, we could use it.

We decided to investigate. The Abdul Rasul Bai madrassah – fronting an ordinary street of squat mud-brick houses – was built at the turn of the 20th century in an unusual shape. A beautiful medallion floret was carved into each front door, which I could already imagine as a suzani. Inside, a large room to the left – once a room for communal instruction – gave way to a small covered courtyard with one other room. Access to the second floor was prevented by a clumsily bricked-up stairwell. To the right was a second, larger courtyard with seven small cells radiating from it and a powerful smell of drains. The place was filthy and derelict but I saw only potential.

Madrim was soon scribbling down the materials we would need for renovation while I made lists of equipment to buy. We decided to appoint Zamireh as our suzani usta. She had no idea how to embroider suzanis but then nor did anyone else, and she'd proved quick to learn and reliable. Rosa would be our designer, and Madrim would oversee both workshops and the dyeing of silk threads for the suzanis as well as for the carpets.

There were still many unknowns. Who would teach us how to embroider suzanis? Where would I find a loom for weaving the cotton cloth backing? And who still knew how to use such looms?

Neville wrote back a few weeks later with confirmation that the British Council had approved our budget. We now had a powerful protector for the new suzani centre, much as UNESCO had been for the carpet workshop – after all, I wasn't sure how long I'd be around for.

I'd be leaving sooner than I realised.

12

Signed with a pomegranate

The suzani – from the Persian word 'suza' meaning needle – hung among many in the Bukharan Emir's summer palace. Peacocks had once roamed the palace gardens while the Emir watched his harem frolic naked in an outdoor pool.

This particular suzani, produced in the Nurata oasis, contained a solid burst of colour and embroidery emanating from a central medallion and surrounded by curling fronds and blooms of lotus and peony blossoms. For the casual observer, the piece was impressive though purely decorative, but there was more to it.

Samovar and teapot motifs, representing hospitality, radiated like spokes from the medallion centre, as did water jugs, representing purity. Abstract birds flitted around the border, able to cross over from the spirit world. Rows of ram-horn motifs – potent symbols of strength – were embroidered to ward off the evil eye. There were other motifs – their original meaning lost. More recognisable were the peacock-feather eyes embroidered in each corner. These were particularly apt, for like the feathers of a peacock, the beauty of this suzani was also designed to attract a mate.

An anonymous embroiderer – a sequestered beauty of fifteen or sixteen – had lovingly worked on this piece. No suitor would ever glimpse her beauty; this privilege was reserved for the wedding night. Instead, potential husbands would content themselves with the beauty of the suzani. A glance was enough for a young man to ascertain that this was the work of a well-bred young lady – her time devoted to embroidery, not menial household chores. The intricacy of her stitches spoke of patience, the ambitious size spoke of endurance, and the symbols within promised a wife pure, hospitable, spiritual and hard-working – qualities eagerly sought after in young women and often sadly lacking in the suitors themselves.

The sheer number and quality of suzanis in the young girl's bridal trousseau reminded any potential match that they were marrying into an extended family of useful connections.

It was impossible for one embroiderer to complete an entire trousseau, so an army of female relatives were enlisted. First, our embroiderer's grandmother – as tradition demanded – drew out the design. The strips of loosely stitched cotton were then pulled apart and parcelled out. Each woman stitched with a different tension and the reassembled suzani often contained mismatched colours and disjointed patterns along the seams. There were other imperfections too; a suzani was never finished – a leaf or flower left untouched – for completion meant the embroiderer could now depart this life. Also, attempts at perfection might rouse jealousy in the evil eye or even the Almighty himself, for surely God alone is perfect.

Despite the help of female relatives, a trousseau still took many months – if not years – to complete. It included larger suzanis for wall hangings, a lavish suzani for the bridal bed, a suzani prayer-mat – an archway facing Mecca. Smaller suzanis were made for wrapping stacks of freshly-baked bread and gifts, larger ones for food cloths, and a special cradle-covering – rich in symbols to ward away evil – in hopeful anticipation of many children.

Had this particular suzani wooed a good husband, or was it squirrelled away by a bitter and disillusioned kelin – a painful memory of her embroidered hopes and dreams?

Rosa, Zamireh and Aina looked closer at the suzani, noting the different stitches and marvelling at its finesse – noticeably better than the commercial suzanis for sale all over Bukhara's old quarter. Aina was with us more for the sake of propriety than anything else. She was a Norwegian nurse and an Operation Mercy volunteer. She was chaperoning us, ensuring that there would be no gossip about young Uzbek girls taken for trips alone with their foreign boss.

During our browsing of stalls in Bukhara earlier that day, I called in favours from one or two hawkers who had done well out of my previous visitors, and furnished myself with phone numbers of suzani workshops in the region. Zamireh contacted a workshop in Shiberhan and arranged a visit for the following day. We spent the evening with my friend Galya, who had invited us to her home for supper.

Whenever I was in Bukhara I would always drop in on Galya, a Tatar English teacher who lived in a beautiful old Jewish merchant's courtyard – a maze of rooms, each boasting exquisitely carved wooden beams. There were few Tatars in Bukhara and the number continued to decline.

Galya's husband answered the door. He rarely spoke – a silent presence behind his easel, lost in his paintings. His bedridden mother lived with them. She praised Stalin at any given opportunity, despite the fact that her husband had died in a gulag under his regime. Suspected of bourgeois tendencies during Stalin's reign of terror, she slavishly devoted herself to the Communist cause and had remained inconsolable since the Soviet Union's disintegration.

Galya escaped her mother-in-law's querulous demands by retreating to her study, where she offered private English tuition. We felt a kinship from our spanning of two cultures, and always enjoyed an opportunity to swap novels or gossip over bowls of green tea. It was through Galya that I had heard about a grisly Bukharan tale to rival Sweeney Todd.

A plastic bag abandoned on a rubbish-tip and torn open by strays had spilled a collection of human body parts. No one knew exactly what had happened, but it seemed that a well-respected couple (he worked at the university and she ran a women's cooperative) had opened an agency assisting those wishing to emigrate to Canada. Unsurprisingly, they were soon inundated with enquiries.

All candidates were given full medicals and those who passed were told to pack their bags and say their farewells. They were then taken to a special flat for quarantine purposes and fed on a diet of lemons. There was one last medical procedure necessary before they could be approved by Canadian immigration, which required a general anaesthetic. Few suspected anything. Once sedated, a trained team of physicians moved in, removing all useful body organs, which were packed in ice and flown on for sale in East Asia. The carcasses were stripped of their meat, which was turned into *kalbasa* – a Russian-style sausage – and sold in the bazaar. Somehow a plastic bag of tit-bits had ended up on a local tip.

The couple had not acted alone. High-ranking members of Bukhara's main hospital were involved; and as an investigation took place, the airport director – afraid of implication – drank a bottle of potent vinegar in attempted suicide. The guilty couple were placed on trial, the wife accepting all blame as there was no death penalty for women.

There was shock and speculation over such terrible wickedness, but the story did little to quell the tide of emigration from Bukhara. Minorities were particularly keen to leave. A few elderly Jews remained, with a handful of Russians, Koreans and Tatars, diminishing Galya's friendship pool considerably.

We were entertained in Galya's study away from her mother-in-law. Rosa and Zamireh picked gingerly at the Bukharan plov ('But it's not how we cook it in Khiva!') while we chatted in English. Galya's son was returning shortly from America where he'd been working. This was a relief, as America was a dangerous place. Her son had worked as a cleaner in the World Trade Center, resigning the day before they were destroyed. His Uzbek friend was nearly caught in the second tower, as calls over the speaker system requested all staff to remain calmly in their seats. Most Uzbeks have a well-founded distrust of institutional authority, and the young man bolted down the endless stairs and out of the building – living to tell the tale.

The following day it took us almost two hours to get to Shiberhan, squeezed into an overcrowded, asthmatic bus that juddered slowly through every village en route. After our previous experience with Fatoulah the Bukharan and Ulugbeg, I instructed the girls to observe always, ask lots of questions, and to assume they would not be taught all they would need to know.

We eventually found the workshop address and were welcomed by a large woman called Mubarekjan. After tea, bread and pleasantries, she gave us a tour of her workshop. Most women worked from home, and Mubarekjan used the tradition of dividing suzanis and parcelling them out to good effect – ensuring that none of her workers could complete a suzani and sell it independently. There were a few embroiderers, hunched over their work. A young man drew circles around a bowl with a pen onto a large suzani backdrop, adding curls, fronds and florets with an ease that suggested much practice. Satisfied at the quality of the work, we negotiated a price for three days' training.

The embroiderers invited us to sit with them and gave us each a sampler with a flower drawn on it, as we began a couching stitch called *basma*. I hadn't expected any training, but thought I should make an effort. After an hour, my cack-handed flower might generously have been described as a cloud or possibly an amoeba. I decided to talk with Mubarekjan instead. She assured me that all the dyes were natural, but after further probing, she grinned guiltily and explained that the silk was ready-dyed and she knew nothing about the dyes themselves – only that tourists liked natural dyes and usually took her word for it.

Rosa and Zamireh – faces furrowed in concentration – were doing well, but it was Aina who proved an effortless natural. Her patch of beautifully embroidered flowers was passed admiringly among the ladies, some disbelieving that this was the work of an apprentice. Aina had moved over to one of the more experienced women and was asking her questions about different stitches, jotting down new words. She would become an integral part of the suzani centre and – as with Madrim – I would look back and try to imagine how the workshop could have succeeded without her.

Our three days of training went well, leaving us one day to visit the Bukhara workshop. None of us was particularly keen, but Barry had asked us to teach the Bukharans how to use metal looms. It seemed fair that in return Fatoulah's daughter Zarina could teach us more about suzanis. But despite our best attempts, Zarina skilfully evaded each of our probing questions on suzani stitches and clearly had no intention of helping us at all.

We taught them all we knew about metal looms, leaving disgusted at their lack of reciprocation. Fatoulah had ousted all the other ustas, including Ulugbeg, installing his own wife and daughter in their place. Fatoulah had amassed a small fortune for himself out of pricey carpet sales and now had plans to build a hotel with the money. Meanwhile, his weavers were paid a measly $15 a month, working for a year and then forced to 'graduate'. Far from empowering the local community, the workshop merely reflected the corruption and oppression around it.

None of this came as a surprise. Without new structures put in place, rigorously enforced and monitored over a long period of time, most locally-run projects would naturally slide back into a corrupt default mode. As most development organisations paid large Western salaries and couldn't afford such a long-term approach, they handed projects over with little true accountability, calling this project-dumping 'empowerment'.

We returned to Khiva, where Madrim had begun work on the Abdul Rasul Bai madrassah. We needed to replace most of the courtyard paving as well as the flooring in some of the cells. While Madrim renovated the madrassah, Aina worked with Rosa and Zamireh practising different stitches, and I prepared for a winter holiday, braving the Genghis Khan Express from Kazakhstan to China in outside temperatures of –35°C. My travelling companion spoke Mandarin and I managed to communicate with the Uighars in Urumchi and Kashgar, who are very similar to Uzbeks in language and culture.

I returned to Khiva laden with cheap, gaudy gifts for the weavers, and a new bike which had turned heads at the airport. My home in Khiva was now a building site, presided over by Koranbeg, muffled in a long padded robe. Keen to expand on our two guestrooms, he was building four more on the roof. To finance this venture he'd borrowed $3,000 at a rate of 10 per cent interest a month. I asked how he hoped to service this debt, and received a vague reply that, God willing, it would be repaid one day. I lent him my rather measly savings, and Uncle Richard, hearing what had happened, offered to stump up the rest, aghast that anyone would borrow at such usurious rates.

Life took on an element of indoor camping, Zulhamar and Malika spending their days cooking plov for the builders. The building site proved a perilous place for my ginger cat, who fell into a large vat of whitewash and almost drowned. Despite the ensuing scratches, I managed to soap him down in a tub. He remained a dusty white, and resentful, for several days afterwards – seldom venturing outside.

Meanwhile, renovation work was nearing completion at the madrassah and we gave more thought to training. As no one in Khiva knew how to make suzanis, we decided to call twenty women from the carpet workshop waiting list and give them all a week of embroidery training. The ten most adept would become our new apprentices.

This approach worked well, and soon our first ten apprentices moved in to the madrassah. They worked in awkward silence the first day, graduating to quiet whispers and eventually becoming just as raucous as the carpet-weavers. At first they simply worked on samples while Rosa drew Timurid, door and majolica tile designs onto hand-woven cloth we'd purchased in Shiberhan. But despite her best attempts, the designs were always wonky and stretched. The problem was solved by tracing the designs onto interfacing and stitching this papery material onto the cotton cloth and then embroidering over it – cutting away the remaining interfacing at the end.

Rather than signing each piece in Persian script as we did with the carpets, I wanted a simple motif that we could secrete in each piece as a hidden emblem. It would make our work identifiable and would provide customers with the challenge of spotting it each time. We needed a motif that didn't already occur in our designs, and something relatively easy to embroider. We settled on a pomegranate.

Aina liked the idea and was soon sketching plump round pomegranates with stalk and leaf attached. The fruit also featured heavily in our diets, as the dye workshop had run out of pomegranate skins and needed considerably more. The previous autumn we'd waited until pomegranates were at their cheapest, before dipping into the ice-cream fund and hitting the bazaar.

'But why do you need so many pomegranates?' asked one of the stall ladies. 'You've bought sacks and sacks!'

'Don't you have Pomegranate Day in Uzbekistan?' I asked, feigning incredulity. There was solemn shaking of heads. 'I thought everyone celebrated International Pomegranate Day.' Madrim smirked as the women discussed animatedly what one might do on such an occasion.

The pomegranate emblem proved popular with our first dribble of tourists, as did the suzanis themselves. In Bukhara and Samarkand there were few places where embroiderers could be observed in action, and a group of women from New Zealand on a textile tour of Central Asia were our first major customers. Following me into each cell, they gasped with delight, marvelling at the bemused apprentices who sat on corpuches embroidering. Each half-finished cushion cover was taken outside for closer inspection, and bartering began among the group so that everyone would end up with something they liked.

Encouraged by our first sales, Aina designed handbags and Rosa drew up more templates from Timurid designs as well as carved doors and majolica wall tiles. Aksana, our guide, learnt the art of suzani embroidery so she could invite tourist groups over to our more secluded suzani centre. Aina also produced a magnificent patchwork suzani which we hung up at the carpet workshop, hoping to attract more visitors.

While Aina worked with the apprentices, I sat down with Madrim to discuss the matter of cloth looms. Our stock of cloth purchased in Bukhara was running out and we needed to weave our own. The only place where cotton cloth was still handwoven in Khorezm was in the blind-factories, and we decided to visit the one in Khiva.

These blind-factories were part of the institutionalised approach taken by the Soviet authorities towards disability. Blind children went to blind boarding schools – invariably marrying one of the other blind students – followed by work at a blind-factory and a state-provided flat in the blind ghetto. There had even been plans during the Soviet era to build a city accommodating all disabled people from throughout the Soviet Union, safely closeted away from the toiling masses.

Blind-factories had worked well under the Soviet system. If quality wasn't always top-notch, that didn't matter, as national institutions such as railways or hospitals were required to order their mattresses from blind-factories, ensuring that no one was unemployed. Independence brought with it the harsh realities of a market economy. Customers weren't interested in hand-woven cotton when better, cheaper fabric was available from other factories. Now, most of the blind-factories were standing idle.

The Khiva factory turned out to be no different – a startled watchman greeting our arrival. The blind director was summoned. He assured us that his factory boasted 50 hand-looms, neglecting to mention that they had stood in dusty obsolescence for almost a decade. Our offers to purchase two were met with astronomical sums and we left, hoping for more success at the Urgench blind-factory.

This factory had fared better, with looms standing idle for just six months. There were no looms for sale, but having purchased 50 metres of cotton, I felt entitled to some help and asked the director for introductions to some of his unemployed workers. A young, one-eyed man emerged from what looked like a shed and the director called him over.

'This is Farkhad,' he explained. 'Talk to him.'

Farkhad smiled shyly and invited us into what was, in fact, his home. We sat in the larger of two cupboard-like rooms where Farkhad lived with his wife and two boys. He was obviously very poor but like most Uzbeks was dressed smartly. We explained our need of looms and training, offering Farkhad the job. He accepted, keen to have something to do.

We returned to Khiva and did battle with the blind-factory director, who eventually offered us two looms at an acceptable price. Heaving open the rusting factory door, we picked our way through bird-droppings and a fallen nest – everything shrouded in thick layers of dust. Farkhad wasn't impressed with the rickety-looking wooden looms, but after some general

tinkering he pronounced two of them fit for use. I persuaded
the director to throw a small bobbin-spinning contraption into
the bargain.

Farkhad began work, producing high-quality, even weaving
with a rich linen feel. He was hard-working and industrious,
and didn't complain about the hour-long commute by trolley
bus from Urgench. He had a beautiful smile and a gentle sense
of humour and I liked him, frustrated that he kept himself so
distant from everyone else. I invited him to lunch at one of the
nearby tea-houses, hoping to get to know him better. Over a
large mound of plov he told me more about his life.

As a child he had been teased for having just one eye but
lived a relatively normal life until the age of six, when teachers
from the Khiva blind-school came to his village, eager to make
their quota for a new class intake. He was put on their list and
became a boarder at the school, preferring to read braille by
sight, and sticking up for classmates who were completely blind
– particularly when bullied on the street by other children. After
graduation, he studied history at Urgench University – his brief
foray into the wider world – before marrying a Karakalpak
student from the blind-school and starting work at the blind-
factory. He applied for a state-sponsored flat but after independence this luxury was no longer available.

'All my friends are blind as well,' he explained. 'Apart from
university, this is the first time I've really been with others. I feel
shy at the workshop. I know the girls must be pitying me and
saying things.'

I took off my glasses and we discovered that Farkhad had
better vision than I did. I told him that people with one eye
in most countries weren't considered disabled, as it hardly

affected them. Surely if he could see clearly, he shouldn't refer to himself as blind?

'No, you don't understand, Aslan,' he replied adamantly. 'I'm a Class 2 invalid.'

This had been the official diagnosis of the department of Defectologia. This Soviet system specialised in disempowering disabled people, keen to stash them away in institutions. Teachers in these special schools were usually the worst perpetrators. During the integration camps we'd run in the Tashkent mountains, a teacher from the deaf-school had refused to translate into sign language.

'But why must I do this?' he'd asked. 'Don't you understand? This boy here, he's deaf, he has no intellect. None of them do. When they first come to us they don't even know the word for *non*. Can you imagine that? They can't even say *non*.'

'Well, do you understand when I say the word *bread*?' I countered. 'Of course you don't – it's an English word. Does that make you lacking in intellect? These children don't know the Uzbek word *non* because it's spoken and not signed, not because they're stupid!'

The teacher – an older man – sighed at my foreign impudence and ignorance. I experienced similar responses from the Khiva blind-school where we'd run fun camps. Sitting with a bright young boy who wanted to learn macramé, I was interrupted by one of his teachers.

'What are you trying to do with those ropes, Aslan? You're not expecting Murat to learn those knots, are you? Can't you see he's blind? He could never learn that, could you, Murat?'

Murat bowed his head and said nothing. I told the teacher to come back in an hour to see how we'd progressed. Murat's skilled fingers felt the knots and with a quick smile he was soon reproducing them. Later that day he proudly presented his sceptical teacher with a plant pot-holder.

Many of the children at the blind-school, like Farkhad, were not blind or particularly visually impaired. However, the school needed to fill its quotas and parents from poor families were keen to gain state benefits. This happy collusion meant that some children grew up learning braille and how to walk with a white stick, when a simple trip to an optician was all they needed.

That said, a visit to an optician could lead to all sorts of unpleasantness. The hocus-pocus of Soviet medicine, slavishly adhered to by doctor and patient alike, perpetuated practices as barbaric as they were bizarre. Umid, a boy from the orphanage where we ran weekly events, was severely shortsighted and needed new glasses. We arranged to take him to the best opticians in Khorezm – a wing of the main eye hospital.

A woman in a lab coat introduced herself to us as the head doctor. Ignoring Umid, she ushered us into her office. A chart of decreasing letters stood at one end, but this was superfluous. The doctor simply gave Umid's eyes a cursory overview and then declared her treatment. We had expected stronger glasses but she had something else in mind.

'He has weak eyes and must stay in this hospital for one week of darkness so that his eyes can rest. During this time we will give him vitamin injections to strengthen his eyes. Then he will be ready for the second week when we will administer two injections daily into his eyes.'

'I'm sorry,' I interrupted, 'do you mean actually into his eyeballs?'

She nodded curtly. 'Of course, because he is an orphan, his stay here will be free of charge.'

Horrified, we returned to the orphanage, requesting permission to take Umid to an excellent Korean optician in Tashkent. Our request was denied and Umid was packed off to the hospital, where he spent a week in darkness and boredom and a further week in excruciating pain.

The same thing had happened to Malika, my Uzbek little sister. She was slightly cross-eyed, and to correct this she spent two weeks at the eye hospital undergoing endless injections into her eyeballs. Returning, unable to see for the first few weeks, she remained cross-eyed. Then there had been the time when Zulhamar got tinnitus. Plagued with an incessant ringing in her ears, she saw the doctor and underwent twenty or so injections straight into her inner ear.

I had never met an Uzbek who shrank away from a needle. Injections – the panacea for everything – were always favoured over mere pills. Drips were also popular and could be purchased from the bazaar and set up at home. The most popular was called the 'heavenly drip' – a mixture of vitamins and glucose.

Bed-rest and drips were popular for both domestic use and hospital stays. Weavers and embroiderers often requested two or three days off from work as they were booked into hospital for a rest.

During the Soviet era, rest and leisure were, in themselves, suspect bourgeois activities and quite counter-revolutionary. Sport was justified and promoted, as it taught discipline and represented the nation at international events. Holiday facilities, however, smacked of indolence and so were rebranded as sanatoriums. Each was owned by a state company and privileged workers came for massage therapy, swimming therapy, mountain-air therapy, hot-spring therapy and anything else suffused with a sense of health-giving.

For those without access to sanatoriums, there was the humble Soviet hospital. Admission was relatively easy and those suffering from stress or exhaustion could enjoy two weeks of bed-rest and telly with a drip stuck in their arm. This proved particularly popular among Central Asian women who rarely experienced the luxury of rest within the home. Ill health became an empowerment of sorts – the one thing that women could control, and a means of escaping the drudgery of daily life.

This tradition continued after independence. Zulhamar regularly disappeared for two weeks of hospital rest and Koranbeg's mother, at 65, had made it her ambition to spend as much time in hospital as possible. This was, it must be said, encouraged by Koranbeg, keen for some peace, leaving Zulhamar and her sisters-in-law to ensure that a regular stream of home-cooked food was taken over.

I got into trouble with Zulhamar for criticising Soviet medicinal practices. After all, was I wearing a white coat? What did I know? I countered that in Uzbekistan I could buy a medical degree, turning up only for my graduation – as many an oligarch's offspring did.

Some traditional medicinal cures worked quite well, even if they were a little unorthodox. My cousin came out as a volunteer for one of the integration camps. She stoically endured the communal pit latrines, perfecting a squatting jig necessary to prevent maggots from crawling onto her sandals. Towards the end of her time, Cathy came down with a severe cold and took to her bed feeling bunged-up and miserable. A young Uzbek teacher promised to help her. A few minutes later I heard a loud shriek from her bedroom. Rushing in, I saw Cathy lying down with the young man leaning over her. He had fitted an upturned teapot lid onto one of her nostrils as a funnel and was spooning onion juice down it. The burning sensation and lack of common language, as a strange man leant over her, had caused her fright, but the onion juice worked and Cathy was soon recommending the procedure to others.

Neville from the British Council came for a visit, with strict instructions from his wife not to buy another carpet. He was a joy to work with and very affirming of the project. As the British Council director, Neville attended endless official functions and ceremonies but was rarely given the opportunity to mingle with ordinary Uzbeks. Consequently, he enjoyed sitting cross-legged on the floor asking questions of the embroiderers and gaining more insight into everyday Uzbek life.

We were now on our second intake of suzani apprentices and were producing more than just samplers. We focused on utilitarian items such as cushion covers and handbags, as these sold well, but were also branching out into more ambitious wall-suzanis and table-runners. I had commissioned a series of embroidered explanations which I planned to hang around the workshop, creating a self-guiding tour. Most of my time was spent in the suzani centre – called to the carpet workshop only when decisions were made or problems needed solving.

I pointed this out to Uncle Richard during another of his trips to Khiva – the carpet workshop was finally becoming self-sustainable.

'Yes, but what about the corruption?' he asked. 'How do you know that the Mayor won't just turn up and demand free carpets whenever he wants them?'

This was a valid point and a concern I'd often discussed with Madrim. We knew that the main reason we hadn't been more aggressively pursued by greedy officials so far was because the UNESCO name gave us an element of protection, but also that it would only be a matter of time before our relative success proved too tempting for someone.

That evening, Madrim invited Uncle Richard, Koranbeg and me for an evening meal. Koranbeg was in the middle of a lengthy toast in honour of Richard when a car sent by the Mayor interrupted us. The driver had orders that Madrim should accompany him with the keys for the workshop, as the Mayor wished to view our carpets. The driver hadn't expected my presence and was obviously uncomfortable when I insisted on accompanying Madrim. We drove through the northern gateway into the walled city where Botir, head museum director, was waiting for us. I realised that something underhand was going on, so went on the offensive.

'What is the meaning of all this?' I demanded loudly. 'Our workshop has been open all day and the Mayor could have come any time. Instead we get summoned to come out in the middle of the night. I've left my uncle – a foreign guest from England – alone at Madrim's house. He doesn't speak any Uzbek. I feel ashamed that he must stay there by himself!'

Botir looked uncomfortable and cast an irritated look at his lackeys. He explained that President Karimov's daughter Gulnora was visiting to open her new hotel in Khiva and that the Mayor wished to present her with a small gift – a couple of carpets. Would we kindly open the workshop for just half an hour so the Mayor could make his selection?

We unlocked the madrassah and laid out the carpets in the dim courtyard light. I explained that some of the rugs were not for sale, as they were orders.

'You'd better put those ones back inside then,' Botir said hurriedly. 'It won't do for the Mayor to be shown something he can't have.'

It was common knowledge that the Uzbek president was grooming his daughter for succession, and officials all over the country were falling over themselves to out-bribe each other in hopes of her favour. In a strange way it was flattering to know that our carpets were considered worthy of such an extravagant bribe. We waited for ten minutes in uncomfortable silence for the Mayor to arrive.

He entered with his usual entourage and I greeted him testily, asking why he was unable to visit during opening hours. Everyone else deferentially watched the Mayor peruse the rugs. I chatted with Madrim, keen to feign lack of interest in the whole procedure. The Mayor asked about prices and I pointed out the label sewn on the corner of each piece.

'Of course, this price ...' – he gestured at a rug – 'we can come to some sort of agreement, yes?'

'That is correct,' I replied. 'The agreed price is written on the label. We have only one price. It is the same price that my own mother paid for one of our carpets.'

A little tic above the Mayor's right eye twitched but he said nothing. After some further browsing he pointed to three carpets. They were rapidly bundled by his henchmen and he turned to me, saying: 'I will take these three carpets. If I wish to purchase them, then I will send you the money tomorrow by four o'clock. If not, they will be returned.'

I was unhappy about this, knowing that possessions were nine-tenths of the law anywhere else – the odds even higher in Uzbekistan.

'Mr Mayor, I'm not sure if this is possible,' I began. 'People usually pay for the rugs first.' I turned to Madrim and asked him what he thought.

'Why are you speaking to him?!' the Mayor exploded. 'Don't you know who I am? I am the Mayor of Khiva!'

'And this is the director of our workshop,' I replied calmly. Madrim blanched and nodded at the henchmen, and we watched our carpets – the equivalent of over $2,000 – being taken away.

'It will be OK,' Madrim said quietly, his tone lacking conviction.

The next day Koranbeg took Uncle Richard fishing at one of the desert lakes. I tried to keep busy. By 4.30, the Mayor had still not returned the carpets or paid for them. I took Madrim aside, explaining my proposed plan of action. Madrim was to go directly to Botir the museum director for a little chat. There, he would explain how obviously this was all a simple misunderstanding and that, or course, he knew the Mayor would pay for anything he took. Unfortunately Aslan – a foreigner – did not understand these matters and was already threatening to call the British embassy and UNESCO and even write to the British press. Surely there was a simple solution to this misunderstanding? If the Mayor could simply return the carpets or pay for them, then the matter would be resolved and we could all be friends again.

Madrim liked this indirect approach, always fearful that I might say something rash or offensive in the heat of the moment. Still, he wanted to give the Mayor until tomorrow before putting our plan into action. I conceded and returned to the suzani centre. An hour later the Mayor turned up there with his entourage.

'I have decided that the carpets did not please me,' he began, 'so we have returned them to your workshop. I just came here to let you know.'

I thanked him, and he left. Madrim was beaming.

'Aslan, did you see that? He's scared of you! He knew that you weren't going to just let him take the rugs and make empty promises of payment soon. Look, he even made a detour to the suzani centre to let you know!'

We both felt a wave of relief and were soon joking about the event with Zamireh and Aina. I would have felt quite differently had I known that the Mayor would soon be deciding my whole future in Uzbekistan.

13

Carpet of corpses

'While people were peacefully airing their concerns, soldiers opened fire from the main street. Everyone tried to save themselves. There was no warning. The people aren't animals. They're human beings. They understand words. But they started firing, hunting us like wolves. Those who could, ran away, and those who didn't run faced death. Men, women, and children ran. There were women running with children in their arms. Nobody cared that people were getting killed. It was so that a handful of leaders can live.'
—A woman from Andijan, Radio Free Europe, 27 May 2006

I no longer thought of Khiva as just a chapter in my life. I could see myself living there indefinitely. My parents offered to help me buy a house; a nice one would cost far less than a garage in England. I imagined myself really settling down and perhaps getting married – maybe even adopting from the local orphanage. There was workshop speculation, not altogether unfounded, that I might enter into wedding negotiations with Aksana's father.

New volunteers joined Operation Mercy, starting a sexual health programme and a solar oven project. Both workshops flourished. The American embassy loved our carpets and their staff became lucrative customers. I made a third trip to Afghanistan with Madrim and Aina. It was to be our last, as the dyes were impounded on our return until we coughed up a hefty bribe or paid a massive 75 per cent import tax.

We tried to grow our own dyes instead, renting a garden and spending two back-breaking days covering it in manure. I had brought madder, indigo and woad seeds from the UK which we carefully planted, topping each with a small mound of sand. A few weeks later, the indigo and madder seeds had failed to grow and the woad seeds, we discovered, were not woad at all but flower-for-an-hour mallows. Having penned a strongly worded complaint to the reputable garden centre where I'd bought the seeds, I considered other options. Buying from Afghanistan still seemed easiest in the short term, but we needed to find a regular trader who already knew who to bribe on both sides of the border and who could buy the dyes in Mazar and deliver them to us in Uzbekistan.

Our house was now officially the 'Meros Family Guesthouse'. My ginger cat – a consummate beggar – grew sleek on the rich pickings to be had from tourists. Koranbeg repaid his loans and Zulhamar bought a satellite dish with her share of the money from the tashkil. Some evenings I watched daytime BBC programmes with my Uzbek little brother, who marvelled at how much money the English paid for old and useless items picked up or sold at auctions.

The carpet workshop weavers were also doing well for themselves.

'Aslan, look at our girls,' Madrim said, looking around him one lunchtime. 'Remember how it was when we first started? No one had new clothes and they were all thin. Now, everyone's looking healthy and wearing nice clothes.'

It was true. Most weavers wore gold rings and earrings – the traditional way of saving money. 'You know,' Madrim continued, 'If you add up all the people in both workshops it comes to around 80. And that makes us the largest employers in Khiva.'

It sounded impressive, but Khiva – a small town of 50,000 – needed more than a couple of workshops to keep it going.

Although there were a conspicuous few who were doing well – petty oligarchs, secret police, traders, and those working in tourism – the majority of people struggled with a dwindling standard of living. Regina, our German occupational therapist, noticed how offers of lunch during home visits became increasingly vegetarian. Many people could no longer afford meat.

Prostitution was on the rise, including furtive housewives who hadn't received remittances from their husbands in Russia or Kazakhstan. The population of Khiva now shrank noticeably each spring as more and more men left in search of work. National propaganda on television merely irritated the masses, who became increasingly outspoken in their dissatisfaction. At first, shortcomings were blamed on the transition to independence. Later, people complained about corruption in government, sad that their beloved president was so unaware of what was really happening in the country. Finally, there was outright animosity towards President Karimov and his cronies.

Apart from some grumbling there was little sign of popular resistance, although Tashkent taxi-drivers proved the most vociferous critics. Most people simply shrugged their shoulders: '*Boshka iloyja yoke* – there is no other way.' This phrase was used as much by women trapped in abusive marriages as by oppressed communities well-practised in helpless disappointment.

Western political analysts had been predicting an uprising of some kind for years and yet it still hadn't happened. The Karimov regime made little effort to stem the tide of its unpopularity. A country tense with pent-up frustration needed only a spark. It came in May 2005.

The flashpoint occurred in the city of Andijan. Greedy officials had been eyeing the few remaining factories in the city, and their owners, all pious Muslims, had formed a loose coalition. Each factory was targeted for tax evasion, but when this proved unsuccessful, the authorities branded the factory bosses Islamist extremists and had them brought into custody. There was nothing particularly unusual about this act of injustice, but employees, friends and relatives of the factory bosses were tired of corruption and began to protest outside the prison. They were joined by curious onlookers and others with grievances and the crowd swelled.

Many of the protesters were women, as the men were mostly away in search of work. The protests were initially peaceful, although it seems that radical elements also joined the crowd. They eventually rushed the prison, breaking out the factory bosses and setting fire to the county hall.

Tanks arrived. Most protesters assumed they were there as a peace-keeping measure. Suddenly the army opened fire on the crowd, mowing down hundreds of protesters and anyone else caught in the main square. Bodies carpeted the square and heavy spring rains mingled with their blood, flowing down the streets. A terrorised crowd fled, heading for the nearby Kyrgyzstan border, hounded by the army who picked off stragglers.

Later I spoke with a foreign friend who was in Andijan at the time and who described the overwhelming shock and fear felt by everyone in the city. No one was allowed near the city morgue. Other parts of the city where hasty mass graves were dug were also off limits. The wounded were taken to hospital until it became apparent that they were being rounded up by the secret police and taken away – never to be seen again. After this, relatives of the wounded cared for them as best they could, terrified of informers or a late-night knock on the door.

Most people in Khiva knew nothing about it. I happened to watch the news breaking on the BBC, but internet sites were blocked, and in Tashkent Russian TV stations on cable were jammed during news broadcasts. The one road into the Fergana valley was sealed off and soon the bazaars were full of anxious rumours over what might be happening. Uzbek television continued its usual blend of dubbed Mexican telenovelas and traditional singing. There was no mention of anything amiss on the news.

While Uzbeks remained unsure of what was going on, the international community responded with outrage. The UN called for an independent investigation into the massacre and there were threats of sanctions. The hasty government response was to invite a plane-load of diplomats to Andijan, assuring them that everything was peaceful, giving them a bus-tour of the recently scrubbed square and then rapidly returning them to the airport. President Karimov appeared on television explaining that wahabis had once more attempted to desta-bilise democratic Uzbekistan, but those who loved peace and freedom had prevented them. The official death toll was 169 people, most of them said to be wahabis. Eye-witness claims put the figure between 500 and 700.

The massacre – worse than that of Tiananmen Square – left American foreign policy towards Uzbekistan in a tricky situa-tion. The US State Department had regularly glossed over the brutality of the Karimov regime, determined not to upset the owners of their important airbase in Karshi (within convenient bombing distance of both Afghanistan and Iran). Despite the outspokenness of the British ambassador and international human rights groups, America had turned a blind eye to the regular use of torture and the repressive nature of the Uzbek government. Now, though, even a master spin-doctor was unable to describe the events in Andijan as anything other than a massacre, and as such, the Americans had no choice but to condemn it. President Karimov, feeling threatened, immediately gave the US forces six months to leave the airbase in Karshi and began battening down the hatches.

Russia and China – keen to exert their own geo-political influence on the country – were both quick to congratulate Karimov on his strong-arm approach to the protests. The Uzbek propaganda machine creaked into action with 'documentaries' explaining the wiles of wahabis trying to break terrorists out of prison, aided by traitors. The people of Andijan were demonised and a new scapegoat was produced.

Western NGOs had claimed an important role in the pro-democracy Rose Revolution in Georgia and Orange Revolution in Ukraine. Now they were accused of destabilising the Great Nation of Uzbekistan, pulling strings in league with traitors and leading young people astray. The ripples from this incident were to affect me far more than I realised.

In Tashkent, strategic roads were dug up and planted with trees overnight, ensuring that protesters couldn't easily collect in one central location. There were even more police on the streets. NGO workers applying for visa renewals found the process dragging on for weeks. The Peace Corps finally got so fed up that they set a deadline for all visa renewals, threatening to leave if these weren't provided. The deadline passed and the Peace Corps shut down. The government became increasingly anti-religious, not only towards Islam but also Christianity. Rustam, the pastor in Urgench, was arrested and released only due to ill health. It was clear that the government were shaken up and were now consolidating their grip on society, anxious to ensure that no other protests took place, or were witnessed by outsiders.

The first ripple from Andijan to affect me in Khiva took place at the orphanage a few months after the massacre. We'd run a number of fun camps there and continued to make visits. In summer, orphanage graduates now away at university or in the army returned, having nowhere else to go. One graduate – a tough-looking lad called Alisher – hadn't stopped smoking since coming back. I asked him how he would complete his army training if he kept smoking; didn't he know that smoking kills? He shrugged and told me he wanted to die.

Alisher, I discovered, had been in Andijan during the uprising and had lost his friend there. We went for a walk and he told me more. His best friend at the training camp was Dilshod, a boy from Bukhara. They were inseparable, always watching each other's backs. Although still in training, they had joined the army stationed at the main square in Andijan.

'We were both responsible for a big gun that was mounted up on the steps. Below we saw all these women protesting and then some people came by with suitcases. They were wahabis and took out guns and grenades. Before we knew it, they were firing at us. I heard a massive explosion next to me. It went through my whole body, knocking me over. I was sure I was dead, but then I opened my eyes and began to feel myself. I was covered in blood and bits of bone but I didn't feel any pain. I sat up and Dilshod's leg was twisted with mine. I pushed him away from me and saw that his head was gone; it was all over my clothes.' He paused, biting his lip. 'So, why shouldn't I smoke? They gave me his tags and I wear them around my neck – look.

He was the only family I had. Now I just want to fight and get myself killed so I can join him.'

Alisher had received no counselling or emotional support. I asked him to describe the things he would miss most about Dilshod, and what he would like to say to his friend. He began to weep and then we sat for a while in silence.

The younger children at the orphanage had been sent to a summer camp and we joined them for a couple of days, running sport and craft activities or jumping off the bridge into the chocolate waters of the canal. I was happy to escape the heat, and had plans to join my friend Ryan in August, trekking in Azerbaijan. He had come for a visit the previous year, having heard about the workshops and keen to start something similar. Now I wanted to see how his project reviving traditional woven kilims of the Caucasus was going. I would also meet up with Ruslan, a good Azeri friend of mine who lived in the capital, Baku. My flight was booked and my passport had sat in Tashkent for the last month or so, awaiting a new visa.

I grew more anxious as my departure date loomed, yet with no word on the visa. I rescheduled my flight twice, no longer merely annoyed that my holiday plans were ruined, but also worried that I might miss an important conference in Turkey. The Operation Mercy office in Tashkent were promised 'tomorrow, tomorrow' on a daily basis. Tiring of this, I decided to leave without a visa, planning to collect my new visa from the Uzbek embassy in Azerbaijan. This was to prove a costly mistake.

There was nothing special about my departure, no tears or fond farewells. I had no idea that I wouldn't be coming back. I asked the tashkil to wait until my return before our next gathering, and discussed which carpet designs to begin with

Safargul – leaving more important matters until I got back. We had a large order of carpets to deliver, so Madrim left with me, planning to combine a trip to Tashkent with a detour down to Termez where we hoped he might find a trader to buy natural dyes for us. There was the usual rush to get to Urgench airport in time, hauling three huge bazaar-bags of carpets to the taxi rank just outside the walled city. I never even turned around as we drove off, for one last glimpse of Khiva.

The developed, cosmopolitan air of Baku made a refreshing change from Khiva and I enjoyed catching up with Ruslan, communicating with his parents through a pidgin of Uzbek and Azeri. Trekking in the lush mountains of northern Azerbaijan with Ryan felt like a real holiday. Soon it was time to head for Baku, pick up my visa and catch my flight back to Uzbekistan. Three aunts and an uncle were planning a trip out just a week or so after my return and I was looking forward to taking them around the Silk Road cities.

My visa was still not ready but promised soon. I phoned or emailed the Operation Mercy office in Tashkent each day, but the message was the same. My return date came and went. Ruslan had to leave for another city and Ryan returned to Gusar in the north. This left me with an accommodation prob-lem. People at the Baku International Church were incredibly kind and hospitable, granting me official waif status as I waited for my visa. Phil, a young Scot with BP whom I'd met only once, offered me a place in his flat which, as it turned out, was situated in a five-star hotel. Exile – I pondered during laps in the pool – could be a lot worse. I was convinced that my visa would arrive soon and considered my two-week sojourn in Baku a bonus holiday.

Finally the Tashkent office got a response, in the form of a letter, referring to Andrea (waiting for her visa in Germany) and myself: 'The research shows that the activities of the above-mentioned persons exceeds the bounds of their professional commission and do not coincide with accomplishing the set aims and goals of the organization. Taking these factors into consideration, The Ministry of Justice of the Republic of Uzbekistan has decided that granting them accreditation will not be expedient.'

There was no mention of what bounds we might have exceeded, nor were we given the opportunity to defend ourselves. I found out later that this standard letter was sent out to all NGO workers who had their visa application denied.

The rug had been pulled from under me. Malika, my little sister, was getting married in a month. I'd miss the wedding. It was my turn to host the tashkil soon, but that would never happen now. My relatives were on their way to visit me and I wouldn't be there. My belongings – apart from a small bag of clothes – were all in Khiva. Soon, short-term concerns were replaced with longer-term ones. There was so much I wanted to do at the workshops before leaving. I'd never really told Madrim how much I'd come to value him as a brother, not just as a colleague. There would be no more wage days, watching the weavers carefully tucking their earnings into their bras. I would never again wake up on my roof and watch the dawn sun glinting on the madrassah portals and minarets of a place I considered home. Did my Uzbek family really know how much I loved them and would miss them? There would be no goodbyes.

The computer screen blurred. I didn't care that teenagers playing *Doom* on the internet café computers next to me were staring as tears splashed on the mouse-pad.

A few days later I left, arriving to a chill British autumn. It was good to see my parents again and to know that I still had one home, at least, that I could lay claim to. My aunts and uncle returned from Uzbekistan having enjoyed the trip immensely despite my absence, couriering some of my warmer clothes back for me.

I felt lost, unsure what to do with myself. In Khiva I thought I'd learnt how to plan for contingencies, but nothing had prepared me for this abrupt exit. Nor was I ready to simply shelve my seven years in Khiva and start job-hunting. Writing a book seemed the healthiest way to think about the past while staying in the present. I began to plan the book's structure.

I kept in touch with the remaining team in Khiva, who were finding life hard without their team-leaders. We all agreed that some kind of team debriefing was essential for handing over roles, responsibilities and luggage. At first this was planned for Kazakhstan but Andrea suggested we apply for two-week Uzbek visas, pointing out the need for proper project handovers. Much to my surprise, our visas were granted. However, the Ministry of Foreign Affairs in Tashkent pointed out that, while we had been granted valid visas, it was still the secret police who controlled the borders.

With this in mind, Andrea made use of her return ticket to Tashkent, buying a follow-on ticket to Kazakhstan just in case. I returned to Baku, planning to stay there for a week if Andrea's return proved futile and then join her in Kazakhstan. If she did get back in, then I would follow her to Tashkent.

Andrea's entry was successful. She was the last in line on a busy evening and managed to keep her hands from trembling as her passport was scanned and she was waved through. I flew out the following day.

Arriving in Tashkent laden with parting gifts for everyone, I was first in line at passport control. I greeted the official in Uzbek. He smiled, surprised, and scanned my passport – the smile vanishing. There was a problem and he told me to stand aside. Someone would come and see me.

I waited until a Russian member of the border police arrived. 'This visa, no good,' he said. 'You, go home.'

I asked for a translator and an Uzbek was summoned.

'The Uzbek embassy in London granted me this visa, so how can there be a problem?' I asked. The official was in no mood for explanations and simply scrawled INVALID across the visa page. I realised then that for some reason I had been blacklisted.

There followed a short discussion about what to do with me. I couldn't be deported straight away, as the plane I'd arrived on terminated in Tashkent. Instead I was to collect my bags and would be escorted to the transit lounge. Vince and Marsha, friends in Tashkent, had come to pick me up. They saw what was happening and promised to call the British embassy.

It was already late by the time I was bundled into the transit lounge, and I'd had nothing to eat. The building had a shabby grandeur typical of Soviet architecture, with a more modern glass front that faced the airport bus terminal and a small bazaar. I'd walked past this building many times without know-ing what it was.

Babies cried, two televisions competed for volume, and bored passengers tried to smoke as much as possible between flights. Most of the transit passengers were British Asians on their way to Amritsar in India from the Midlands. I found a quieter corner where four young Chinese were already camping. They didn't speak English but managed to convey that they had been in the transit lounge for three weeks. They were obvious pros at transit lounge camping, so I mimicked their practice of laying out newspaper on the grubby carpet. I was just falling asleep when a Russian voice bellowed over the tannoy: 'Aleksandr! Aleksandr! Telefon!'

I ran over in my socks and answered the phone. It was the British embassy. They had been denied permission to visit me but promised to follow up on my visa renewal. I fell asleep naively imagining that they might be able to help.

The following morning the lounge was almost empty. I took my bags to the window, staring at the autumn leaves outside as an old woman swept the street. A young boy passed by wheeling a pram full of freshly baked bread and meat *samsas* for sale in the small bazaar. A few Uzbeks stood at the bus stop spitting sunflower seed shells and waiting. The sound of Uzbek pop drifted across from a shashlik stall and a gypsy woman with a pan of smoking isfan and a ragged baby pawed at people in the bus queue, hoping for money. I was in Uzbekistan, and yet I wasn't. Beside me was a discarded copy of the *Economist* and a water dispenser, and nearby was a small, locked duty-free kiosk. I felt trapped between worlds.

A little while later Vince and Marsha arrived at the glass window and peered in. We established contact and moved to the glass door. It was locked, but if we both pressed up against the crack and shouted, a conversation of sorts was possible. A guard, convinced that this was forbidden, came up and told me to stop talking.

I refused, challenging him to arrest me, as at least I'd get visiting hours in prison. He backed off. There was no news from the British embassy, but Marsha had brought a generously packed bag of food for me. It was to be the first of many, and I soon learnt the complex routine needed for their procurement. It involved retracing the chain of command, with permission granted over a walkie-talkie by someone higher in the echelons of power who dispatched a staff member outside to collect the food bag, search it, and pass it on to me. The system failed when Russian staff members were on duty, as they weren't obliging like the Uzbeks. 'We are busy!' they would pout, varnishing their nails or looking at the pictures in *Hello!* magazine.

I passed the first day waiting for news from the British embassy. It was a Friday, so I held out hope that my case might be resolved before the weekend. I heard nothing, and the following day – having established that I was allowed to make local calls – I asked Neville from the British Council if he could find out more. He assured me that the embassy could do nothing and that I should leave as soon as possible. There didn't seem anything to stay for.

I asked at the information desk for flights to Kazakhstan. There were no seats available until Sunday evening. I made a reservation, accepting that I would spend two more nights in the transit lounge. I read for a while, wrote, chatted with Uzbek staff members, spent an hour walking up and down the staircase, and managed to teach the four Chinese how to do Sudoku puzzles. I found out that they were illegal immigrants who'd been deported from Italy and were on their way back to China in four days.

The ebb and flow of the transit lounge seemed random. Sometimes it was filled with people, noise and smoke and at other times it was virtually empty apart from myself and the other flotsam. The Khiva team called to cheer me up, and I spoke to Madrim and my Uzbek family. Speaking to the latter proved too painful and ended in tears. Bakhtior the wrestler was in Tashkent and came to visit. We had five minutes at the door before a guard on his side told him to leave, but at least we had a farewell of sorts.

Madonna's new video appeared regularly on Russian MTV. The refrain was, 'Time goes by, so slowly, time goes by, so slowly'. Finally the time for my departure loomed. I had been so desperate to return to Uzbekistan but now I couldn't wait to leave, focusing on the freedoms I'd enjoy in Almaty – no more food parcels; fresh air; and a much-needed trip to the opulent public baths, as I was beginning to smell. Someone from Operation Mercy Kazakhstan would meet me at the airport and sort out any potential problems with my Kazakh visa, which became valid only in three days' time.

The plane was delayed for an hour and then another hour and then indefinitely, due to fog in Almaty. I bedded down for a fourth night, but was woken at four with a boarding announcement.

Almaty was bitingly cold, the first glimmer of dawn showing behind the Tien Shan mountains that dominated the skyline. A Russian woman checked my passport and called over her boss, pointing to the date. I asked a passenger who worked for the human rights group Freedom House if she could translate from Russian for me. I explained that someone was supposed to be waiting for me who could explain the situation, but that they hadn't come due to the plane delay. Surely I could apply for a transit visa? The immigration official suggested instead that I could pay him $300 and he would allow me through. I had only $100 left and offered this.

The official immediately lost his friendly demeanour and told me that I must return to Uzbekistan. My visa wasn't valid, so I must be deported. The lady from Freedom House tried to reason with him, but he paid her no attention. The idea of returning to Tashkent and the transit lounge was something that hadn't even occurred to me. I blanched, refusing to return and foolishly pointing out that I couldn't be deported back to a country that had already deported me. This was the wrong thing to say. The official seized my passport, flicking through to the offending Uzbek visa, now more determined than ever that I must be expelled. The woman from Freedom House began to cry helplessly and was told not to meddle. A guard began dragging me towards the exit.

I protested, demanding to speak to the embassy. But the guards and others who had accumulated by now merely jeered. Did I have a phone and did I know the number? I shouted at a group of incoming passengers, asking if anyone knew the British embassy phone number. Most hurried on, clearly alarmed by my wild-eyed appearance.

I asked to use the toilet, where I stared at a greasy-haired reflection of myself, unshaven and unkempt, with large bags under my eyes. I looked like a crack addict. Resisting the urge to somehow break out, I splashed water on my face, took a few deep breaths and returned, hoping to reason with the guards. Surely I could just stay in the Almaty transit lounge for two more days until my visa was valid?

The more I reasoned, the angrier they became. They enlisted a Kazakh policeman who ended up siding with me, further infuriating the guards. Finally, they dragged me forcibly outside and bundled me onto a plane that had been grounded – waiting half an hour for my presence. My passport was given to the captain and a guard stood beside me until take-off. I could hear the passengers behind me whispering and wondering who I was and what I had done wrong. I was back in the Tashkent transit lounge before breakfast.

Nargisa, one of the Uzbek staff on duty, stood speechless as I returned, wondering why I'd come back. She clucked in sympathy as I explained what had happened. The four Chinese deportees offered me back some of the food I'd left for them. I realised that in the scuffle with the Kazakh guards, they had left my baggage behind. I had just my small rucksack and wondered numbly whether I would ever see my bags again.

The men's toilets were a long way from the luxury of the Almaty bath-house, but I was in need of a wash regardless. At this point – inured to degradation – I stripped off, filling a toilet water jug usually reserved for other purposes and untangling hairs from a piece of discarded soap. After washing myself, I washed my socks, T-shirt and underwear and then sat in just my trousers and jacket by the radiator, waiting for them to dry.

I wasn't sure what I was supposed to do next. Jeremy called from the Tashkent office of Operation Mercy. He'd heard from Almaty that the airport guards were furious with me and refused to allow me back at the airport. He reminded me that elections were taking place the following week and that security was particularly tight. I was desperate to see my team-mates again and for this disastrous experience to still have some kind of purpose. However, my only hope of getting to Kazakhstan was to fly to Bishkek in Kyrgyzstan and then travel overland across the border.

This seemed like a good plan, and I enquired about tickets. The next available place was in two days' time. I was about to make my purchase when Jeremy rang again. On further investigation, he had discovered that the airport guards had blacklisted me. Entry from any direction into Kazakhstan was impossible. I sat back wondering what else could possibly go wrong. I had been deported and blacklisted from two countries in less than a week and was now stuck in what amounted to a prison.

My one consolation was the arrival of my luggage on the evening flight from Almaty. An influx of passengers from India to Birmingham brought with them an aggressive drunk. I was called upon by the staff to act as translator and asked to explain why he was forbidden to fly unless sober. He responded with a lunge and lurched back to the duty-free kiosk. Other arrivals included two Chinese girls in new clothes with new luggage and a seedy-looking American Vietnamese. They sat as far from each other as possible, avoiding all eye contact, and were individually summoned for interrogation. I found out from staff that he was suspected of trafficking them to Europe.

The other four Chinese had finally left. I asked Nargisa if they held the record for transit lounge longevity. At three weeks, they weren't even close. A few years previously, she explained, a Syrian man married to an Uzbek woman had arrived without a valid visa. His wife was heavily pregnant and gave birth six weeks later. Her family bribed the staff to allow the baby inside so the new father could hold him. Another six weeks later, mother and child were ready to travel again and the Syrian ended his three-month sojourn. An African of unknown origin had stayed in the transit lounge for nine months. He refused to disclose his nationality and survived on the generosity of other transit lounge passengers until an interrogator discovered his country of origin and deported him there.

I had no intention of joining their ranks and made plans to return to Azerbaijan. The next flight to Baku left exactly one week after my arrival. The plane was full apart from business class, but at this stage I was willing to pay whatever it cost, and Jeremy had sent me additional funds in one of the food parcels. I was then told that there were no available seats in business class either. The idea of staying any longer than a week in the transit lounge was too much. I was close to cracking and appealed to Habibullah, the shift-leader on duty. I had served the people of Uzbekistan for seven years, and had done nothing to warrant this treatment. He had seen me sleeping on the floor for the last week, he had appreciated my help with translation. Was there nothing he could do?

I was close to tears, and Habibullah assured me that the following morning when his shift ended he would do everything possible to get me on that plane. I thanked him and bedded down for the night. The two televisions blared loudly – one in Russian and one in Uzbek. The fluorescent lights were never turned off and the air was thick with cigarette smoke and chatter. I lay on my newspaper, feeling claustrophobic, praying feverishly for a seat on the plane. I could feel myself unravelling, and despite exhaustion, sleep was impossible.

Another unceremonious jug-shower in the men's toilets the following morning did little to improve my appearance. I spent the rest of the morning nagging the staff on duty for news from Habibullah. At midday he returned triumphant with a plane ticket in his hand. He smiled in embarrassment as I hugged him and presented him with chocolate originally intended for the team. I had just one more night to go and then I could leave.

Aina had come to Tashkent and brought me my last food parcel. She was the only person from Khiva I'd seen since returning from Almaty. We shouted at the door for a while, talking about the workshops and the responsibilities she would shoulder with Madrim. I didn't want to say goodbye, but in the end we both placed our hands against the glass door, and then she left.

I sat alone with my food parcel. Aina was the only person from the team I'd said goodbye to, and I felt the weight of all the farewells that would never happen. Now that the end was in sight, I closed my eyes and different faces swam before me. Zafar, Madrim, Zamireh, Koranbeg, Zulhamar. I no longer cared what anyone thought about me and just sat there crying for a very long time.

The following day my flight was on time. Nargisa even came to wave me off. My only thought as the plane took off was a deep but irrational fear that I might be deported from Azerbaijan. I felt a wave of panic as I remembered that two passport photos were needed for the visa application form. I rooted around in my bag, tearing a photo from my Uzbekistan ID document and fretting that the only other picture I had was a black and white photocopy.

At Baku airport I tried to appear normal as I handed over my application form, hoping my smile looked relaxed and not crazed. Wild feelings of joy at my visa stamp were immediately followed by paranoia that some other obstacle would prevent me leaving the airport. It was only as I made it through the barrier that I felt a wave of relief. Ruslan was waiting and we hugged, no glass door between us. We walked outside – it was allowed now – and I felt sun against my skin. I was back in a world of rights and freedoms and I took deep breaths of fresh air.

14

My mother's friend the warlord

Childlessness is better than a son who flees the battlefield.
—Pashtun proverb

I spent a week in Azerbaijan recuperating, trying to laugh at comparisons with the recently released film *Terminal*. I wanted to put my time in the transit lounge behind me but I found myself lying awake at night, remonstrating over all the things I should have done differently, replaying the moment when I wrote down the dates for my visa at the Kazakh embassy in London and thinking how easy it would have been to apply for one that started three days earlier. If I did sleep, I'd wake up in a cold sweat with the panicky feeling of being trapped again.

I tried to settle back into English ways, but still found my head bobbing and my hand placed on my heart whenever I thanked someone. I seemed unable to sit properly on sofas, ending up cross-legged, and was mortified whenever guests strode into my parents' house with their shoes on. I was told off for asking a friend how much they earned. Trying my best to refer to the bazaar as the market, I still found myself haggling, and discovered an embedded compulsion to offer food to strangers if eating on a train or park bench. Communal mealtimes also felt incomplete without a prayer at the end, hands cupped to receive blessing.

News from Khiva was mixed. Aina helped Madrim manage both workshops – a set-up that worked well. Malika, my Uzbek little sister, got married, and Uncle Richard flew out to attend the wedding in my stead, returning with bags of my stuff. Aksana the guide managed to get into university without paying a bribe – a highly unusual event. The Operation Mercy team struggled. They experienced increasing governmental harassment, as did most NGOs. They were forbidden to work in schools or orphanages – the children in both feeling bewildered and abandoned. Soon, entire NGOs were closed down and within six months the number dwindled to just six foreign development organisations, including Operation Mercy. These last few organisations hadn't been shut down, but nor were they granted new visas, and it seemed just a matter of time before the government won a war of attrition.

March the 21st loomed and I knew that it would be an ordinary working day in England with no one to celebrate Navruz with, so I called my Uzbek family, Madrim and Zafar. Each conversation ended with the traditional invitation to come and visit soon, and I wished I could. I focused on writing, and decided that 2006 would be an unexpected sabbatical of sorts.

In the short term, I took up an invitation to visit Afghanistan as a consultant for two textile projects there. I would assist a carpet cooperative in Kabul and an embroidery project in Kandahar. They also wanted me to run a natural dye-making workshop, so I suggested that Madrim might join us, hoping for a reunion.

Leaving the gleaming glass architecture of Dubai's international airport for an older terminal nearby, I immediately felt at home in the scrum of Afghan traders with their flowing beards and turbans, heaving cloth-wrapped bales of merchandise and bargaining with harried check-in staff over luggage weight allowance. Passengers on the plane were neatly segregated, Afghans at the back and Westerners at the front. The latter were either earnest laptop-carriers or burly private security muscle, sporting crew-cuts, tight vests and an extravagant variety of tattoos. My three travelling companions were all Americans – of Chinese, Japanese and Cuban extraction – and had been invited along as a business consultant, web-page designer and journalist respectively.

We arrived at Kabul's Soviet-built airport – the faded and dated modernist architecture jarring with the timeless faces of passengers who would have looked more in keeping unloading their goods from camels than conveyor belts. Outside the weather was warm but pleasant, the heat kept at bay by the high altitude. The city sprawled without a clear centre, ringed by dusty, barren mountains.

We drove through teeming bazaars of colour and squalor – the air alive with the shouts of hawkers and the smell of sewers and spice. My colleagues craned their necks for photo opportunities among the exhilarating chaos. I just sat back and enjoyed the feeling of returning to where I belonged.

We drew up outside a modest compound where Dave, our host and the project leader, greeted us. He looked Afghan with his white beard, portly stature and shelwar kamiz – an effect that dissolved as he pronounced how 'real neat' it was to finally meet us. Dave had identified an impoverished and squalid suburb of Kabul called Dashti Barchi as a place of particular need. His aim was to provide income generation opportunities among the local population – mainly returned Hazara refugees.

The Hazaras – descendants of Genghis Khan – still retained flat Mongolian features and were despised by the dominant Pashtun clans. They had suffered greatly under the Taliban, considered lowest in the ethnic pecking-order. They had now returned from exile in Pakistan, where many had learnt to weave carpets, and their previous employers were keen to maintain a monopoly on the carpet trade. They provided the Hazaras with designs, buying their completed carpets at bargain prices and attaching a 'made in Pakistan' label along with a large mark-up, and then shipping the carpets internationally.

Dave had started a carpet cooperative in Dashti Barchi. He hoped to establish a direct link with American buyers by using the internet to bypass Pakistan. Direct exporting would mean the weavers themselves would see more profit, with an opportunity to work themselves out of poverty.

We drove out to Dashti Barchi along unpaved roads, the air choked with a fine dust spewed up by every van, donkey-cart and bicycle that jolted along it. Turbaned men and young boys squatted at the roadside stalls flicking blackened water from the open drains onto the road in vain attempts to settle the dust. Most stalls displayed bales of wool – spun and un-spun – and rows of hook-knives hanging from strings beside piles of carpet combs. Ornate Pakistani trucks – a celebration of colourful excess – drove past laden with untrimmed carpets, their decorative metal tassels jangling along the pitted road.

We lurched down a side-street, arriving at the cooperative headquarters, and were introduced to three local staff workers. There wasn't much to see, as the cooperative was still in its infancy, but we visited a home nearby where boys as young as eight perched on their benches busily weaving – their tiny, practised fingers flying across the loom.

That evening we discussed the issue of child labour with Dave. On the one hand it was important for weaving families to apprentice their children and pass on skills to the next generation. On the other, these children weren't receiving an education or much leisure time. Effectively monitoring child labour within a domestic context was impossible, but we agreed that all families partnering with the cooperative should send their children to school, allowing them time to weave in the afternoons.

I asked Dave why the cooperative was producing ubiquitous Turkish *oshak* designs rather than something both Afghan and unique. I was sure we would find some interesting designs – as we had with doors and tiles in Khiva – at the Kabul museum, and planned a visit there.

The museum was situated beside a bombed-out hulk that was once an opulent palace. We were frisked on entering, passing a marble placard that stated: 'A nation stays alive when its culture stays alive.' It seemed more of an epitaph than anything else. We wandered through empty halls. Laminated sheets of photographs were all that remained of many priceless artefacts, captioned with the inevitable 'destroyed in 2001 by the Taliban'.

Fortunately for us, what had survived the iconoclastic Taliban was mainly non-figurative arabesque work. We discovered a 19th-century marble door, and traced the intricate border and field designs. The lotus and peonies that entwined the border were a similar, simpler version of one of our Khiva tile designs, and I found myself longing to know more about the history and migration of the patterns we discovered. There were marble tombstones outside with delicate filigree, and upstairs a fascinating collection of carved wooden items from Nuristan, known previously as Kafirstan. The wild mountain people of Nuristan had been forcibly converted to Islam in the 19th century and most of the artefacts on display were strongly tribal and pre-Islamic in terms of motifs. Totem poles, fertility doors and thrones were covered in simple patterns which would work well as modernist carpet designs.

For the rest of the week, we scoured the Kabul bazaars for natural dyes and discussed internet marketing strategies and publicity. The structure of the cooperative concerned me, as power was concentrated in the hands of one Afghan whom Dave seemed to trust implicitly. The rest of us found him downright shifty. We researched the market price for wool in Dashti Barchi and discovered that this man had produced receipts for a considerably higher sum, pocketing the difference. Dave reluctantly fired him, and the working atmosphere within the cooperative improved considerably. We prepared for a natural dyeing workshop and Madrim made plans to join us via Tajikistan, as the Uzbek/Afghan border was now closed.

I was keen to meet up with a warlord friend of my mother's. She'd insisted that I not refer to him as a warlord, as technically he had been general to a warlord and was now involved in politics. I prefer not to use his name, so will refer to him as the General. He had served Ahmed Shah Massoud – the head of the Northern Alliance – until Massoud's assassination by Al Qaeda just before the World Trade Center attacks. Grief-stricken, the General had left Afghanistan and spent time in Holland with his family before enrolling on an English course at a language school in Cambridge. My mother had been one of his tutors, treating him with honour and respect. He regaled her with tales of war and strategy, turning the classroom desk into a battleground map and enjoying a subject he was well versed in.

Lonely in Cambridge and accustomed to status and deference, the General felt lost and unappreciated. His family came to visit, and my mother invited them all for Sunday lunch. The General was impressed that my father prayed before the meal and decided that my parents were people he could trust his wife with. My mother then visited them in Holland. Now, armed with a letter, a parcel of posh tea and a phone number, I hoped to track the General down.

We finally made phone contact on the day before I travelled down to Kandahar.

'Please Mr Chris, what can I do for you in Afghanistan? What is your need? You just must say it. I will look to everything. Also please to must be careful. It is still little interesting in Kandahar,' he explained.

I thanked him for his kindness, looking forward to our meeting on my return to Kabul, and passed on warm 'Salaams' from my mother.

I just had time to visit the tailor and collect my new shelwar kamiz – the one permissible item of clothing in Kandahar – before leaving the following morning. We'd been told to do everything possible to blend in, which worked well for my ethnically ambiguous travelling companions who all looked passably Afghan. I, however, was far too tall and blond, wore glasses, and was clearly a foreign fake. Even the large headscarf I wore, covering as much of my face as possible, did little to disguise my foreigner status.

We woke before dawn and made our way to the main bus station, where ageing German buses and tarted-up Pakistani vehicles left in the cool of the day. Travel by bus was considered the safest, as foreigners were assumed to travel only in gleaming SUVs. Once outside Kabul, we passed arid hills emblazoned with lush green settlements where orchards and fields of poppies were carefully irrigated. A camel caravan passed us laden with goods to sell in one of Kabul's bazaars. Peasant girls in bright dresses and headscarves tended the fields and boys in dusty shelwar kamiz led flocks of sheep and goats to pasture. The 21st century rested lightly here.

A new arrival to our group was an intern at the Heritage Foundation – a conservative think-tank in Washington. I sat next to him and we struck up a whispered conversation, keen to avoid attention. I listened to his views on American foreign policy, President Bush (not conservative enough) and his support of Israel, before launching into my own opposing views. Soon turbaned heads craned round to see what the foreigners at the back were shouting about. We were reprimanded over greasy eggs and long flat *naan* at a tea-house stop by our Afghan minder.

'It's not just you they will kill if they know there are foreigners on the bus,' he explained, referring to Taliban elements. 'They hate Afghans who work with foreigners. They will find my papers and then it is all over for me.'

We apologised and spent the rest of the journey in a sweaty stupor as the day warmed and we drove to the lower, hotter Afghan plains. Kandahar felt more Pakistani, with motorised rickshaws weaving between cars and lorries. The faces of all visible adults were heavily bearded. We passed a large poster providing a helpful contact number for those observing suicide bombers. We learnt later that a suicide bomber had blown himself up on the airport road half an hour before our arrival. Suicide bombers were commonplace. Many were poor ethnic Pashtuns from Pakistan, taken in by madrassahs and groomed – their families generously provided for in the event of their martyrdom.

One of the General's friends was another general from Kandahar, and he told me this story after I'd returned to Kabul. A taxi driver picks up a fare and drives to the airport, half an hour away. His passenger waits silently in the back seat for twenty minutes and then tells the driver to return to the city centre. They stop in the bazaar, beside the main bank, and outside the import shops. After two hours of random driving, the passenger gets out and pays.

'What's this?' the driver demands. 'We've been all over Kandahar. You should be giving me at least ten times the amount.'

The passenger looks deep into the driver's eyes and tells him: 'Go home, embrace your mother, then go to the mosque and thank Allah for your life.' He lifts his vest enough to reveal explosive devices strapped to his torso. 'It was not the will of Allah for me to find foreigners today, so we both live to see tomorrow.'

Understandably, there weren't many international NGO workers in Kandahar, and those there chose to keep a low profile. Our hosts asked to remain anonymous. They were looking for ways to empower Kandahari women, hoping to establish an embroidery cooperative exporting overseas.

Our hosts explained how embroidery was one of the few avenues of employment open to Kandahari women, who rarely left their home more than once a month, and even then were always under the supervision of their husband or mother-in-law. Within the home, the segregation continued. Two sons and their respective wives might live under the same roof, yet neither son would know the name of their sister-in-law, much less see her face uncovered. The outside world was almost exclusively male. While visiting a local gym – trying not to get weights tangled up in the baggy folds of my sweat-stained shelwar kamiz – I was chatted up and offered orange juice, watching young men preen and flirt with each other, for who else could they flirt with? This complete separation of the sexes seemed to benefit no one, and I struggled to understand it.

'You have to stop thinking of men and women as the same species,' I was told. 'Women are like sheep and men are like wolves. Everyone knows that it is in the nature of sheep to be led astray and that sheep make a tasty meal. You never trust sheep – what a notion! – nor do you leave your sheep unguarded, because men are like wolves and the nature of a wolf, given the chance, is to prey upon unguarded sheep. If sheep and wolves freely mingled together, it would lead only to bloodshed.'

I realised that our challenge was trying to empower sheep within the sheep-pen. We might not free women from their cloistered existence – any attempt to do this would result in the inevitable male backlash – but we could at least liberate them from the bonds of boredom. Embroidery gave women something creative to do, earned them an income, and brought them status and favour with their husbands and mothers-in-law.

We discussed embroidery designs. The traditional *khamak* that graced the collars and breast-pieces of men's shelwar kamiz was extremely detailed but unlikely to sell well abroad. Instead, we focused on textiles embroidered with tiny mirrors, and more utilitarian items like cushion covers, handbags and bed-spreads. The women in our group all wore burkas when visiting the embroiderers, knowing that they were more likely to be tolerated if they showed respect for local traditions. I asked one of the single foreign women how she managed to survive.

'It's true, Pashtun culture is a challenge and Pashtuns can be hard to love, but by God's grace, we try.' She was later abducted along with her driver, and at the time of writing it's still unclear whether she's dead or alive. Five hundred Pashtun women protested for her release.

Even before this abduction, security measures were tight and we scurried in our vehicle from one compound to another. It was frustrating when all I wanted was to wander through the bazaar, my internal danger-ometer seriously dulled by a childhood growing up in war-torn Beirut where I had a shell collection that had nothing to do with the sea. We made one or two furtive trips to mosques and mausoleums, looking at tilework and other potential sources of design inspiration. A tomb – one of the few pilgrimage sites permissible for women – was surrounded by a metal fence covered in votive rags and rows of padlocks. The latter represented locked curses placed by women, usually against particularly abusive mothers-in-law.

The night sky lit up with shelling between the resurgent Taliban and Western forces, reminding us that the political situation was far from peaceful. Taliban entered the city for the first time since their retreat in 2002, and our hasty departure was considered prudent. The roads were too dangerous, so we booked seats on a tiny plane laid on for development workers.

Airport Road was notorious for suicide bomb attacks and I spent most of the journey with just my eyes peeking from under my headscarf, hoping to look as inconspicuously foreign as possible. We turned off the main road where the airport and its surroundings had mushroomed into a giant army barracks – aggressive Western teenagers in uniform eyeing our vehicle with visible hostility. These were the NATO peace-keeping forces.

Posted signs all over the airport politely reminded us, 'No weapons please'. Our plane waited on the runway. One of the pilots – an American – lounged against a wing, wearing shades, his fingers curled around a belt sporting a large buckle with 'No more gun laws' emblazoned on it. Incensed that anyone who actually lived in a place with no gun laws could really be stupid enough to wear something like this, I was about to engage in 'dialogue' but thought better of it, remembering the journey down – and also that this plane was our only option for getting out of Kandahar.

After Kandahar, Kabul seemed positively Western. Young men loafed in buttock-hugging jeans and tight T-shirts. In place of the beards a mandatory fist long required under Taliban rule there were trendy sideburns and slicked-back hair. Before Kandahar I'd noticed only the women in burkas. Now I realised how many women wore just a headscarf – teenage girls wearing it Iranian-style, so far back as to be a token gesture. I wondered how the powerful Pashtun tribes of the south felt when visiting the capital, and whether such rapid change would provoke a conservative backlash.

The General called, inviting me for supper. I was to meet his driver outside the parliament building and could bring a friend. I wore my sweat-stained shelwar kamiz, determined to show my respect for traditional garb. The General greeted us, clean-shaven and wearing a dapper designer suit, smiling indulgently at my dishevelled clothing. I introduced him to my English friend Will, who spoke some Dari, and the General asked after my mother.

'You know Mr Chris, your mother, is also like to my mother. She is a very good, very kind, very wonderful person. Come, I will show you the room I am building for her.'

We walked next door with an entourage of armed soldiers covering us from every angle. The General was building an opulent mansion which he had designed himself. He would rent out this mansion but was building a second, smaller mansion where he planned to live. I was shown my mother's room.

'She is very good and trustworthy person,' he explained, 'so she can to stay up here in the family quarters with my wife and with my childrens.'

We were driven to the General's current home, full of mock-baroque furniture and gilt-framed paintings of shepherdesses, in marked contrast with the ethnic Afghan rugs and Nuristani chests found in the homes of most Kabul expats. I'd mentioned on the phone that I was vegetarian, just in case the General was planning to slaughter a sheep in my honour. The entire banquet was meatless, and the General insisted on serving us food personally, playing the role of host to perfection as course followed course. Both Will and I felt slightly overwhelmed and humbled by the effort he had gone to. Afterwards we sat replete, drinking green tea with cardamom, and asked the General about Massoud and what he was like.

Smiling dreamily, he described the dead Northern Alliance leader – a man he loved more than his own father and would happily have died for. Massoud was fearless, wise, humble, strong, and the future of Afghanistan. News of Massoud's assassination by Al Qaeda reached the General in the Panjir valley where he'd been fighting the Taliban. At first it was unclear whether Massoud was dead or badly wounded. Overpowered by grief, the General was entrenched in the battlefield and unable to return to his commander. He never saw Massoud again, and had not been present at his deathbed – a fact that grieved him greatly. For days afterwards the General avoided journalists, unable to control his emotions, afraid of what he might unleash.

Talking about it now was still painful, and the General's eyes flicked up regularly to the gilt-framed portrait of Massoud, incongruous among the shepherdesses. I changed the subject, asking the General about his escapades against the Red Army, and he was soon entertaining us with tales of bloodshed.

'I am not so tall, which is also very good if bullets flying at your head. It is also very nice for approaching the tanks and putting the bomb and then running. I don't know how many Russians I killed. Many, many. But I am not a murderer. I never killed prisoner or torture. On the battlefield, it is different. It is like the race – you both trying to kill the other and who will be first?'

We left late that night, with promises to visit again and an armed escort back to our accommodation.

Three days later the General called to say that some friends of his were having an evening of concert music. Would Will and I like to come? This time I dressed in my least scruffy Western clothes. We were picked up by the General's driver and taken to the home of another distinguished general. Four or five other generals were already present, and we'd barely sat down before three more arrived. Our General wasn't among them, but we managed stilted conversation over green tea, feeling conspicuously aware of our un-generalness. It became clear on our General's entrance that he was held in the greatest esteem by the others. It was only after he arrived that we were ushered upstairs, to the quiet rustle of women hurriedly vacating the dining area.

Here a huge banquet had been laid out on a giant dasturkhan. The layout was much the same as in Uzbekistan, although here it was permissible to step on a corner of the dasturkhan and there were no bottles of vodka congregated in the middle.

After the banquet, we were led to the basement. This was the best place to host domestic concerts – a new tradition established during Taliban rule when music was outlawed. A *tabla* player adjusted his two drums and began a hypnotic beat. One of the generals played the accordion and another sang mournfully.

'It's about love,' the General whispered to me, somewhat superfluously. The song was followed eventually by another and another. The lilting melody combined with a recently consumed banquet created a powerful soporific effect and I soon found my eyes growing heavy. Our compound's curfew time came and went and the music continued. Finally, at around midnight, one of the generals begged leave.

'Please excuse to my friend,' the General requested. 'Now he must to sleep. Tomorrow he will be to Kandahar to fight Taliban.'

I explained that we too should leave, as our nightwatchman would worry at our absence, having missed curfew. The night drew to a close.

The following day Madrim arrived in Kabul, exhausted and traumatised. He had been stripped naked on the Uzbek side of the Uzbek/Tajik border. The guards then discovered $200 he hadn't declared, taking this from him without a receipt and relieving him of his remaining 50,000 som as a 'fine'. I had yet to witness such rapacious border guards anywhere else. He had to borrow money from the Operation Mercy office in Dushanbe to continue his journey.

Seeing Madrim again was wonderful. It felt like a triumph over the Uzbek government that borders couldn't contain our friendship. For the first hour or so I had to reach for words, my Uzbek rusty, but soon we were chatting away as I caught up on the goings-on in Khiva. My Uzbek family were doing well and sent their greetings. Malika, my Uzbek sister, was expecting her first child. The workshops were running OK, but there were still lots of problems and Madrim missed me, finding it lonely being a director, shouldering most of the worries and stresses. Aina had also been told to leave by the authorities. But hearing news from home was exhilarating. Every now and then one of us would break off our conversation just to sit and grin at the other, still amazed at our reunion.

I still didn't know why I'd been deported, and speculated on this with Madrim. He thought it was because a guide I'd upset had connections with the secret police. Equally possible was that an informer had been present at an illegal gathering of Uzbek Christians in Urgench where I'd led the singing. There was no way of knowing for sure. What I hadn't known was that the Tashkent authorities had demanded a letter of recommendation from the Mayor before considering my case. Koranbeg and Madrim waited outside his office for hours, hoping for an audience. He finally emerged and they chased him to his car, begging him to sign a letter of recommendation, but he refused.

～

We began our dye workshop in Dashti Barchi with the assistance of a local Uzbek boy who translated into Dari. A few days previously I'd bought huge copper cauldrons perfect for dyeing. It had taken us months to find just one of that size in Uzbekistan, but in Kabul these cauldrons were sold in towering stacks. It was our first time dyeing with wool, but the resulting colours were vivid and strong and the six apprentices seemed keen to learn.

I had just three days left before my ticket expired, and I wanted to extend it to spend more time with Madrim. This proved impossible, but while I was in downtown Kabul I decided to visit Chicken Street one last time. This was where most of the carpet shops were, and I also wanted to pick up some necklaces for my mother. I was rooting through a pile of kilims in one shop when the owner suddenly appeared, urging me to leave immediately as he began frantically packing down his stock. Confused, I left the shop to see the scene repeated up and down Chicken Street. Shop-owners feverishly slammed metal grilles shut and fled. I tried to ask why. No one knew, but they'd learnt to flee first and ask questions later. A sense of fear hung in the air as the street emptied.

Clearly something was wrong. But I wanted to know what before deciding what to do. I'd arranged to meet friends in the Shah bookshop, so I headed that way, aware that the anxious crowds were all fleeing in the opposite direction. I was wearing Western clothes and a backpack and looked painfully foreign. Passers-by glanced up with looks of pity and bewilderment, clearly aware of my imminent demise. A young man stopped me.

'Don't you know what's happened?' he asked. 'It's very bad for you foreigners now. You must get out. Go and hide!'

Before I could thank him or ask him any questions, he was gone. I offered up a quick prayer and wondered what I should do. A nearby school was emptying and there were fewer and fewer cars on the streets. I retreated back past the entrance to Chicken Street, which had been a popular target for anti-Western feelings in the past. All the shops were now shut up, and it was clearly not a good place to be caught. I tried the next street along but my way was barred by a soldier.

'You must let me pass,' I pleaded. 'Please, I'm a foreigner!'

A nod from his commander and I was through. Scurrying along, scrabbling in my bag for the phone Dave had lent me, I just wanted to know what was going on. I stopped to put the backpack down and rummage properly. A passing Afghan, or possibly an angel, assumed I couldn't find the doorbell for the building next to me and rang it. A burly, bearded Afghan peered out as I tried to apologise for the misunderstanding.

'What are you doing out here? Are you crazy?' he asked with an American twang. 'Get in here now!'

He beckoned me into a spartan hall, offering me a seat before running off to attend to urgent business. I waited and was offered a bottle of water. He returned fifteen minutes later to introduce himself properly. He was an Afghan American who had recently returned to Kabul as a cultural advisor for the American embassy, and he had just been briefed by the embassy on the unfolding events. I'd found someone who knew exactly what was going on.

Early that morning, fighting had broken out in a suburb of Kabul and a convoy of American soldiers was dispatched to quell it. They drove in formation, until one of the soldiers – either stoned, drunk, or crazy – broke ranks and drove his vehicle over several civilian cars. As mangled bodies were dragged from the wrecks an angry crowd formed, exchanging insults, stones and then bullets. Whoever fired the first bullet, the Americans were soon firing into the crowd, which dispersed but returned with weapons. The Afghan police, sent to aid the Americans, turned on them once they saw what had happened. As the Americans retreated, the crowd – now a violent mob – began its rampage through the city, targeting anything or anyone connected with the West.

'When will these guys learn?' he asked wearily. 'The Soviets actually helped us. All our electricity still comes from the dam and hydro-electric plant they built up in the mountains. Still, the moment they started to behave like they owned the place, we turned on them. Now these kid soldiers think they can run over anyone they like. Kabul is pissed and it's people like me who are gonna get it. Guests we treat with respect, but occupiers …' He made a slicing motion across his throat.

We heard gunfire approaching. My host led me away from the exposed hallway to a courtyard garden sheltered by tall buildings. The walled garden was full of pomegranate trees and flower-beds, with a carefully manicured lawn – an American lawn, I was told proudly by my host. Echoing around the walls were the sounds of gunfire and the angry screams of the mob out on Chicken Street. Soon, bursts of gunfire were punctuated by shattering glass, exploding cars and the deep-throated 'thump' of rocket-propelled grenades. Wreaths of gunpowder smoke filled the garden – this tranquil image at odds with the jarring sounds of violence all around us. We took shelter inside.

It was clear that I'd be there for some time, and my host kindly invited me to lunch with the male members of his family. We watched BBC News report that the riot was over as the sounds of warfare continued around us. The phone networks were jammed. No one knew where I was or that I was OK. My host's nephew – around my age – looked bored and I presented him with some DVDs I'd just bought on Chicken Street, asking if he wanted to watch one. He chose *Munich*. Soon, explosions and gunfire could be heard both on and off screen. I couldn't watch, and went out to the garden where the sound of fighting was beginning to recede. I managed to send a text to say I was alright, and another giving the address I was staying at.

They promised that a van would come and pick me up. Madrim called from the cooperative, oblivious to the rioting which hadn't affected Dashti Barchi, wanting to know why I hadn't turned up. I held up the phone so he could hear the gunfire and asked him to be careful when returning to our compound. The General also called to check that I was safe.

The gunfire died down and the van arrived. I was given a turban to wear and instructed to sit away from the windows. I thanked my Afghan American hosts for their unexpected hospitality. We drove past blackened hulks of cars, looted shops, broken glass and pock-marked walls. I tried not to think what might have happened had a fleeing Afghan not taken time to ring the doorbell on behalf of a foreign stranger – if I hadn't been offered a garden of sanctuary in the middle of the riot. I offered up a prayer of profound gratitude.

There was a city-wide curfew that evening. A number of Western compounds had been destroyed in the looting, including Oxfam's. Local staff at the Serena Hotel had been dragged out and gunned down, and this was declared the worst riot in Kabul since the fall of the Taliban. There was nothing in media reports about the Americans opening fire on the protesting crowd, or about the Afghan police siding against them.

The next day, back in my shelwar kamiz with my face obliterated by a headscarf, I headed to the still-peaceful suburb of Dashti Barchi with Madrim to continue our workshop on dye-making. We purchased more weaving combs and hook-knives for Madrim to take back to Khiva, and I spent an hour in the bazaar finding gifts for my Uzbek family, returning to a rainbow of dripping wool skeins. Madrim was drawing up a couple of new designs taken from the Kabul museum, and I felt we had succeeded in equipping the cooperative as best we could.

The General insisted on one more visit, despite my protests that a curfew was still in force. He waved aside this objection, declaring that he knew the password. We enjoyed another enormous feast and I left laden with gifts for my mother and each member of my family, promising to encourage my mother to visit soon.

We drove back through deserted streets, an armed soldier accompanying us. At each checkpoint, nervous Afghan soldiers aimed their weapons at the driver's head – particularly disconcerting as I sat directly behind him. The soldiers barked out the first part of a password, to which our driver responded with the second. Hostility abruptly dissolved into banter, backslapping and wishes for a safe journey. We relaxed until the next checkpoint, where the process would repeat itself.

As I was to leave the following day, I spent the morning with Madrim. We went for a roadside banana milkshake – a rich blend of bananas, almonds, dates and cream, and our traditional treat in Afghanistan. Everything had already been said, but I repeated the greetings he should pass on and tried to avoid saying anything that might cause emotion. Dave drove us to

Dashti Barchi and I said my farewells to the dyers we'd trained. Finally it was time to say goodbye to Madrim. I wanted to say something positive, about my hopes that we would meet again and that we would still keep in touch, but we just embraced without words, only tears. I thought about all the carpets we'd created together, the jobs we'd provided, and the lives that had been changed as a result. I thought about the interweaving of my life with all the people I'd never been allowed to say goodbye to: the weavers and dyers, my Uzbek family and friends, even my ginger cat. This tapestry was far more meaningful to me than our most extravagant carpet or ambitious suzani. Somehow Madrim, my one living link with Khiva, embodied all of this, and I realised that I wasn't just saying goodbye to a close friend, but also to Khiva and a whole chapter in my life.

Dave was waiting in the van and smiled sadly at me as I tried to compose myself. The dust from Dashti Barchi mingled with my tears, leaving brown streaks down each cheek.

Epilogue

September 2009

Out of my window I can see the Afghan mountains, close enough to reach on foot in half an hour – plus a bracing swim across the Panj River which separates the Afghan and Tajik Pamirs.

I've been living in the Pamirs for two years now. The region is known as Badakshan and covers bits of four different mountainous countries: Tajikistan (where we are apparently semi-autonomous), Afghanistan, China and Pakistan. The people are Ismaili and speak a variety of obscure and complicated mountain languages. The one I'm learning and writing a textbook for is called Shugni.

I live with a local family and try not to draw comparisons with my Uzbek family in Khiva. In fact, life over this past year has been a conscious effort not to make comparisons, and to live in the present, not the past. The town of Khorog itself is shabby and uninspiring, and I still yearn for the spectacular view of madrassahs and minarets that I had from my balcony in Khiva. Still, the enormous mountains that surround Khorog are full of natural beauty.

I'm in contact with friends in Khiva and plan another dye-buying trip with Madrim to Afghanistan, once this year's tourist season is over. I still get to use my Uzbek a bit here, when talking with the Kyrgyz who live in the high plateaus to the east of us. I'm working with yak-herders there, introducing yak-combs and buying up yak-down – traditionally thrown away

– to be knitted into luxury sweaters here in Khorog. So I'm about to start another workshop, and I'm hoping that my experience in Khiva will help with that. We've established a brand name, Yak-yak (www.yakyakstory.com), and I've just visited a traditional Pamiri house for sale that, with a bit of work, would make a great workshop. I've had some adventures already: a misguided swim that ended in Afghanistan; being gored by a yak; and being confronted at gunpoint while soaking in a hot-spring on the Afghan–Chinese border.

I'd love to write more about this, but it's a new chapter, and first it needs to be lived.

Glossary

Abke   Literally 'older sister' in the Khorezm dialect, but also used as a generic term of respect towards older women.

Abrash   The mottled effect created by subtle differences that affect anything dyed naturally. This can also be more noticeable in a carpet where different dye batches with different shades have been used.

Achik   Spicy or sharp-tasting; also a description of objects or substances which can ward off the evil eye.

Agha   Literally 'older brother' in the Khorezm dialect, but also used as a generic term of respect towards older men.

Aksakal   A white-beard.

Amin   Similar to 'Amen', and said at the end of prayers.

Arabesque   Intricate swirling patterns, often incorporating floral motifs.

Beshik   A Central Asian cradle into which swaddled babies are strapped.

Beshik toy   Literally a 'cradle celebration', similar to the christening of a new-born baby.

'Boshka iloyja yoke'   'There is no other way.'

Caravanserai   A huge courtyard for trading and bartering large quantities of merchandise, surrounded by storage facilities, the upper storey functioning as an inn.

Chowkidor   A guard, often called on to perform other household duties, in Afghanistan and Pakistan.

Corpuche   A long, narrow, cotton stuffed mattress for sitting on.

Dasturkhan A tablecloth laid on the floor on which food is placed. The same rules apply as if it were on a table, so walking on it is a big cultural faux pas.

Field and frame Both carpet terms, the field refers to the main design within the central rectangle of a carpet, and the frame is the border of the design that frames it.

Frontispiece A detailed painting or geometric design that appears on a double spread at the front of antique, handwritten books.

Gok Literally 'green', describing the first shoots of clover that emerge in spring and are minced and cooked, tasting much like spinach.

Gul Flower, both literally and as an abstract floral motif in textiles.

Halpa Either the female folk Islamic equivalent to a mullah (presiding over spiritual gatherings of women such as funerals) or a female singer of folk songs.

Hoja A title of respect given to someone who has made the pilgrimage to Mecca.

Homom Public bath-house (pronounced 'Hamam' in Turkish). Older ones are communal with steam rooms and hot marble to lie on. Soviet ones are just shower blocks with the possible addition of a sauna.

Ichan Kala Literally 'inner city', referring to everything within the city walls of Khiva.

Ikat A style of dyeing in which warp threads carry the pattern, having been resist-dyed.

Isfan A dried herb which gives off a pungent smoke when burnt and is reputed to drive away evil spirits or microbes, depending on your worldview.

Iwan   A tall, three-sided building that faces north, usually with a carved wooden pillar or two holding up the side without a wall. This open-air room is shaded from the sun and captures the northern breezes, circulating them and acting as a simple air-conditioner. All traditional dwellings include an iwan.

Jinn   A devil or demon.

Kilim   A flat-woven floor covering which, unlike a carpet, has no knotted pile.

Kelin   A term used to describe both a bride and her position of daughter-/sister-in-law within her husband's family.

Kufic   An ornate stlye of Arabic calligraphy.

Laghman   Thick, hand-stretched noodles, usually served in a meat and vegetable broth.

Madder root   Madder is a straggling weed, known as *royan* in Uzbek and *Rubia tinctorum* in Latin; the roots, once matured, give a pinkish/brick-red colour that can be enhanced by the use of mordants and tannins, such as oak gall.

Madrassah   An Islamic school of learning, usually based on a courtyard layout with residential cells for studying and living in.

Maidan   A central square or plaza.

Majolica   Tiles using a colour palette of white, turquoise and blue, originating from the island of Majorca.

Medallion   Used in carpet terminology to describe a large, irregular, central pendant design surrounded by smaller, floral designs.

Namaz   A Muslim prayer, recited five times a day facing Mecca.

Naqsh   A generic term used to describe patterning or design that can apply to anything from tiling to carved wooden inlay, etc.

Nashallah   A blend of beaten egg-whites, sugar and cream of tartar, eaten raw with bread during Ramazan.

Navruz   One of the largest festivals; celebrated on 21 March, marking spring and the New Year, with Zoroastrian roots.

NGO   Stands for 'non-governmental organisation' – usually doing development work of some kind.

Non   Traditional flatbread baked in an earthen oven.

Oak gall   Nut-sized round nodules formed by certain types of oak in reaction to wasp eggs laid in their trunks. High in tannin, they work with madder root to create vivid reds.

Paranja   An all-enveloping covering worn by women in Central Asia along with a horse-hair veil, until banned under Communism.

Plov   The greasy national dish of Uzbekistan, consisting of rice, carrots and mutton.

Ramazan   The Uzbek name for Ramadan – the Muslim month of fasting.

Remont   A Russian term used to describe the continual patching and mending of buildings and cars.

Resist-dyeing   A form of tie-dyeing in which parts of a fabric or warp threads are bound to prevent dyeing and other parts are left open to receive the colour.

Samovar   A large urn for boiling water and brewing tea.

Samsa   A pastry parcel filled with meat, potato or pumpkin, similar to a samosa.

Sericulture   The rearing of silkworms for silk.

Shashlik   Skewers of mutton or beef on a stick and cooked over charcoal.

Shelwar kamiz Cotton baggy pants covered in a long top, commonly worn in Afghanistan and Pakistan.

Sumalek A brown paste made from mashed wheat-shoots, stirred continually for hours and cooked primarily at Navruz.

Suzani Literally means 'needlework' in Tajik and describes the embroidered tapestries of southern Uzbekistan and Tajikistan.

Tanish bilish 'Useful connections'; similar to the proverb 'It's not what you know, but who you know that counts.'

Turkestan A historic term used to describe the area of Middle Asia now occupied by the former Soviet Central Asian states, northern Afghanistan and western China.

Usta Master at something (of either sex) but also a generic term for a handyman.

Vellum Skin from the stomach of a sheep or goat and superior to paper in book-making.

Wahabi The term used to describe Islamist fundamentalists, referring to the strict Saudi Wahabite sect which advocates jihad.

Warp A weaving term describing the vertical threads that make up the backbone of a carpet.

Weft A weaving term describing the horizontal threads that weave between the warp threads.

Further Reading

Colonel Bailey, *Mission to Tashkent* (1946)

Frederick Burnaby, *A Ride to Khiva* (1876)

Ella Christie, *Through Khiva to Golden Samarkand* (1925)

Victoria Finlay, *Colour* (2002)

Peter Hopkirk, *The Great Game* (1990)

R. Jefferson, *A New Ride to Khiva* (1899)

Gustav Krist, *Alone Through a Forbidden Land* (1938)

Chris Kremmer, *The Carpet Wars* (2002)

T. Lentz, *Timur and the Princely Vision* (1989)

Lady Macartney, *An English Lady in Chinese Turkestan* (1931)

J.A. MacGahan, *Campaigning on the Oxus, and the Fall of Khiva* (1874)

Ella Maillart, *Turkestan Solo* (1933)

Ethel Mannin, *South to Samarkand* (1936)

N. Muraviev, *Journey to Khiva* (1871)

Paul Nazaroff, *Hunted Through Central Asia* (1932)

Orhan Pamuk, *My Name is Red* (2001)

Arminius Vambery, *Travels in Central Asia* (1863)

Monica Whitlock, *Beyond the Oxus* (2002)

Acknowledgements

Firstly I'd like to thank my parents, who kindly allowed me a year of rent-free living in order to write this book. Special thanks to Pat Alexander, whose editing skills helped me enormously at the start, and to Rachel McKinley for your diligent proof-reading. Thanks also to Jane Hepburn, Tim and Sheila Stevenson, Will Beharrel, Lis and James Woods, Iain Pickett, Lauren McGill and David Lewis for your helpful comments.

Tatiana Wilde, thank you for your constructive criticism and helping the book take shape. Simon Flynn, Duncan Heath and all at Icon, thanks for taking a chance with a first-time author; your professionalism, your polishing of the manuscript and your commitment to seeing the book do well, have been a huge encouragement.

Finally, thanks to Endre Medhaug for your unfailing, prophetic optimism that this book would ever come to be!

Picture credits
Colour plate 8: Arthur M. Sackler Gallery, Smithsonian Institution, Washington, DC. Purchase: Smithsonian Unrestricted Trust Funds, Smithsonian Collections Acquisition Program, and Dr Arthur M. Sackler, S1986.160.

Colour plate 10: © British Library.

Index

329